IT CAN HAPPEN HERE

It Can Happen Here

White Power and the Rising Threat of Genocide in the US

Alexander Laban Hinton

NEW YORK UNIVERSITY PRESS

New York

NEW YORK UNIVERSITY PRESS
New York
www.nyupress.org

© 2021 by New York University
Paperback edition published 2022.
All rights reserved

References to Internet websites (URLs) were accurate at the time of writing. Neither the author nor New York University Press is responsible for URLs that may have expired or changed since the manuscript was prepared.

Library of Congress Cataloging-in-Publication Data
Names: Hinton, Alexander Laban, author.
Title: It can happen here : white power and the rising threat of genocide in the US / Alexander Laban Hinton.
Other titles: White power and the rising threat of genocide in the US
Description: New York : NYU Press, [2021] | Includes bibliographical references and index.
Identifiers: LCCN 2020040792 (print) | LCCN 2020040793 (ebook) |
ISBN 9781479808014 (hardback) | ISBN 9781479808052 (paperback) |
ISBN 9781479808021 (ebook) | ISBN 9781479808038 (ebook other)
Subjects: LCSH: Unite the Right Rally, Charlottesville, Va., 2017. |
White supremacy movements—United States—History—21st century. |
Political violence—United States. | Trump, Donald, 1946- —Political and social views. |
Right-wing extremists—United States. | United States—Race relations—21st century.
Classification: LCC F234.C47 H56 2021 (print) | LCC F234.C47 (ebook) |
DDC 973.933—dc23
LC record available at https://lccn.loc.gov/2020040792
LC ebook record available at https://lccn.loc.gov/2020040793

New York University Press books are printed on acid-free paper, and their binding materials are chosen for strength and durability. We strive to use environmentally responsible suppliers and materials to the greatest extent possible in publishing our books.

Manufactured in the United States of America

10 9 8 7 6 5 4 3 2

Also available as an ebook

For N, M, and A

CONTENTS

PREFACE

Donald Trump's presidency took the United States to the brink. If the situation seemed to be getting increasingly dire as I wrote this book, and especially as I finished the epilogue in July 2020, it got even worse as the 2020 US presidential election approached. Trump ramped up his demonization of people of color through racist "law and order" messaging. He refused to commit to a peaceful transfer of power while questioning the integrity of the election. And, during the first presidential debate with Joe Biden, Trump told white power extremists to "stand by."

By the time the November 3, 2020, election arrived, the United States faced a serious risk of atrocity crimes. I wrote an October 2020 op-ed that made this case.[1] Others sounded the alarm as well, warning about both the threat of violence and the collapse of a US democratic system that Trump had been eroding since the start of his presidency.

In a radio interview, I was asked how the United States could avoid such a situation. The best way to prevent election-related mass violence from happening in the United States, I replied, would be for Biden to defeat Trump in a landslide victory that would be difficult to contest. If Biden did not quite reach that threshold, he did win the election decisively. Nevertheless, Trump still sought to contest Biden's win, tweeting lies and misinformation to inflame his followers, filing lawsuit after lawsuit, and refusing to concede. In the end, however, he had little choice but to leave office after being widely condemned for inciting an insurrection at the Capitol on January 6, 2021, an event that took place as this book was going to press.

I have no doubt that, had Biden's win been narrow, the situation in the United States would have become even more volatile and there likely would have been mass protests and violence in the streets. White power extremists and far-right militias, many heavily armed, had signaled that they were ready to fight. And Trump had already indicated that he was willing to invoke the Insurrection Act and use military force to quash dissent. We will never know whether he would have done so or whether military officers would have complied. But, one way or another, there were realistic scenarios in which atrocity crimes could have ensued, as vividly illustrated by the violence of the Capitol insurrection.

The pages that follow underscore an important lesson learned from the Trump presidency. If dramatic, Trump was not exceptional. His presidency was a symptom of a long and enduring history of systemic white power in the United States, one filled with moments in which genocide and mass violence took place. During Trump's administration, white power merely became more visible, and some of its more extreme and violent aspects were put on public display. Trump's presidency, especially in its tumultuous final months, underscored the key point about genocide and atrocity crimes in the United States that this book takes as its title. It can happen here.

Introduction

The Snake

"I want to read you something."

Presidential candidate Donald Trump stands before a raucous audience at a campaign rally at the Youngstown airport in Vienna, Ohio. It is March 14, 2016, the day before the state's Republican primary. Trump's ascent to the Republican Party presidential nomination looks likely after his Super Tuesday victories two weeks earlier.

Trump had arrived on his personal jet, featuring gold-plated seatbelts and Rolls-Royce engines.[1] It is painted red, white, and blue and emblazoned with Trump's name, which is also printed in thick, bold letters on each of the ramp stairs he descended before walking to the nearby podium, while the crowd cheered and recorded his entrance on their phones.[2]

Some hold "Make America Great Again" signs. Trump invokes this slogan several times during his Vienna stump speech, homing in on the country's allegedly dismal state of affairs: job losses, bad deals, manufacturing decline, decrepit infrastructure, and the lack of a "winning" military strategy in the Middle East, underscored by the failure to defeat ISIS.

"We're becoming third world," Trump laments.

The solution is to vote him into office. "We're going to do things the country isn't used to doing," Trump explains. "It's called we're going to win. Win!"

To underscore the point, Trump offers a story. "I want to read you this because I love it," Trump tells the crowd. The story, he continues, is based on a 1968 song by Al Wilson, an African American soul singer. As with most things he discusses, Trump suggests his version will be "an upgrade."

"It's called 'The Snake,'" Trump tells the crowd. He underscores his disgust by wrinkling his nose and saying, "Ew! The snake!" Reading from a sheet, Trump begins:

> On her way to work one morning
> Down the path along the lake
> A tender-hearted woman saw a poor half-frozen snake.
> His pretty colored skin had been all frosted with the dew
> "Oh well," she cried, "I'll take you in, and I'll take care of you."
> "Take me in oh tender woman
> Take me in, for heaven's sake
> Take me in oh tender woman," sighed the broken snake.
>
> She wrapped him up all cozy in a curvature of silk
> Then laid him by the fireside with honey and some milk
> Now she hurried home from work that night as soon as she arrived,
> She found that pretty snake she'd taken in had been revived. She was
>   happy.
> "Take me in, oh tender woman,
> Take me in, for heaven's sake,
> Take me in oh tender woman," sighed the broken snake.
>
> Now she clutched him to her bosom, "You're so beautiful," she cried.
> "But if I hadn't brought you in by now, heavens, you might have
>   died."
> Now she stroked his pretty skin and then she kissed him and held
>   him tight.
> But instead of saying thank you, that snake gave her a vicious bite!
> "Take me in, oh tender woman,
> Take me in, for heaven's sake,
> Take me in oh tender woman," sighed that vicious snake.

"I saved you," cried that woman,

"And you've bit me heavens why?

You know your bite is poisonous and now I'm going to die!"

"Oh shut up, silly woman," said the reptile with a grin.

"You knew damn well I was a snake before you took me in."

When he finishes, Trump looks up and throws his hands out, as if to say, "See!" In response, the crowd cheers. "Right?" Trump eggs them on. "Right?" The audience begins to chant, "USA, USA, USA . . ." After the crowd settles down, he adds, "So we don't know what we're doing, folks, as we have to learn [the lesson of this story]. We're going to make America great again!"

It is not the first time Trump has related this parable, which is becoming a staple at his campaign rallies. "The Snake" speaks to the heart of his campaign message: the danger malicious outsiders (the "vicious" snake) pose to the United States (the "tender-hearted" woman who takes it in). Usually, as is the case in Vienna, Trump precedes the parable by warning his audience about the dangers posed by terrorists and immigrants.

"We need borders," Trump had stated after telling the Vienna audience he was going to tell them the story. "We're going to build the wall!" He prompted the crowd to chant, "Build that wall! Build that wall! Build that wall! . . ." Then he asked, "Who's going to pay for the wall?" The crowd screamed, "Mexico!" And indeed, during the 2016 presidential campaign, Trump frequently depicted Mexico, China, and a host of other (snake-like) countries as taking advantage of the United States in bad trade deals that resulted in massive economic decline, particularly in states like Ohio.

"The Snake," however, most directly refers to threatening nonwhite others. If, echoing earlier conservative populists like George Wallace and Patrick Buchanan, Trump's political oratory was sprinkled with racist allusions, he constantly harped on immigration and weak borders while invoking the trope of the Islamic terrorist and Latino criminal epitomized by the MS-13 gang.

This language of borders, dangerous outsiders, and a nation besieged is familiar to me. My research focuses on genocide and mass violence. Indeed, on the day of Trump's Vienna campaign speech, I was on the other side of the world testifying on precisely these issues at an international tribunal in Cambodia, where I would have a direct exchange with Nuon Chea, the highest-ranking Khmer Rouge leader still alive. If Trump had the snake, Nuon Chea and the Khmer Rouge had the crocodile, an imagined enemy invader threatening their revolutionary body politic. Such connections between the past and present are a central plank of this book, which argues that the danger of genocide and atrocity crimes in the United States looms much larger than most people realize. My testimony at the Khmer Rouge tribunal underscored the stakes.

* * *

Nuon Chea. Khmer Rouge ideologue and propagandist. If Hitler had Himmler, Khmer Rouge leader Pol Pot had "Brother Number Two." Together they rose to power against the backdrop of the Vietnam War. Then they launched perhaps the most radical socialist revolution in history, one in which roughly a quarter of Cambodia's eight million inhabitants perished in less than four years, from April 1975 to January 1979.

The Khmer Rouge banned money, markets, private property, and religion. They targeted those who might dissent, especially the rich, educated, and powerful. They eliminated basic human rights, including freedom of speech, movement, and assembly. Having soft hands, wearing glasses, or using foreign words could be a death sentence. Meanwhile, they forced the masses to work day and night on meager rations. Some starved to death. Others fell sick. Perhaps a million were executed.

No one knows for sure since bodies were dumped in unmarked mass graves, victims of the Khmer Rouge hunt for "hidden enemies burrowing from within." Many were targeted as imagined pawns of "the Crocodile," Vietnam, which the Khmer Rouge believed was seeking to subvert their revolution. Nuon Chea would place the crocodile at the center of his defense, arguing that Vietnam and its agents, not the Khmer Rouge, were responsible for genocide and atrocity crimes.

My expert witness testimony, which began the day Trump delivered his Ohio speech, challenged this contention. I had been called to provide insight based on my years of anthropological research in Cambodia, my expertise as a comparative genocide scholar, and a related book I had written, *Why Did They Kill? Cambodia in the Shadow of Genocide*.[3] As the title suggests, *Why Did They Kill?* explains why the genocide took place and what motivated Khmer Rouge, ranging from the low-level perpetrators to leaders like Pol Pot and Nuon Chea, to participate in a project of mass murder.

When I took the stand, the prosecution questioned me about the dynamics that fueled this process. Ideological genocides, I explained, often emerge in a context of upheaval as buffers—the economy, moral safeguards, and traditional ways of life—come unglued. This was certainly the case in Cambodia, which was caught in the currents of the Vietnam War and suffered through civil war, foreign incursion, socioeconomic tumult, a coup, and US carpet bombing.

Amid such crises, ideologues offer a blueprint of renewal, one that plays upon grievance and distinguishes between a pure "us" and a contaminating "them"—an invasive outgroup that is scapegoated as the source of contemporary woes and therefore must be eliminated as part of the process of national revitalization. To effect this process of "purification," a genocidal regime will reorganize society and revamp its security apparatus to seek out, confine, and eliminate these alleged "internal enemies," who are marked, stigmatized, devalued, and dehumanized.

Euphemisms further facilitate this genocidal process. So, too, does state propaganda, which uses hate speech, incitement, and the language of borders, threat, and invasion to legitimate mass murder by depicting it as a sociopolitical necessity and moral good.

Not surprisingly, Nuon Chea's defense took issue with my testimony, which undercut their "crocodile" defense that sought to place blame on Vietnam. For two days, I countered the defense attacks. This made Nuon

Chea upset. And so, at the end of my three and a half days of testimony, Nuon Chea asked to address me directly in court. This request was unusual given that Nuon Chea had long been engaged in an unofficial boycott of the court. I was startled. A notorious ringleader of an infamous genocide, someone I had read and heard about for years, wanted to confront me in court.

My testimony concluded with this dramatic exchange, during which Nuon Chea posed two questions to me. The first focused on the crocodile. "Has Vietnam ever abandoned its ambition to swallow Cambodia?" he asked.

His second question sought to turn the tables and place the blame on me as a citizen of the United States, which had carpet-bombed Cambodia during the Vietnam War, wreaking havoc on the countryside and resulting in many deaths. "Do you consider that a war crime and genocide?" he queried.

I was face to face with genocide denial and, spotlight on, had to respond. I agreed that the damage caused by US bombing had been devastating and may have reached the threshold of war crimes. And there was also no doubt that Vietnam had long meddled in Cambodian affairs. But, I emphasized, it was Pol Pot, Nuon Chea, and the top Khmer Rouge leaders who made decisions, incited hate, chose whom to target, and gave the orders to "smash" these supposed enemies. They held command responsibility. They were the ones directly responsible for the genocide.

With these words, my testimony was finished. Little did I know that the same issues I was addressing at the Khmer Rouge tribunal—the origins and dynamics of violence and hate, seeking truth in the face of denial, and the lessons of the past—would be front and center in the United States after Trump's election. The man who depicted nonwhite others as snakes at his rallies became president. Hate speech proliferated, and white power views moved closer to the mainstream.

Suddenly, people everywhere began to ask the question that stands at the center of this book and became a focal point of my university teaching: "Can it happen here?" It is a question Nuon Chea's defense attorneys had suggested during my testimony when they pointed to events like Japanese internment and the US carpet-bombing of Cambodia. It is also a question people in the United States have pondered previously.

* * *

During the 1930s, for example, the United States faced extreme socioeconomic stress after the 1929 stock market crash and the Great Depression that followed. At the time, Mussolini led a fascist government in Italy. Hitler would create one after taking control of Germany in 1933. With fascism on the rise abroad, people wondered if a fascist leader could also seize power in the United States. Indeed, in 1934, the *Modern Monthly* published a 1934 symposium titled "Will Fascism Come to America?"[4]

Such fears were amplified by domestic events.[5] The previous decade had seen a resurgence of the Ku Klux Klan (KKK), widespread anti-immigrant sentiment that led to the Immigration Act of 1924, and increased antisemitism underscored by Henry Ford's mass publication of the infamous antisemitic conspiracy theory screed, *The Protocols of the Elders of Zion*. More recently, William Dudley Pelley, a Hollywood screenwriter, had established a fascist-inspired "Silver Shirt" white-power-extremist group that had as many as fifteen thousand members by the mid-1930s.

Meanwhile, Huey Long, the populist and autocratic governor of and then senator from Louisiana, was gaining prominence and was rumored to be preparing for a presidential run. Some have noted the similarities between Long and Trump even as they rose to power on opposite ends of the political spectrum. And like Trump, Long was sometimes called a fascist.[6]

Within this 1930s context, Nobel Prize–winning US novelist Sinclair Lewis wrote a bestseller, *It Can't Happen Here*, published in October 1935, just a month after Long was assassinated.[7] In it, Buzz Windrip—a populist demagogue thought to have been inspired by Long and perhaps Pelley as well—rises to power on a fifteen-point platform that includes militarization, disenfranchising Blacks, returning women to "feminine spheres," and investing the new president with dictatorial powers. On the campaign trail, Windrip is supported by the League of Forgotten Men and paramilitary Minute Men, likely modeled after Hitler's Brownshirts and Pelly's Silver Shirts.

Following his election, Windrip strips the other two branches of government of power, bans opposition, executes political enemies, discriminates against nonwhites and Jews, and establishes labor and concentration camps. Windrip's Minute Men militia wreak havoc as they enforce the new order. Eventually, the Minute Men arrest the book's hero, liberal journalist Doremus Jessup, who is sent to a concentration camp and tortured. He later escapes and joins a resistance movement.

Earlier, a friend had dismissed Jessup's concern that Windrip's election would lead to a "Fascist dictatorship" by saying, "That couldn't happen here in America, not possibly!"[8] Lewis's novel warns against such naive assumptions about "American exceptionalism," or the idea that the United States occupies a unique role as the moral leader of the world and has an unparalleled democratic system that could never permit an authoritarian demagogue to take power or allow genocide and atrocity crimes to take place. Like Lewis's novel, this book questions this assumption that "it can't happen here."

* * *

Of course, just a few years after Lewis published his book, it did happen in Europe, the "citadel of Western civilization" and cradle of the Enlightenment, which valorized Reason. Although they hinted at it, the concentration camps and violence Lewis depicted in *It Can't Happen Here* paled in comparison to the Nazi system of industrialized mass murder.

Afterward, people sought answers to the question, *Why?* If some, like the poet and critic Aimé Césaire, argued that Nazi atrocities were linked to the logics of modernity and colonialism, many more depicted the violence as exceptional.[9] One current of thought held that the Nazis were atavistic, a regression to an earlier, barbaric stage of national being.

Others turned to psychology, viewing the Nazi violence in terms of deviance and pathology (as the work of madmen, sadists, and sociopaths) or attitudes like antisemitism and prejudice.

In this latter regard, a major research initiative examining the roots of intolerance was launched in 1944 by the American Jewish Committee. The project resulted in a five-volume series, *Studies in Prejudice*, edited by a US psychologist, Samuel Flowerman, and Max Horkheimer, a leader of the Frankfurt School of critical theory and its Institute of Social Research, which had relocated to the United States in the 1930s as Hitler came to power.

Another member of the institute, Theodor Adorno, collaborated with the Berkeley Public Opinion Study to examine whether and how personality predisposed people not just toward prejudice but toward antidemocratic ideologies such as those espoused by the Nazis. Drawing on surveys and interviews with over two thousand people, the researchers developed an "F-scale" to measure susceptibility to fascism.

The results of their study suggested that there existed a "new anthropological type," which was named in the title of their book: *The Authoritarian Personality*. Informed by early childhood experience, the authoritarian personality was linked to characteristics such as conformity, conventionalism, submissiveness, aggression, projection, rigidity of thought, and uncritical, stereotypic thinking.

In a *New York Times Magazine* article publicizing the findings, Flowerman noted that roughly 10 percent of the US population had this personality type while another 20 percent were somewhat predisposed toward authoritarianism. The article, titled "Portrait of the Authoritarian Man," warned, "It is he, an anonymous fellow in the crowd, and not the dictator who menaces democracy."[10] These finding clearly suggested that it could happen here.

The goal of the *Studies in Prejudice* research project, however, was not just to understand the origins of intolerance and antisemitism but to seek ways to prevent it. In their foreword to *The Authoritarian Personality*, Horkheimer and Flowerman explain that the project's objective was to explain prejudice in order to eradicate it. Eradication, in turn, "means re-education, scientifically planned on the basis of [scientific] understanding."[11]

At times, the authors liken prejudice to a social disease that has symptoms and is in need of cure. *The Authoritarian Personality* suggests remedies. Instead of focusing on particular manifestations of group discrimination, Adorno and his coauthors argue, educators should focus on countering the dispositions linked to this personality type, including "stereotyp[ing], emotional coldness, identification with power, and general destructiveness."[12] Such interventions would help make people aware of the psychological and social forces that mold them.

These recommendations wove together overlapping currents that informed *The Authoritarian Personality* and the larger *Studies in Prejudice* project. Most immediately, the research was undertaken as part of a larger attempt to reckon with the origins of the Nazi atrocities and seek ways to prevent its recurrence. Even as the research project got underway, major human rights initiatives were being launched, including the 1948 promulgation of the Universal Declaration of Human Rights and the United Nations Genocide Convention, the establishment of the Nuremberg and Tokyo trials, and the 1946 creation of the UN Commission on Human Rights.

Against this backdrop, the American Jewish Committee, the sponsor of the study, was concerned with combating antisemitism, which was conceptualized more broadly in terms of bigotry, ethnocentrism, and prejudice. Launched at a 1944 workshop, the *Studies in Prejudice* project brought together more empirically oriented US social scientists with critical theorists from the Frankfurt School.

Flowerman, the series coeditor, was particularly interested in improving the efficacy of efforts to combat prejudice, which he conceptualized as the "antidote" of "mass protolerance propaganda." Such propaganda, Flowerman argued in a journal article, might ideally be used to "modify the standards of the in-group" and change "anti-tolerance group values"—even if this was very difficult to do.[13]

Ironically, contemporary white power extremists point to such statements as proof that Flowerman, the Frankfurt School, and other Jewish "cultural Marxists" were secretly plotting to destroy white culture and identity.[14] In response, white power extremists see themselves as engaged in a race war being fought on a "metapolitical" level that will reveal the truth of this attempt at "white genocide" and mainstream their white power views. They sometimes refer to this process as changing "the narrative" or shifting the "Overton window," a metaphor coined by conservative analyst Joseph Overton to refer to altering the boundaries of cultural language and public opinion and thereby bringing into the mainstream ideas and policies that were previously considered fringe or unacceptable.[15] I discuss this white power "metapolitical" battle later in this book.

Like the American Jewish Committee and Flowerman, the Frankfurt School participants shared a concern with combating prejudice through cognitive and emotional restructuring. But they ultimately approached this objective from a different direction, critical theory. Just a few years earlier, Horkheimer and Adorno had published *Dialectic of Enlightenment*.[16] This landmark volume argued that, far from being an aberration, fascist authoritarianism was an outcome of the instrumental reason that drove the Enlightenment.

If reason could liberate (through critique, demystification, and enhanced self-awareness, autonomy, and creativity), it could also dominate through an ordering impulse that extended not just to the natural world but to human beings who were subject to categorization, administration, mediation, standardization, commodification, and alienation. This dominating tendency of instrumental reason, manifest in capitalism, bureaucracy, popular culture, and science, had been taken to an extreme by the Nazis even as it was a fundamental part of modern society—including its expression in antisemitism.

For Horkheimer and Adorno, then, the authoritarian personality was not exceptional but a reflection of domination and ultimately rooted in history and social structure. As Adorno put it in a chapter he wrote for *The Authoritarian Personality*, "The world in which we live is typed and 'produces' different 'types' of persons. Only by identifying stereotypical traits in modern humans . . . can the pernicious tendency toward all-pervasive classification and subsumption be challenged" through interventions that enable people to recognize and resist their "standardization."[17] Adorno expanded on such comments in "Remarks" that were not included in the volume, perhaps because of his view that, more than being the outcome of personality predispositions, fascism and intolerance were related to the social and economic forces that produced such forms of "blind" subjectivity.

Although revolutionary change to the social order was unlikely, it was possible to make modest interventions to combat this "blindness" and "ticket" thinking by increasing critical self-awareness. Education was essential in this regard, as Horkheimer and Flowerman's foreword to *The Authoritarian Personality* had underscored by linking explanation to "eradication" via "re-education" that effected change on the "personal and psychological levels."

Adorno elaborated on these ideas in "Education after Auschwitz," an essay based on a 1966 radio broadcast that opened with the line, "The premier demand upon all education is that Auschwitz not happen again."[18] Prevention first required understanding and then raising awareness about the mechanisms that led to the Nazi horrors. Such educational efforts would lead to "critical self-reflection" and awareness that would help people resist the social forces that dominated their lives and could result in "blind identification with the collective" and fascist totalitarianism. "The single genuine power standing against the principle of Auschwitz," Adorno argued, "is autonomy . . . the power of reflection, of self-determination, of not cooperating."[19]

Although couched in the language of critical theory, Adorno's essay takes up a number of themes from *The Authoritarian Personality*, ranging from emotional coldness to thoughtlessness. Indeed, *The Authoritarian Personality* spawned an enormous amount of research, becoming

a foundational text in fields like political psychology. It also had its critics, including those who, overlooking the less obvious critical theory
inflections of the book, critiqued it for psychological reductionism.[20]

More broadly, the idea of the "authoritarian" or "fascist" personality
has also had a public life, surfacing in response to charged historical moments such as McCarthyism, the Cold War, the rise of far-right populists
like George Wallace, the Vietnam War, and Nixon's impeachment.[21] In
such popular usages, the idea of authoritarianism (suggesting central-
ized elite control with severely restricted freedoms) often mixes with
fascism (suggesting militaristic far-right ultranationalism promising renewal) and totalitarianism (suggesting authoritarian control over most
aspects of a society) and is used to characterize regimes on both the
Right and the Left, including "left-wing authoritarian" socialist governments like the Khmer Rouge regime in Cambodia.

As Adorno himself had noted, such terms are often deployed with a
"democratic bias" that, in the US context, dovetails with American exceptionalism to suggest that mass human rights violations occur in these
sorts of regimes, not liberal democracies.[22] As this book underscores
and Nuon Chea's remarks about the US carpet-bombing of Cambodia
suggest, this is clearly not the case.

* * *

Not surprisingly, these notions—and especially the fascist trope—gained
new currency with the rise of Trump, whose path to power was very
much intertwined with demagoguery, hate speech, the demonization of
nonwhite others, and the increased visibility of neofascists and other
white power actors who supported him.

Days before the Vienna campaign rally, Trump came under fire after
asking supporters at a rally to raise their right hands and pledge their
votes, an action reminiscent of the Nazi salute. "This Donald Trump
Rally Looks like a Scene from Nazi Germany," headlined a *Huffington
Post* story. Others focused on Trump's animus toward nonwhites, with

some likening his proposed Muslim ban to Hitler's treatment of Jews. On March 11, National Public Radio dubbed the Trump-Hitler comparison the "#MemeOfTheWeek."[23]

Meanwhile, *Time* magazine featured a black-and-white photograph of Trump's face on its cover with a row of checked boxes placed just beneath Trump's eyes: "Bully." "Showman." "Party Crasher." "Demagogue." Trump stares, stern, but with a trace of a smirk. A fifth box, "the 45th President of the United States," remained unchecked.

Amid the controversy, critics were checking different boxes in their minds: "racist," "Nazi," "fascist," "Hitler." Donald Trump: the anti-Obama. His candidacy hinted at what had seemed unimaginable just months before. White power. Extremist hate. Openly expressed and in the streets. The seeds of Charlottesville.

Trump played directly to white power sentiments and beliefs ("this is our country"), sometimes with hypermasculine and misogynistic language that valorized white male virility and idealized female beauty and sexuality. Even before becoming president, Trump repeatedly objectified women, as his infamous "grab 'em by the pussy" remark underscores. He has been accused of sexual misconduct and assault.[24] And on many occasions, Trump has demeaned women on the basis of their appearance and bodies, referring to them as "pigs," "disgusting animals," and "dogs."

Sometimes he has done so in racially inflected ways. If he famously referred to former Miss Universe Alicia Machado as "Miss Housekeeping" (invoking a stereotype of Latinas as housekeepers) and "Miss Piggy" (a comment on her body), Trump later doubled down by calling her "disgusting" while simultaneously invoking her sexuality (claiming she was in a sex tape and had "a past"). Trump's comments conjured the stereotype of hypersexual Latina women in particular and hypersexual—and by implication more emotional and less rational—people of color in general.[25] Machado, in turn, referred to Trump as a Nazi and alleges he sought to have sex with her while she was a teenager.

More broadly, Trump has aligned himself with light-skinned feminine beauty. He has dated and married actresses and models. He re-

quired his female staff to "dress like a woman."[26] His wives, past and present, have blonde hair or Eastern European ancestry, both of which are idealized by white power actors.

In such respects, Trump's asserted hypermasculinity dovetailed with the white power gender ideology that posits essentialized differences between men and women. For some, such as the Proud Boys and other "alt-lite" white power groups, gender differences are often construed in patriarchal, heteronormative terms, with men and women having their "natural roles."[27] From this perspective, feminism has led women astray—a notion that is taken to an extreme by highly misogynistic male empowerment groups like the "incels" (involuntary celibates).

While also informed by such gender essentialism, other white power extremists seek to regulate the white female body to ensure that white women fulfill their "duty" of propagating an imperiled white race.[28] Male white power actors, in turn, are positioned as the guardians of this white female purity (and therefore race survival) and charged with protecting white women from threats ranging from predatory Black and Brown male others to Jewish-orchestrated plots to enable race mixing and miscegenation. "The Snake" played directly on such gender essentialism and racial fears as an unprotected and innocent woman is violated by a dangerous predator representing, in Trump's framing, non-white immigrants.

As we shall see, these sorts of gender concerns are among a number of white power grievances to which Trump spoke and part of the reason many white power extremists and male-empowerment groups supported him. Already, in the summer of 2015, the neo-Nazi editor of the *Daily Stormer* website, Andrew Anglin, had backed Trump. Anglin was joined in his endorsement by KKK leaders David Duke and Thomas Robb and a growing number of other white power extremists.[29]

They often appeared at Trump's rallies, where Trump sometimes read "The Snake." There were moments of real or potential violence between such Trump supporters and protesters, often cast in racial hues of white versus Black and Brown. In the past, politicians, left and right, would call for such violence to stop. Trump egged it on. "Knock the crap out of them," Trump urged at one rally, then offered, "I'll pay the lawsuits." White power extremists were directly involved.

While overt violence was episodic and minor, Trump's strategic use of hate speech, which helped incite it, was constant in his campaign. As illustrated by the Vienna rally, Trump's rhetoric often pandered to white socioeconomic anxieties, which found targets such as "illegal aliens," Latino rapists and murderous gangs, and Muslim terrorists.

This sort of incitement had been a focus of my three and a half days of testimony at the Khmer Rouge tribunal as well. It connects Trump, white power extremism in the United States, and the Khmer Rouge regime through the politically savvy use of hate speech and its shadow, fear mongering. Both Trump and the Khmer Rouge used a common extremist formula. Inflame grievances. Cast blame. Name targets. Legitimate a new political order. Claim it will defeat the bad in the name of the good while righting wrongs. The lessons of the past teach us about this formula, which has long been used by populists, demagogues, and fomenters of violence—including figures like Hitler, Mao, Stalin, and Pol Pot, who committed some of the worst crimes in history.

Of course, extremists operate on a spectrum: Trump's MAGA with its imagined enemy, nonwhite "snakes"; the white power apocalyptic vision and desire for racial purity and survival; and the Khmer Rouge revolution and attempt to turn the wheel of history and reinvent society even as it was threatened by a host of imagined enemies. As president, Trump was a man of moderate ambition compared to ideologues like Pol Pot and Hitler. Nevertheless, he pandered to white power interests, a situation that could have had disastrous consequences—even genocidal ones—if circumstances had fully aligned.[30] That is a key first lesson from this book and the warning in its title, which echoes Lewis.

Indeed, during Trump's campaign and especially after his unexpected election, there was also a dramatic resurgence of interest in Lewis's book and the question it poses—as well as thematically related books such as *The Authoritarian Personality*, George Orwell's *1984*, and Hannah Arendt's *Origins of Totalitarianism*.[31] Some drew connections between Windrip's League of Forgotten Men and the "forgotten" Trump voters who cheered so loudly at his rallies. Others noted the similarities between Trump's more extreme supporters—including contemporary white power groups holding extremist beliefs that echo the 1930s Silver Shirts—and Windrip's Minute Men. Many more made a straightforward link between Trump and Windrip in terms of their authoritarian tendencies, populism, and inflammatory oratory—the sort on display in Vienna, Ohio. Such concerns were greatly amplified by the August 11–12, 2017, "Unite the Right" rally in Charlottesville.

* * *

Charlottesville looms large in this book. Many people had been shocked by Trump's election in 2016. The first African American president, who supposedly signaled a postracial age, was being replaced by a man who trafficked in fear and hate. Just months after Trump's inauguration, white supremacists, neo-Nazis, Christian Identitarians, and the Klan were massed, torches in hand, chanting "Blood and Soil!" and "Jews will not replace us!" The Unite the Right marchers clashed with counterprotesters. Fists flew, then finally bodies, as James Alex Fields smashed his car into a crowd, killing Heather Heyer and injuring dozens.

If dramatic, this event, like Trump's election, was nevertheless dismissed as an aberration—the momentary appearance of haters who did not represent the real United States. This book argues that this view has it backwards. Rather than being exceptional, these events are symptoms of a reality most people do not want to face: the United States is a postgenocidal country long premised on systemic white supremacy that continues in the present and creates the potential for further atrocity crimes. Awareness of this fact has been pushed out of sight by political obfuscation, assumptions about "American exceptionalism" and the "postracial society," and the reductive lens through which white power extremism is filtered.

Too often, white power actors are dismissed as "racists," "neo-Nazis," and "haters." These individualizing discourses divert attention from the structural dimensions of white power extremism, including its relation to history, structural inequality, systemic white supremacy, and the country's brutal past. The United States was founded on genocide. It has repeatedly committed atrocity crimes. And there is a high likelihood that such violence will occur here again, a point the Trump presidency underscored as a symptom—not an exception. This book makes the case as its title teases: it can happen here. This ongoing danger, this book contends, is a key lesson we learned from the Trump presidency.

Indeed, the motif of lessons learned directly informs the structure of this book. Narratively, the book is centered around my experience of teaching during Trump's presidency at one of the most diverse universities in the country. The students in my classes on genocide, mass violence, and human rights, many of whom experience racism regularly, considered the questions that were being asked throughout the country after Charlottesville. How do you ascertain the truth in the face of lies and distortions of the sort Trump made by claiming that there were "very fine people on both sides" at Charlottesville? Who are the white power extremists who suddenly became visible in Trump's USA, and how do they fit into the country's history of systemic white supremacy? Given Trump's seeming support and the white genocide frame that drives many of these actors, could it happen here? If so, how can genocide and atrocity crimes be prevented? And what can we do as individuals and as a society?

The book's penultimate chapter is framed around the November 2018 verdict in Nuon Chea's trial, which I attended, and President Trump's politics of fear ahead of the 2018 midterm elections, which included warnings of nonwhite immigrant "infestations." With this backdrop in mind, it considers different prevention strategies. Some interventions, like the Khmer Rouge tribunal, are more long-term, including education, memorialization, accountability, and projects of redress. Reparations or a truth commission, I note, could be used to address the history of white supremacy and settler-colonial genocide in the United States. Other interventions are more proximate, such as those that seek to turn people from extremism through methods ranging from dialogue and deradicalization to exposure and financial sanctions.

In undertaking these considerations, this book also explores the global dimensions of the white power movement, in which white genocide fears loom large. If the Trump presidency underscored the fact that there is an ongoing risk of genocide and atrocity crimes, I conclude by noting that there are multiple strategies that can be used to prevent this from happening, including, as Adorno had emphasized, genocide education of the sort I used in my classes while teaching during the Trump presidency.

The book also delineates the qualities of moral compass: Discernment, Orientation, Perspective, Prudence, and the center rose of the Awareness of Grace. Each dimension helps restore the rich context that is stripped away by the abstract, violent ideologies of extremists and that is necessary to understand a situation and envision paths forward. This emphasis on awareness and critical reflection, I note, resonates with the work of the Frankfurt School. The idea of moral compass, informed by the lessons of the past and demanding moral imagination in the face of impending atrocity crimes, backlights the book's argument that "it can happen here."

To underscore this point, the volume finishes with a discussion of the "bird-in-the-hand" parable that Toni Morrison, who died the day after Nuon Chea in August 2019, recounted during her 1993 Nobel Prize speech. Her metaphor and emphasis on dialogue, tolerance, and the consideration of alternative perspectives serves as a concluding juxtaposition and counter to Trump's campaign rendition of "The Snake," the moment with which the book begins.

The theme of lessons is woven into the book's narrative structure and overarching "it can happen here" argument. In several respects, it echoes the idea of lessons implicit in the Frankfurt School's critical theory approach to *The Authoritarian Personality*, one made explicit in Adorno's

"Education after Auschwitz" radio address and essay. On the one hand, I discuss the "mechanisms" that cause genocide and atrocity crimes as well as how an understanding of them can be used as a diagnostic and to help prevent recurrence—all key goals of the Frankfurt School and reflected by the mechanisms-education-prevention triad they espoused.

On the other hand, the "lessons" of *It Can Happen Here* are likewise informed by a critical approach that begins with the unpacking of a "Charlottesville Teach-In" I taught and continues with examination of the historical and social forces underlying Charlottesville, including systemic white supremacy and the white genocide frame. As noted above, the concluding discussion of moral compass and individual awareness very much dovetails with the ethical and self-reflexive concerns of Adorno and his colleagues.

The motif of lessons is also reflected by some of the disciplinary literatures that inform this book. It is written within the tradition of comparative Holocaust and genocide studies with its assumption that the lessons of the past have relevance for the present, a point underscored by my testimony at Nuon Chea's trial. This comparative interest intersects with my professional discipline of anthropology, which is comparative and, like the Frankfurt School, has long combated ethnocentrism and racism with research and pedagogy.

Finally, much of this book is written in lesson form. In response to Charlottesville, I changed my teaching, reworking my classes to explore the interconnections of genocide, race, and white power extremism. The chapters of this book are set in the classroom and discuss the questions and issues my students raised as they sought to understand Charlottesville, Tree of Life, and other expressions of racism and hate that were spiking in Trump's USA. Drawing on my syllabi, notes, and recollections, I recount these conversations in first-person narrative and dialogic form while masking the identity of my students, given the sensitive topic.

The answers that emerge from these lessons from Trump's USA are deeply troubling. There are white power extremists in the United States who, to prevent what they refer to as "white genocide," are preparing for a race war and willing to perpetrate ethnic cleansing and the mass murder of Jews and people of color. Rather than being exceptional, their views are continuous with and reflect, albeit in extreme form, a long tradition of white supremacy. Millions of people in the United States sympathize with this white power perspective, one that has been mainstreamed through coded language used by conservative media hosts and far-right politicians.

The Trump presidency underscored how readily white-power-extremist interests can align with the levers of power. Indeed, Trump directly appealed to the white power movement through inflammatory racial allusions, hate speech, populism, and anti-immigration policy, even as he openly admired demagogues and eroded democratic safeguards. As a result, the threat of genocide and atrocity crimes spiked during Trump's presidency even as it continued into the future. This book makes the case, chronicles the moment, and sounds the alarm. It has happened here before. It came close to happening during the Trump presidency. Some say it did happen on the southern border. And it can happen again. Indeed, genocide and atrocity crimes often stand just one crisis away.

1

Charlottesville Teach-In

I see the hater.

There's a torch in his hand, rage in his eye. "Jews will not replace us!" he and his fellow marchers scream from my computer screen. "Blood and Soil!" "White Lives Matter!" One wears a "Radical Agenda" shirt. He is packing guns and knives—as well as lots of hate. Fists fly, then clubs, and finally bodies, a person killed by a car, dozens injured, and a nation in shock.

The Unite the Right rally. A new stain on US history. Charlottesville transforms the conversation about race and hate in Trump's USA. It is also a moment that underscores just how relevant the lessons of the past are to the present. Charlottesville catalyzes my decision to write this book. It also changes my teaching as I consider, *How do you teach in Trump's USA?* The next four chapters, set in the classroom, relate my answer.

* * *

Roughly two years after the Khmer Rouge tribunal contacted me about testifying at Nuon Chea's trial, I receive another e-mail summons. This one, which arrives on the last day of August as I am finalizing the syllabus for my Fall 2017 course on Human Rights in a Global World, comes from the president of my discipline's largest scholarly organization, the American Anthropological Association (AAA). "It is a most maddening and deplorable fact of our times," the message reads, "that in 2017 there is still the need to denounce the symbolic and physical violence of white supremacists, neo-Nazis, the Ku Klux Klan, the 'alt-right,' and their sympathizers in the seats of power, on the streets or wherever they may be. Yet this is what we are up against."

"We call on each and every AAA member," the message continues, "to participate in a collective action to stand up for a just world in the weeks leading up to Monday, September 18, 2017, when we will hold 'Understanding Race after Charlottesville,'" a collaboration with the national academic history and sociology associations. The goal of the initiative, the message states, is to provide "accurate information and knowledge" necessary for a just world, especially with regard to race, since there is a "state of utter confusion being promulgated by the least responsible of leadership and disseminated by the least accountable of sources."

The message is referring in part to Trump's statement that there are "very fine people on both sides" of Charlottesville, which suggests a moral equivalence between the white power actors and counterprotesters. While Trump claims he is referring to "innocent" people protesting the removal of Charlottesville's Robert E. Lee statue, his message also suggests his approval of white power extremists, as they clearly recognize.[1]

To change the narrative, Trump seeks to "gaslight," or manipulate popular perception of the racialized reality of Charlottesville by mixing truth (the ostensible protest of the statue's removal and the involvement of Antifa, or loosely organized and sometimes militant antifascist activists)[2] with distortions and lies (the clear white power focus of the event evident in its "Unite the Right" title, the large number of white power extremists present, and the event's connection to a long history of racism and white supremacy in the United States).[3]

It is the same tactic of denial Nuon Chea used, one the American Anthropological Association is asking its members to critically examine. Indeed, truth, moral compass, human dignity, and combating hate are at stake in this post-Charlottesville moment, just as they were at Nuon Chea's trial. Once again, I am being summoned to make a small contribution to help set the record straight, this time in the classroom without cameras, media, or a livestream. My class will have to grapple with the issue of truth from the start.

* * *

Trump had been distorting and denying the truth for years. His early political rise was bound up with a major lie, "birtherism," as Trump repeatedly questioned whether President Obama was born in the United States.[4] Birtherism played to white power actors and others who regarded Obama's presidency as a symbol of white displacement.[5]

The birtherism "controversy" presaged what was to come. Trump's obsession with undoing Obama's policies and his anti-immigrant rhetoric pandered to white power undercurrents in the United States, part of Trump's larger populist messaging that harped on themes of socioeconomic dispossession and victimization by allegedly threatening Black and Brown others.

Trump had learned that populism, distortion, and lying are politically effective, particularly in a news cycle he can move at a blistering pace, trading controversy for headlines and vice versa, one after another. His presidency had begun on this note with the controversy about his inauguration crowd size. Despite clear evidence that his crowd was smaller than Obama's, Trump insisted on the opposite.

His advisor Kellyanne Conway explained that the White House had a set of "alternative facts."[6] On *Meet the Press*, Chuck Todd told her, "Alternative facts are not facts. They are falsehoods." But she had introduced a euphemism for lying into the US political lexicon.

And indeed, sales of George Orwell's *1984* surged in the wake of her comments.[7] So, too, did interest in the work of philosopher Hannah Arendt. Arendt warned that assaults on the truth—like "gaslighting"—serve the interests of power and endanger a society by atomizing people and undermining the grounds upon which public dialogue takes place and critical judgment is made. "The result of a consistent and total substitution of lies for factual truth is not that the lies will now be accepted as truth, and truth be defamed as lies," she wrote in the shadow of Hitler,

Mussolini, and Stalin, "but that the sense by which we take our bearings in the real world—and the category of truth vs. falsehood is among the mental means to this end—is being destroyed."[8]

Conway's "alternative facts" dovetailed with Trump's increasing frequent dismissals of "fake news."[9] There was shock when, just a week before his inauguration, Trump told a CNN correspondent, "You're fake news,"[10] an act that foreshadowed his almost nonstop castigation of journalists and news outlets he views as adversarial. "Fake news" quickly became one of Trump's favorite terms, appearing often in his political rhetoric and presidential tweets. Soon Trump was tweeting "Fake News Awards," led by CNN and the "failing" *New York Times*. The phrase itself won a distinction: "fake news" was recognized as the 2017 *Collins Dictionary* word of the year.

Trump would take his demonization of perceived opposition media even further, labeling the "fake news" media "enemies of the people." Just a month after Conway invoked "alternative facts," Trump tweeted, "The FAKE NEWS media (failing @nytimes, @CNN, @NBCNews and many more) is not my enemy, it is the enemy of the American people. SICK!"[11]

Trump's use of this term shocked observers, who noted that the phrase "enemies of the people" had been invoked by Stalin to justify the repression and killing of political enemies. Mao and Pol Pot did the same. Even members of Trump's party became alarmed.

Republican senator Jeff Flake took to the Senate floor to warn about Trump's assault on the free press and the truth, including the use of terms like "alternative facts," "fake news," and "enemies of the people." "The President has it backward," Flake stated. "Despotism is the enemy of the people. The free press is the despot's enemy, which makes the free press the guardian of democracy."[12]

Trump's assault on the media had a pernicious effect, undermining a democratic safeguard and eroding public trust in the media. By April 2018, half of the Republicans interviewed viewed the media as "enemies of the people."[13] Trump, in turn, positioned himself as the teller of truth, the one who could combat the enemy "fake news" and provide the facts—despite his frequent use of distortion and denial. He dismissed any contravening narratives—allegations of Russian interference, the Mueller investigation, impeachment charges, and even the outbreak of the coronavirus—as a "hoax" or "witch hunt," positioning himself as the victim of lies and conspiracy. At the time of Charlottesville, Trump had made more than a thousand false or misleading claims since taking office—an already shocking statistic that would rise twentyfold by July 2020.[14]

* * *

SEPTEMBER 5, 2017, FIRST DAY OF CLASS, RUTGERS UNIVERSITY, NEWARK, NJ

How do you teach in Trump's USA? The first hurdle is to deal with this relentless assault on the truth. What is truth in a "post-truth" age?

Post-truth. The *Oxford English Dictionary* selected the term as its 2016 word of the year. An adjective, it denotes "circumstances in which objective facts are less influential in shaping public opinion than appeals to emotion and personal belief."[15] The stakes are high. Insipidly, the term suggests that the search for truth is fruitless, misguided, insignificant, or irrelevant. In its toxic form, the "post-truth" perspective lays the basis for denial and lies. Alternative facts. Fake news. Hoaxes. Enemies of the people.

My own pedagogy is well suited to grapple with such contentions and the issues they mask. First and foremost, I seek to teach students to think critically. My approach is partly informed by critical theory, and I sometimes assign Adorno's "Education after Auschwitz" to start classroom conversations regarding the importance of critical self-reflection and awareness about the social forces that shape our assumptions and identifications—and to underscore the dangers of remaining ignorant about them.

Such critical thinking can be difficult when passions run high and people have taken sharp sides. A number of universities lean to the left;

I teach at one that does so a bit more than most. Rutgers–Newark: the United States' most diverse national university for more than twenty years. It is evident each day I walk in the classroom. The undergraduate population is just under a quarter white, the majority Black and Brown. Many students and their families come from different parts of the globe.

This diversity is reflected by the larger Newark metropolitan area community. Indeed, New Jersey was one of the exit ramps off Ellis Island, a history that is in part responsible for the enormous diversity of surrounding parts of northern New Jersey. The chancellor has made it her mission to anchor the university in this urban context, a mission reflected in initiatives large and small.[16]

The diversity inflects many discussions, including those invoking a monolithic "us" or "we"—the sorts of pronouns politicians like to use. Indeed, the diversity offers a first quick path to critical thinking, destabilizing such taken-for-granted categories and offering a range of perspectives.

This diversity also offers an important perspective on politics in Trump's USA. Rutgers–Newark has a number of students enrolled in the Obama-era Deferred Action for Childhood Arrivals (DACA) program, which protects youths who entered the United States as undocumented immigrants from being deported. The university proclaimed its support for DACA students after their status and futures were threatened early in the Trump administration. Other students are from first- or second-generation immigrant families, including those from countries Trump has disparaged. Many students have grown up experiencing discrimination and racism in their daily lives.[17]

Forget "post-truth" for the moment. How does one even begin a classroom conversation about Trump's USA given such experiences, let alone the broader context of political polarization and sometimes outright hate?

Critical pedagogy provides one path forward, shifting discussion away from opinion and toward analysis. If the Frankfurt School was partly informed by Marxist thought, the larger method of critique is a tool that can be used broadly to examine the social structures and histories that shape our lives and subjectivities, particularly when the work of later critical theorists, who inflected critique in different directions, is kept in mind.[18]

The method of critique provides a way to take up not just identity issues like race, ethnicity, class, and gender but also phenomena such as colonialism, capitalism, bureaucracy, mass media, and so forth. For Horkheimer, Adorno, and the Frankfurt School, critique was emancipatory, providing a pathway to self-awareness, autonomy, and, when necessary, resistance. Their ideas about education influenced the field of critical pedagogy and the work of related scholars like Paolo Freire, Henry Giroux, bell hooks, and Gayatri Spivak, who reimagined education in ways that grappled with issues like imperialism, postcolonialism, Eurocentrism, Blackness, and gender that had not been a focus of the Frankfurt School.[19]

Ironically, and as noted earlier, white power extremists also sometimes deploy critical theory—and indeed the person who is the public face of the alt-right even wrote a master's thesis on Adorno—even as they deride members of the Frankfurt School as "cultural Marxists."[20] Their usage illustrates the point that people from a range of political perspectives can use the method of critique—even as Adorno and his colleagues would have viewed white-power-extremist attempts at critique as manifestations of the very sort of instrumental reasoning and "coldness" that produced the Holocaust.

With regard to the classroom, critical pedagogy focuses on analysis and thereby provides a space where people who have different opinions and political orientations may dialogue, particularly when such discussions proceed in a "warm" manner that is empathetic and predicated on respect for the dignity of others. The conversations may vary depending on class composition. Some students in a predominantly white classroom, for example, may be uncomfortable or even defensive when talking about systemic racism or the advantages and privileges of being identified as white in a supposedly color-blind and multicultural society.

In these different classroom contexts, "warmth" is one key strategy for teaching about charged issues like race in Trump's USA.

* * *

I begin the first class with critical thinking.

"Take out your pens, please," I ask my forty undergraduate students on the first day of class.

"What is critical thinking?" I continue, then add, "and don't worry—the assignment won't be graded!" We go through their answers. A hand rises. "It means 'thinking outside the box.'" Heads nod. "Examining the strengths and weaknesses of an argument," another student offers. And so the discussion continues.

"Critical thinking will be at the center of this class," I tell them. "We're going to focus on global human rights, but we'll also look at the connections to race and hate."

"So what's critical thinking?" a student suddenly asks.

"We'll discuss that throughout the semester," I reply. "But one way to start is with the origins of the word 'analysis.' It comes from a Greek term, *analusis*, meaning 'to unloosen.' Analysis involves an unraveling, taking something apart to understand how it is composed from its constituent parts."[21]

I hold up my fist. "Here's a way to visualize it." The students are quiet. I slowly open my fist, revealing the flat of my outstretched palm. "Critical thinking happens in the same way," I tell them. "It involves revealing what's taken for granted, masked, hidden, and assumed to be 'natural.' Critical thinking is about unpacking our tacit assumptions and always asking, 'Why?'"

I pause, let them consider the metaphor for a moment. "Critical thinking," I continue, "provides a path to greater autonomy and self-awareness. It involves examining your own biases and preconceptions, remaining open to alternative perspectives, and withholding judgment while you assess and seek to understand the backdrop of an idea, institution, practice, identity, or issue.

"It's important to also examine why and who gets to define the issue," I add. "Critical thinking involves being aware of power and persuasion, the propaganda and ideology that block things from sight, obscuring how what is viewed as 'natural' supports systems of power and domination, frequently in the name of 'the good.' That's often the case in genocide. It's also true of global human rights as well as race in the US.

"Do you see other connections to the world around you?" I ask.

"Fake news!" offers a student. "Charlottesville!" says another. One shouts, "Trump!"

"Those are all issues we're going to be exploring," I reply. "But we need space in the room for everyone to express their thoughts, including those who support President Trump." There is a pause; people look around.

"This isn't a class to argue about our different political opinions," I continue. "It's a place for analysis and critical thinking about some of the most important human rights issues of our day. We're going to hold a Charlottesville Teach-In the week after next, so we need to be able to have a civil conversation."

"What's a teach-in?" a student asks.

"That's a great question," I reply. "The idea was actually pioneered by an anthropologist as a form of engaged pedagogy during the antiwar protests of the 1960s. While it retains this sense of urgency and action, the term 'teach-in' is now used more generally to refer to a teaching unit used to raise awareness about a topic of public interest. I think of it as a class session that brings critical thinking to bear on the most urgent public issues of our day."[22]

"Like taking a deep dive behind the headlines," the student adds.

"Exactly," I respond, "and Charlottesville has certainly been dominating the news."

* * *

Critical thinking remains very much on my mind as, over the next two weeks, I develop the lesson plan for a "Charlottesville Teach-In" in response to the American Anthropological Association's (AAA) call for members to incorporate lessons on Charlottesville into their classes the week of September 18, 2017. I consider ways to link Charlottesville to my human rights course.

One connection is to examine how race and enslavement are bound up with the emergence of human rights, as a worldwide movement arose to ban the slave trade. I could also center our discussion on how white power is linked to long-standing debates in the United States about what it means to be both a person and a citizen, with rights long denied to women and nonwhites. Still another path could be to look at how, even as Eleanor Roosevelt and the United States were playing a key role in the promulgation of the 1948 Universal Declaration of Human Rights, Blacks in the United States suffered from Jim Crow, segregation, and discrimination.

Amid the post-Charlottesville confusion, the AAA is calling on its members to have "open and fact-based conversations about race" based on "accurate information and knowledge." The AAA summons adds, "Misinformation, disinformation, and distortion are the enemies of social justice."

I decide to focus my teach-in on Trump's controversial remarks about Charlottesville. The students will critically assess his "two sides" contention. The first step is to discuss critical thinking. The second is to consider what happened during Charlottesville, including the groups and people involved. This understanding can then be used to critically unpack Trump's remark and the complexities it obscures: white power extremism and ideas of race that informed "Unite the Right."

The AAA has created a website related to its initiative. Its resources are primarily related to race, ranging from the AAA Statement on Race to "An Introductory Guide to Teaching about Race after Charlottesville."[23] The guide suggests three key teaching objectives: "1. Introduce students to the biological myth of race and the facts about human variation. 2. Explain the historical construction of race in the United States. 3. Discuss how the historical framing of race has led to the creation and persistence of racism." Much of this material is covered in the AAA statement on race, which I assign along with a related online tutorial.

Less than a month out, Charlottesville has not yet been historicized, as will happen later. So the class reads newspaper summaries and background articles with titles like "Moments of Rupture: Confederate Monuments and a Southern Town's Search for Its Identity," "Why Richard Spencer Matters," "The People, Groups, and Symbols of Charlottesville," "What the Alt-Right Really Wants," and "Psychology of Hate: What Motivates White Supremacists." And so, two weeks after our initial discussion of critical thinking, our "Charlottesville Teach-In" begins.

* * *

TUESDAY, SEPTEMBER 19, 2017, RUTGERS UNIVERSITY, NEWARK, NJ

"How many of you have seen the *VICE News* video on Charlottesville?" I ask. A few students raise their hands. "We're going to start class with it before we open the discussion for today's teach-in on Charlottesville," I continue. "The reporter embedded with the white power marchers." I cue up "Charlottesville: Race and Terror" and press "Play."[24]

The documentary opens on the night before the official Unite the Right march as a column of white power extremists marches, torches in hand, toward a statue on the University of Virginia campus. "You will not replace us," they chant, their white faces stern.

When they arrive at the statue, the marchers, almost all of whom are white males, are met by a small group of counterprotesters. Their arms are locked as they encircle the statute. "VA Students Act Against White Supremacy" reads a sign. "No Nazis! No KKK! No Fascist USA!" the counterprotesters chant.

They are outnumbered by the white power marchers, who surround them. "Black Lives Matter!" the counterprotesters shout. "White Lives Matter!" the marchers respond. Some make monkey hoots as they glare at Black counterprotesters. Tensions rise, then there are punches and shoves, mace sprayed, and injuries. The police fail to intervene. And the formal Unite the Right protest is not even scheduled until the next day. A first skirmish with the promise of more to come.

The documentary shifts to an earlier interview the *VICE* reporter, Elle Reeve, did with one of the Unite the Right speakers, Christopher Cantwell. He wears a black t-shirt emblazoned with "RADICAL AGENDA," the name of the alt-right radio talk show he hosts with the same swagger he displays now.

"So how did you get into the racial stuff?" Reeve asks. "Little Black assholes behaving like a savage" is Cantwell's reply. He names Black shooting victims Trayvon Martin, Tamir Rice, and Michael Brown, whose August 2014 killing led to widespread protests after the police officer who fatally shot him was not indicted.[25] White people are different, Cantwell tells Reeve. Society needs to be accordingly arranged. And so the interview goes, watched by a small group of Cantwell's comrades.

Cantwell admits to being a racist. He says he likes Trump though he complains that Trump allowed "that Jewish bastard Kushner" to marry his beautiful white daughter. Cantwell adds, in passing, that he is currently armed. He wants a white ethnostate. A quick check of his past statements confirms that the views he is expressing are nothing new, as he has elsewhere complained, among other things, about the immigrant replacement of whites, the low IQ of Blacks, Jewish conspiracy, and a coming race war.[26]

The morning of the official march arrives, ostensibly a protest against Charlottesville's decision to remove a statue of Confederate general Robert E. Lee. The documentary's next scene opens with counterprotesters chanting, "We're here. We're gay. We fight the KKK." White power marchers retort, "Fuck you, faggots." One makes a white power ("WP") hand signal, which resembles the "okay" sign: three raised fingers making a "W" with the index finger and thumb pressed into a circle, representing the top of the letter "P."

Signs and symbols of hate and antihate are everywhere, with large numbers gathered on both sides. The students have been joined by Charlottesville residents, local activists, and antifascists. A church group sings "This Little Light of Mine," while white power marchers chant, "Our blood, our soil." Armed and in camouflage, a militia group arrives, claiming they have come to "keep the peace."[27]

"They're supposedly here to protest the removal of the statue of Robert E. Lee," Reeve says as the camera pans white power extremists in the crowd. They wear helmets and carry signs, shields, and flags. "But they're really here to show that they're more than an Internet meme. That they're a big real presence that can organize in physical space." Scuffling soon begins, as people hit each other with fists, poles, and clubs. There are more injuries. Cantwell pours milk over his face after being maced. "Commies!" he complains. "Heil Cantwell!" fellow marchers shout in support. The police again fail to intervene.

Meanwhile, Reeve piles into a van with Cantwell and others as they head to Emancipation Park, the site of their rally. She turns and interviews Robert Ray (aka "Azzmador"), a feature writer for the popular neo-Nazi website, the *Daily Stormer*. "What do you hope to get out of today?" Reeve asks. Azzmador is ready with his reply. "Well, for one thing," he says, "it means that we're showing to this parasitic class of antiwhite vermin that this is our country. This country was built by our forefathers and sustained by us. And it's going to remain our country."

Azzmador speaks more excitedly. "We are stepping off the Internet in a big way. For instance, last night at the torch walk, there were hundreds and hundreds of us. People realize they are not atomized individuals. They are part of a larger whole." Like Cantwell, Azzmador stresses how their march reveals the scope and support for the white power movement. "We have been spreading our memes," Azzmador continues. "We have been organizing on the Internet. And so now they're coming out. And now, as you can see today, we greatly outnumbered the anti-white, anti-American filth." Azzmador concludes with a warning, shaking his finger in the air, "At some point, we will have enough power that we will clear them from the streets forever. That which is degenerate in white countries will be removed. . . . We're starting to slowly unveil a little bit of our power level. You ain't seen nothing yet."

The marchers soon learn that the Emancipation Park rally has been canceled. They are outraged. Former KKK grand wizard David Duke complains to Reeve that the organizers had a court order and speaking permits. "They don't want our speech because we're telling the truth about the ethnic cleansing of America and the destruction of the American way of life."

Matthew Heimbach, leader of the neo-Nazi Traditionalist Worker Party and another featured Unite the Right speaker, reports that the governor has declared a state of emergency. The decision, Heimbach tells Reeve, demonstrates that "the radical Left, the corporations, and the state are all on the same Jewish side." When Reeve asks about his group's organizational tactics, Heimbach replies that they are following the model of European white power groups "who are at the vanguard of nationalists organizing in the world." Heimbach adds, "This is the largest nationalist rally in over two decades in the United States. It's incredibly exciting."

After a segment that focuses on the car that struck counterprotesters, killing Heather Heyer and severely injuring others, the *VICE* video shifts to Trump's first response, given the day of the violence, when he states, "We condemn in the strongest possible terms this egregious display of hatred, bigotry and violence on many sides." He repeats, for emphasis, "on many sides." The controversy was immediate, leading him to issue a scripted response two days later, in which he denounced "the KKK, neo-Nazis, white supremacists and other hate groups."

Trump apparently regretted doing so, calling it "the biggest fucking mistake I've made."[28] And so, when a reporter asked why he had waited so long to make this denunciation, Trump replied angrily that his first statement "was a fine statement" that had been distorted by the "fake news." Later in the presser, Trump stated that there were "very fine people, on both sides," singling out those protesting the removal of the Robert E. Lee statue as opposed to "neo-Nazis and white nationalists" who, he said, should be condemned. Trump would then use the ambiguity of his statement to gaslight, saying he had responded "perfectly" while complaining of the "Charlottesville Hoax."

The next segment of the *VICE* documentary considers counterprotester responses to the violence. In a grass field, people light candles, lay flowers, and speak during a healing ceremony. "I have a great-grandfather who has literally told me the same stories as what I've experienced here today," a Black student activist states. He is appalled by Trump's remarks that fail to condemn Unite the Right marchers, including people Trump "has notably and knowingly incited."

Others express their outrage at City Hall, as Jason Kessler, one of the co-organizers of Unite the Right, readies to give a statement complaining that the white power marchers' First Amendment rights had been violated. "Shame!" people in the crowd chant. Some give him the finger. One yells, "Filth!" A group slowly approaches, encircling Kessler. "Indict for murder now," screams a man. Another person throws a punch and Kessler flees, state police protecting him. "Nazi go home!" the crowd chants.

The documentary concludes with an interview at Cantwell's hotel. "So I came pretty well prepared for this thing today," Cantwell says to Reeve with a chuckle as he begins tossing guns on the bed: an AK rifle, then 9mm handguns, including one strapped to his lower leg. "Oh, and here's a knife." Cantwell tells Reeve that the marchers were restrained. Heyer's death was unfortunate but the justified result of a man terrified when "animals attacked him." The video concludes with Cantwell noting the high rates of Black crime, a reason the marchers want a white homeland. Next to Cantwell, a computer screen displays a swastika.

* * *

"So how do you explain Charlottesville?" I ask the class as I flip on the lights.

"Cantwell's a sick dude!" a student offers. The remark breaks the ice, generates light laughter. The hatred in the video was hard to watch.

"Didn't he break down and cry?" another student asks, referencing a short video Cantwell had posted shortly after Charlottesville in which he sobs as he tells viewers that his group had followed the law and yet he now faced arrest. The fearsome face of white power hate at Charlottesville gained a new nickname, the "Crying Nazi."

"Was President Trump right?" I ask as our conversation turns to our first key unpacking. "What did he mean when he said that there are 'two sides to a story' and that people weren't paying attention to the fact there were good and bad people on both sides of the Charlottesville conflict?"

"Good ol' Robert E. Lee," a student replies, sardonic. "Trump wants to focus on that racist statue and the 'peaceful' marchers. I didn't see any."

"Why is the statue 'racist' and what's the dispute about?" I ask. "Critical thinking involves historicizing and unpacking. So when and why was the statue built, and why is it controversial now?"

We turn to the readings.[29] Originally commissioned in 1917, Charlottesville's towering Robert E. Lee memorial was built in 1924 as a tribute to the legendary Confederate general. At a March 2016 press conference—set amid a larger national debate about Confederate flags and monuments sparked in part by Dylann Roof's attack on a Black church in South Carolina the year before—Charlottesville's African American vice-mayor called for the statue to be removed. A special commission recommended relocation or signage with historical contextualization. In February 2017, the City Council voted to remove the Lee statue and change the name of Lee Park to Emancipation Park.

Lawsuits and demonstrations followed, with Charlottesville resident and white power extremist Jason Kessler leading the charge and accusing the vice-mayor of anti-white bias. Kessler and Richard Spencer—the alt-right leader known, among other things, for his "Hail Trump" salute after Trump's election—held a May 13 rally that included shouts of "Jews will not replace us." The KKK held one of their own in July that was met by a strong counterprotest and injuries.

Prior to Unite the Right, then, the "two sides" Trump was foregrounding were already visible. On the one side stood heritage and history advocates, who argued that the statue should not be taken down because it was part of history or southern heritage. Some had strong white power leanings, others less so. These were the "innocent protesters" and "fine people" Trump sought to highlight. He pointed to the "quiet" Friday night march as proof, ignoring the Nazi-like torches, hateful chants, and violence that became iconic images of Charlottesville.

The other "fine people" Trump referenced may have included church groups, local residents, students, civil rights advocates, and antiracism activists.[30] Trump said little about them so it is hard to know. Instead, he focused on their counterparts, "the alt-left," presumably Antifa, Black Lives Matter activists, and anarchists. Dressed in black, Trump stated, these violent "troublemakers," who were "very, very violent," had charged the Unite the Right marchers while "swinging clubs" and baseball bats.

If, in his scripted comments, Trump condemned the violence and hate of the neo-Nazis and white supremacists who were among the heritage and history advocates, he excoriated the alt-left. And it was true that Antifa was present and fought with the Unite the Right marchers, just as they often clash with white power extremists. Even as Trump condemned the "alt-left," a term he did not define, Trump questioned the use of "alt-right," challenging a journalist at the press conference to "define 'alt right' to me." When a reporter tried to speak, Trump chastised, "I'm not finished, fake news."

"There's blame on both sides," Trump emphasized before defending the marchers by asking if statues of George Washington and Thomas Jefferson, who also owned slaves, should be taken down. Trump's moral equivalency argument was complete. He had even turned the tables, suggesting the marchers had good cause while the alt-left had precipitated the conflict with their "charge" and did not even have a permit.

"So is President Trump correct that there was equal blame on both sides?" I ask the class.

"Look at who organized the rally!" a student says. "That guy Cantwell was involved."

"If it was about history," another student notes, "why didn't they just call it the 'Lee Statue Rally' instead of 'Unite the Right'?"

As the students parse the threads of Trump's argument, it unravels, revealing a gaslighting attempt forged from truth and lies. Trump's suggestion that, some bad apples aside, there were many "very fine people" among the Unite the Right marchers ignored basic facts about the event's objectives and composition. It was organized by white power extremists—not a local historical society or branch of the United Daughters of the Confederacy. The lead co-organizers identified as alt-right, an umbrella term referring to those who reject traditional conservatism in favor of white identity politics inflected through the lens of race and civilization.[31] Those identifying as alt-right include many younger, educated white males who dress well and use the Internet and social media to interact and promote their views.

Unite the Right, as several marchers had suggested on the *VICE* video, was their breakout moment. Richard Spencer, the rally co-organizer and a graduate of the University of Virginia, is said to have coined the term "alternative right" in 2008. A believer in racial difference and the greatness of Western civilization, Spencer inveighs against the threat posed by immigration, multiculturalism, and political correctness. He calls for the creation of a white ethnostate.

Spencer and the alt-right fall in the middle of a spectrum of far-right extremist orientations, which ranges from the more explicitly racist and violent ideas expressed by KKK, Christian Identity, skinhead, and neo-Nazis groups (who form what might be called the "hard far Right") to the softer and somewhat more politically palatable ideas promoted by the "alt-lite," which includes groups like the Proud Boys that, if at times expressing views that overlap with those of the alt-right, more often focus on white pride, heritage, immigration, and fighting political correctness.

As the *Daily Stormer*'s Azzmador noted, all of these groups now mobilize and propagate on the Internet. Besides utilizing websites, podcasts, and social media, the far Right at times finds sympathy with more mainstream media outlets like *Breitbart*, which openly embraces alt-right views, and political actors such as its former executive chairman,

Steve Bannon. And indeed, it is the softer ends of the far Right that most clearly intersected with the Trump administration—though Trump sent veiled messages to alt-right and other white power extremists as well.

Many of the featured speakers at Unite the Right identified as alt-right. But Unite the Right was explicitly meant to bring together a broad range of white power actors, including those warning of race war. Unite the Right rally posters were revealing in this regard. One played on Benjamin Franklin's famous "Join, or Die" cartoon, published in 1754. Meant to advocate for colonial unity, the cartoon depicts a snake cut into segments representing a colony or, in the case of the head, a region (New England). Below, a caption reads "JOIN, or DIE."

The Unite the Right poster version replaces the initials of the colonies with those of participating white-power-extremist groups, filling each segment with the group's logo or symbol. "A-R" (alt-right) is placed above the head of the snake, a sign of the movement's importance and leadership. It is followed by "N.S." (Nationalist Socialists, with the symbols of Vanguard America and the Traditionalist Worker Party), "S.N." (Southern Nationalist/League of the South), "I" (Identitarian/Identity Europa), "N." (Nationalist/White Nationalist), "L." (Libertarians), "A.C." (Anti-Communist Action), and "K." (Kekistani, with the flag echoing the Nazi war flag).[32]

While the poster refers to the event's location at Lee Park (the park's former name), it otherwise makes no mention of the Robert E. Lee statue. The emphasis is on unifying white power groups to take collective action and achieve common goals despite their differences—just as had been the case with the North American colonies. The primary goal of the rally, self-evidently stated in its name, was to unite white-power-extremist groups. The organizers and attendees stated this explicitly, as illustrated by comments made in the *VICE* video. While an issue of concern, the Robert E. Lee statue controversy was a pretext to achieve this primary and more important goal.

Trump ignored this critical fact even as he praised the Unite the Right marchers and suggested that their cause was noble. His message was clearly heard. After Trump's press conference, Richard Spencer, Andrew Anglin, David Duke, and other white power extremists applauded Trump not just for supporting their cause but for helping make its case by stressing the importance of white heritage and blaming the "alt-left" for the violence.

* * *

"Why is it important to think critically about President Trump's remarks on Charlottesville?" I ask next. Our classroom discussion becomes more heated.

"Because he's protecting racists," a student says, clearly frustrated. "The supremacists were making monkey hoots! And the guy with the guns called Blacks 'savages.'"

"It's awful," another student replies, "but they have free speech rights."

"What about when 'free speech' incites violence?" a third student asks. "Like when Trump uses racist language."

"Trump doesn't care about people who are Black and Brown," a different student contends. "He should be dealing with DACA students and the toxic water in Flint," which is majority Black.

Most of my students are speaking from experience. Racism is part of their lives just as it is for the Black community of Charlottesville. "This is the face of supremacy," a Charlottesville resident said during the *VICE* documentary. "This is what we deal with every day being African American. This has always been the reality." And indeed, it is a reality Trump's remarks mask, naturalizing assumptions about race, history, and white supremacy.

〜

We turn to a discussion of race, the focus of the second half of our critical-thinking Charlottesville Teach-In exercise. Monkey hoots were the tip of the iceberg. The language and symbols of racial hate were everywhere at Charlottesville, directed against immigrants, Blacks, and Jews.[33] Some of the symbols were neo-Nazi: the chants of "blood and soil," the torchlight procession, the use of the Nazi flag, colors, and symbols like the swastika, and, of course, the demonization of Jews. While some white power marchers obscured their hate in pseudo-intellectual language while wearing ties, other participants were direct. People affiliated with the neo-Nazi website *Daily Stormer*—named after the antisemitic Nazi journal *Der Stürmer*—provide an illustration.

Even before Azzmador, the *Daily Stormer* staff writer, ranted about race war in the *VICE* documentary, he and the website's founder, Andrew Anglin, posted a revealing message encouraging readers to join the website editors at Unite the Right.[34] Their messages on *Daily Stormer* inveighed against the machinations of the "evil Jew mayor and his Negroid Deputy," "the ruling kike/Negroid powers," and Black Lives Matter "baboons" and "denizens of dozens of monkey cages" planning a "chimpout." They used images to reinforce this language: a Unite the Right poster urging readers to help "end Jewish influence in America," a photo collage juxtaposing apes, Blacks, and Muslims ("Behold: the opposition!"), and a concluding black-and-white photo of Nazis with a "Hail Victory!" caption.

This *Daily Stormer* post also clearly stated the white power goals of the rally. If Unite the Right had initially involved the Lee statue, Azzmador and Anglin wrote, it had become a historic and unifying "rallying point and battle cry for the rising alt-right movement." Later the post added, "We are there for a fundamental reason: We must secure the existence of our people and a future for white children!" Beneath, a bronze poster emblazoned with this slogan featured an Aryan-like couple protecting their two small children with a swastika shield. A caption read, "Remember this, and let nothing get in the way of it."

~

"So it's clear that race was central to the language and symbols of the white power groups and actors in Charlottesville," I note in class. "But what, exactly, is race? And how is the idea of race related to racism? What do today's readings say?"

The students have reviewed the American Anthropology Association's (AAA) online module, "RACE: Are We So Different?" and read the AAA "Statement on Race."[35] Anthropology has a complicated relationship to race. If anthropology emerged amid Enlightenment attempts to understand human similarity and difference during New World explorations, this disciplinary endeavor also helped legitimate colonial rule through the classification of human diversity in hierarchical racial terms—the same ones the white power extremists at Charlottesville assume are real.

Such notions of racial hierarchy sometimes drew on earlier ideas about the "Great Chain of Being" and later the concept of biological evolution to argue that groups evolved from "primitive" to "civilized." This idea helped legitimate the "civilizing mission" in which the disempowerment and enslavement of "savages" was justified in the name of uplift and natural order. In the second half of the nineteenth century, race was increasingly biologized, as scientific racism held that each race had different characteristics, inclinations, and aptitudes. Drawing on Darwinian notions, some scholars argued that human races, like other species, are locked in a competition for survival.

If early anthropologists were involved in the formation and institutionalization of racism, others were among the first to argue that race was a social construct, a mobilization of "nature" used to support white-supremacist ideology and rule. Anthropologist Franz Boas and his students, Margaret Mead among them, argued that human behavior was determined by language and culture, not race. "Given what we know about the capacity of normal humans to achieve and function within any culture," the AAA statement my students read emphasizes, "we conclude that present-day inequalities between so-called 'racial' groups are not consequences of their biological inheritance but products of historical and contemporary social, economic, educational, and political circumstances."[36]

While anthropologists have done important work demonstrating the social construction of race, however, they have less frequently explored the issue of white power. There is little ethnographic research on white power movements in the United States, with somewhat more focus on European far-right groups. And there has been too little consideration of how white power, past and present, is global, colonial, and systemic and even informs contemporary anthropology and other academic disciplines.[37]

In the United States, ideas of race were woven into a racist ideology used to legitimate enslavement, a socioeconomic institution that came with a host of derogatory caricatures asserting the lower intelligence and more animalistic "nature" of nonwhites. Native Americans, Blacks, and, later, immigrants were imagined through this racial lens, informing stereotypes ranging from savage Indian "redskins" to the "Yellow Peril" threat allegedly posed by Asian groups like Chinese immigrant laborers in the late nineteenth century.

Perhaps most perniciously, these white-supremacist ideas were applied to Blacks to legitimate their servitude, first through enslavement and then through Jim Crow and segregation. They are also the source of some of the hate language and symbolism invoked by white power extremists in Charlottesville, including the monkey hoots directed at Black counterprotesters. This racist monkey trope has deep roots in US history, simultaneously asserting the animalistic inferiority and "bestial" threat of Blacks, ideas also expressed through related caricatures of Blacks as "coons," "golliwogs," "rapist brutes," "pickaninnies," and more.[38] Jews are the other group white power actors extensively target with racist stereotypes, even if such vitriol is also often directed against Muslims, immigrants, and members of the Latinx and queer communities.

Such racist caricatures do not just circulate in the extremist fringes. They can be seen on driveway lawns and in movies, and they appear in casual conversation at the highest political levels—such as when Ronald Reagan referred to Africans as "monkeys" in a 1971 phone call with Richard Nixon, who laughed in response.[39] Nixon himself, like earlier US presidents, did much the same. Woodrow Wilson, who held a range of bigoted views, even screened the notoriously racist film *Birth of a Nation* in the White House.

Such racist tropes are sometimes publicly invoked by politicians, albeit usually indirectly through "dog whistles" or coded racial allusions.[40] GOP gubernatorial candidate Ron DeSantis's 2018 "monkey this up" comment, made in reference to his Black Democratic opponent, Andrew Gillum, provides one illustration of such a racist dog whistle. But there are many more examples, including Trump's use of "Pocahontas" to refer to Senator Elizabeth Warren, his suggestion that prominent Blacks like Don Lemon, LeBron James, and Maxine Waters lack intelligence, and his references to "shithole" countries, "rat-infested" US cities, and warnings about Latinx criminals and rapists as well as a southern border "infestation."[41]

Trump's gaslighting of Charlottesville, in turn, demonstrates his alignment with the white power cause—as white power extremists have openly remarked. It also served to mask and naturalize white supremacy and racism. By suggesting that the Unite the Right marchers had just come for a heritage and history protest, Trump further obscured the primary white-power-extremist focus of the event: unifying the broader white power movement.

Even within the terms of the secondary Lee statue controversy, Trump made the case for preservation, which usually glosses over how such Confederate monuments are directly linked to racism. The Lee statue, for example, was commissioned in 1917 and built in 1924, a period when Jim Crow was firmly in place and xenophobia and anti-immigrant sentiment were on the rise. The year 1924 marked both the passage of legislation that greatly restricted immigration and the peak of the second wave of the KKK, catalyzed in part by the 1915 release of *Birth of a Nation*. Indeed, days after the Lee statue unveiling, the KKK lit crosses and bombed a Black church.[42] If ostensibly intended to commemorate fallen Confederate soldiers, then, the Lee statue and other Confederate monuments built during the period were also meant to symbolize white supremacy and instill fear in Black communities, who had no say at the time. Moreover, the monument was built to honor a renowned Confederate general who fought to maintain the institution of enslavement in a city where segregation and racism have a long history.

Trump did not mention this history. Instead, he suggested that the "very fine" marchers were innocents trying to exercise their First Amendment rights despite the violence of counterprotesters—an idea that suggests the savagery of the counterprotesters, which included many people of color. Azzmador and Anglin's pre-Charlottesville post made this association directly, juxtaposing a photo of an ape with mouth agape to a Black youth in a similar pose. So, too, did Cantwell and other white power marchers at Charlottesville.

* * *

"Let's pull the strands of our Charlottesville Teach-In together," I say as the three-hour class draws to a close. "What emerged from our critical unpacking of President Trump's statement that there are 'very fine people' on both sides?"

"He's hiding the real purpose of the rally," a student replies. "It was about 'uniting the white-supremacist right,' not the Lee statue. It's a pretext. All you need to do is look at their posters and listen to what people like Cantwell and the *Daily Stormer* guy said."

"And even if you just focus on the Lee statue, it's still a racist symbol," another student adds. "Trump's pandering to the white supremacists. He's hiding the racism in this country. He doesn't talk about enslavement or Jim Crow. He's gaslighting history in the name of hate."

"And using claims of 'fake news' to do it," a third student finishes.

"Has Trump said anything else about Charlottesville?" a student asks.

"He's been focused on his 'America first' speech at the UN," I respond. "But I'm sure Charlottesville will be back in the news again."

～

And indeed it would be, especially after Joe Biden launched his 2020 presidential campaign bid with a video centered on Charlottesville. "We are in the battle for the soul of this nation," Biden contended, a fight that would be lost with Trump's reelection.[43]

On the one hand, Biden stated, Charlottesville was the home of Thomas Jefferson, who was responsible for an idea—"all men are created equal"—that is a foundational part of what the United States stands for. On the other side, Charlottesville was the site of a "defining moment" in US history, when "Klansmen and white supremacists and neo-Nazis [came] out in the open, their crazed faces illuminated by torches, veins bulging, and baring the fangs of racism. Chanting the same antisemitic bile heard across Europe in the thirties."

Biden went on to critique Trump's remarks about the marchers: "Very fine people on both sides? With those words the president of the United States assigned a moral equivalence between those spreading hate and those with the courage to stand against it." It was then, Biden stated, that he realized that the country faced a "battle for the soul of this nation" in which its "core values" and "very democracy" were at stake. "Folks, America's an idea," Biden concluded, one that is "more powerful than any dictator or tyrant. . . . We can't forget what happened in Charlottesville. Even more important, we have to remember who we are."

Trump answered with more gaslighting. "If you look at what I said," Trump stated in response to Biden's video, "you will see that that question was answered perfectly. And I was talking about people that went because they felt very strongly about the monument to Robert E. Lee, a great general."[44]

Meanwhile, Trump's supporters attacked the "fake news" lies behind the "Charlottesville Hoax."[45] They pointed out that Trump had specifically condemned white supremacists and neo-Nazis and suggested that Trump was solely referring to the Lee statue protesters when he spoke of "very fine people."

They ignored Trump's gaslighting of Charlottesville and how the narrative they were promoting masked the explicit "unite the right" white-power-extremist objectives of the marchers and how Unite the

Right was deeply bound up with racism past and present—the issues my class critically unpacked and discussed during our Charlottesville Teach-In. Along the way, my students touched on other key issues that informed the Charlottesville debate: freedom of speech and assembly, equality, citizenship, immigration, DACA, antisemitism, social justice, civil rights, and the long, twisted road of race, power, and violence in the United States.

These issues, so central to US politics past and present, were also fully on display on the one-year anniversary of Charlottesville, when Jason Kessler organized Unite the Right 2, an event I observed first-hand and discuss later in this book.

~

"What happened to the white power people after the rally?" a student asks.

"There's actually a lot of continuing controversy beyond President Trump," I say. "Lawsuits have been filed. And Kessler, the organizer who was hit at the end of the *VICE* documentary, tweeted that the woman who was killed by the car was a 'fat disgusting communist' and that her death was 'payback.'"[46]

The students are silent. "Kessler later claimed he posted while drunk and on prescription drugs when he said that," I note. "He says he's now getting death threats. Meanwhile, his co-organizer, Richard Spencer, and other white power actors are condemning Kessler's remarks. So there's some in-fighting going on. And we already talked about what happened to Cantwell, the 'crying Nazi.' And there's a lot more."

I pause, then say, "The story of Charlottesville is still being written, though it's part of a much longer history that dates back to the origins of this country. I guess Azzmador was right when he warned, 'You ain't seen nothing yet.'"

I believe our discussion is finished. Then a student who has not spoken says, "I can see that President Trump is whitewashing what the supremacists did. And I understand that their ideas about race are ideology and false. But I still don't quite get *why* people like Kessler and Azzmador believe this racist stuff. What makes them tick?"

"That's a great question," I reply, "but a big one for another teach-in on a different day. Actually, I'm thinking about making it the focus of my course next semester."

Teaching in Trump's USA. "What makes them tick?" Another connection to Nuon Chea. A second Charlottesville lesson to be taught.

2

The Hater

"What makes a man start fires?"

It is the first thing I ask a dozen students, most Black or Brown, on the first day of my Spring 2017 undergraduate anthropology seminar. The question is related to an article I have asked them to read, a *New York Times* feature story on a white power extremist who marched in Charlottesville.

A hand shoots up. "It starts with things like calling places 'shitholes'—pardon Trump's language," a student says. "Trump's inciting the haters."

Trump remains front and center in the news. A few days before our class, during a closed-door meeting on immigration, Trump stated that he prefers immigrants from Norway and Asia to those from places like Haiti, El Salvador, and Africa. "Why do we want all these people from 'shithole countries' coming here?" he had complained.[1] Several people present confirm the vulgarity, which Trump denied.

His remark has not been well received. Critics complain that he is again making racist comments, ones that resonate with his "very fine people on both sides" Charlottesville statement. This time Trump is invoking global racial hierarchy privileging whites and Asians over Black and Brown people from "shithole countries."[2] White House staffers suggest the remark plays to Trump's base. The chairman of the Congressional Black Caucus, in turn, has tweeted that Trump's vulgarity is further proof that "Make America Great Again" really means "Make America White Again."

Meanwhile, white power actors are praising Trump's remark, with the *Daily Stormer* editor, Andrew Anglin, telling his readers that it demonstrates that "Trump is more or less on the same page as us with regard to race and immigration. . . . The real issue is all these shitty brown people who come to the country exclusively to parasite off us."[3] Anglin's colleague Azzmador responds to Trump's remark by invoking the monkey racist trope, saying Haiti is full of "gorilla niggers." White power actors have added various other inflections, ranging from antisemitic allusions to references to immigrant "infestation."

"These are strange times, indeed," I tell the class. "But even if President Trump could be blamed for incitement, what else 'makes a man start fires'? What did the *Times* article on the Charlottesville marcher suggest?"

"'Hate in the heartland,'" a student states. "The article's title says it all."

"Haters gonna hate," another student agrees.

Hate. A one-word answer to that enduring question, *Why?* The question I discussed at Nuon Chea's trial. The question that haunts the United States after Charlottesville.

Two months earlier, *New York Times* reporter Richard Fausset had taken up the quest for answers. His November 25, 2017, feature story, which my students have read,[4] centers on Tony Hovater, a white power extremist from Ohio who sometimes does podcasts on Radio Aryan. Hovater marched at Charlottesville with other members of the neo-Nazi Traditionalist Worker Party, including its leader, Matthew Heimbach, who appeared in the *VICE* video and had been nicknamed "the Little Führer" by the Southern Poverty Law Center.

"A Voice of Hate in America's Heartland," headlined Fausset's article. Fausset wanted to know why Hovater, a "committed foot soldier" in the white power movement, had turned to hate. "Why," Fausset asked, "did this man—intelligent, socially adroit and raised middle class amid the relatively well-integrated environments of United States military bases—gravitate toward the furthest extremes of American political discourse?"

But try as he might, Fausset could not find a "silver bullet" explanation for Hovater's extremism. Hovater seemed to be an "ordinary" American, a welder who lived in a white house, watched *Seinfeld*, ate at Applebee's, and had included a muffin pan on his wedding registry at Target. "He is the Nazi sympathizer next door," Fausset wrote, "polite and low-key."

Fausset's piece provoked enormous controversy, including condemnation from other media outlets and many *New York Times* readers for normalizing hate.[5] "How to normalize Nazis 101," tweeted one reader. "Instead of long, glowing profiles of Nazis/White nationalists," a *Washington Post* editor wrote, "why don't we profile the victims of their ideologies?" A small number of people praised the piece, such as a reporter who stated, "People mad about this article want to believe that Nazis are monsters we cannot relate to. White supremacists are normal ass white people and it's been that way in America since 1776." The *New York Times* apologized for offending people.

In a follow-up article—"I Interviewed a White Nationalist and Fascist. What Was I Left With?"—Fausset wrote that he had sought to explain Hovater's radicalization. "What prompted him," Fausset wondered, "to take his ideas beyond his living room, beyond the chat rooms, and on to Charlottesville, where he marched alongside [extremist] allies?" Invoking a famous metaphor for missing explanation from the 1941 film *Citizen Kane*, in which a journalist seeks to understand why a tycoon whispered "Rosebud" on his deathbed, Fausset asked, "Where was [Hovater's] Rosebud?"[6]

Despite interviewing Hovater for hours, Fausset acknowledged that he was unable to answer this question and find an explanation for Hovater's extremism. "I could feel the failure even as Mr. Hovater and I spoke [for the last time]," Fausset wrote. "Sometimes a soul, and its shape, remain obscure both to writer and reader." Fausset concluded his follow-up article by invoking a Minutemen album title, "What Makes a Man Start Fires?"—the Rosebud question about Hovater to which Fausset had been unable to find an answer.

This question captures what many people in the United States, my students included, have been asking since Charlottesville. So I have made it the focus of my anthropology seminar, "What Makes a Man

Start Fires?" Blood, Soil, Genocide, and the Origins of Hate. My students will give the class an informal title, "The Hater."

For their final essay, each student will explain what led a perpetrator to "start fires" of violence and hate. It is the question I had been asked to answer at Nuon Chea's trial. And during this course, Nuon Chea will at one point again stand center stage. So, too, will the issue of hate.

"In this course," I tell my students at the end of the first class, "we're going to examine the origins of hate and try to answer the question everyone's been asking since Charlottesville: 'Why?'"

What makes a man start fires? Charlottesville lesson number two. Once again, a pair of rules guide us: critical analysis, not opinion; respectful dialogue—no matter your political persuasion.

* * *

TUESDAY, JANUARY 23, 2018, RUTGERS UNIVERSITY, NEWARK, NJ
The Hater lurks everywhere during our class. The label is pinned on Trump. Trump pins it on others. Mass shootings are becoming routine: Las Vegas (October 2017), Sutherland Springs, Texas (November 2017), and Parkland, Florida (February 2018). The violence is explained with one-word answers—"Evil!" "Crazy!" "Heartless!" "Sociopath!"—just as they are applied to ISIS fighters and those responsible for Rohingya suffering and Syrians tortured, gassed, and bombed.

And so the second class focuses on Charlottesville and hate. The students read Fausset on Hovater, background material on Unite the Right, and texts on hate. We start class by watching the *VICE* documentary, then turn to discussion.

"What motivates a person like Hovater or Cantwell," I ask, "to espouse white-power-extremist and neo-Nazi views and participate in an event like Charlottesville?"

"That dude's crazy," says one student, referring to Cantwell. "Demented." "Racist." "Power hungry." "Twisted." "Haters." Trump's USA. The labels flow fast. More one-word explanations. Chris Cantwell. Richard Spencer. Donald Trump. The Hater seems everywhere.

"Several of you mentioned hate," I say. "What, exactly, is hate? For example, during our first class the phrase 'hater's gonna hate' was mentioned. What does that mean? Is that an explanation or, to use Fausset's term, a 'Rosebud' answer?"

"What's a 'Rosebud' answer again?" a student asks.

"It's from a famous film, *Citizen Kane*, in which a journalist tries to find out the meaning of the last word a dying tycoon whispers, 'Rosebud.' People sometimes use the term as a metaphor for a missing explanation or what we can call a 'Rosebud answer' for the purposes of our discussion. So by asking if hate is a 'Rosebud answer' I'm asking if it provides an adequate explanation for why a person like Hovater marches in Charlottesville and joins an extremist group."

Silence. Then some comments, but they come more slowly.

"Hate's an emotion," a student offers. "It makes you want to hurt others."

"It's extreme anger," suggests another.

"Is that what the readings tell us?" I say as we begin our exercise in unpacking "hate." We look at the dictionary definition ("intense dislike, strong aversion"), then examine how the concept individualizes and masks.

"What sort of explanation of Hovater is implicit in the title of Fausset's *Times* article, 'A Voice of Hate in America's Heartland'?" I ask.

"Rosebud!" a student interjects. "It suggests Hovater's a supremacist because he hates. Especially since Fausset didn't find any answers. That's what the reader's left with."

"Does calling him, Cantwell, or other people in the *VICE* documentary, or Trump for that matter, 'a hater' tell us much then?" I query.

"Not really," the student says. "Hate isn't much of a Rosebud answer."

"So what does the use of 'hate' obscure?" I continue. "What if we turned it around and thought of hate not as a cause but as a consequence—or as a lens that filters the way we understand the world? Where might we find a Rosebud answer, then?"

The lesson of the day emerges. By labeling a shooter, a Charlottesville marcher, or even Nuon Chea a "hater," we individualize their actions, suggest that they act on the basis of emotion, not reason. This move distances "them" from "us." It obscures the deeper structures underpinning violence and hate, including the long history of race and racism in the United States my students had discussed during the Charlottesville Teach-In.

Several readings for today underscore this point. One essay looks at the history of debate about what it means to be "American" and therefore who should be welcomed as immigrants and future citizens.[7] These discussions are often intertwined with racism, the exclusion not just of Blacks but also of people from Europe, Asia, and Latin America who are perceived as "invaders" and contaminating "threats." Ongoing debates about Trump's "Muslim ban" and southern border "wall" fit this pattern.

A second reading focuses more on the present.[8] The text argues that everyday ways of speaking about hate mask structural violence against people of color and those who face discrimination based on gender, class, sexual orientation, and disability. By calling people "haters," we render them exceptional, explaining away their hateful behaviors as bigoted or deviant. Doing so masks the deep histories, social structures, and discourses that underpin racism, discrimination, and prejudice. A similar argument can be made about discussions of "Charlottesville" that regard it as a singular event—exceptional as opposed to being part of a long history of race, power, and history in the United States.

"If 'the hater' misdirects us," a student says, "then what about 'racists' and 'supremacists'? Don't these terms do the same thing?"

"That's a good point," I say. "They can misdirect in the same way—as can calling someone like Hovater a 'white supremacist' versus a 'white nationalist' or a 'white power actor.' We can speak of white supremacy as a system of racial hierarchy and domination, past and present. A 'white supremacist,' then, could refer to someone who believes in white domination and seeks to perpetuate this system. In more popular discussion, however, the term conjures images of crazed racist haters and so masks white power's contemporary forms that don't clearly align with racial domination."

"How so?" a student asks.

"Some white power actors," I reply, "claim they are advocating for white rights or a white ethnostate—and that people of color should have one of their own. And they claim to disavow racism and racial hierarchy. Others claim to want to prevent their victimization and diminishment through replacement. Of course, critics claim such discourses mask their underlying racist and white supremacist views.

"Instead of 'white supremacist,'" I continue, "a lot of people are using the term 'white nationalist' to talk about the Charlottesville marchers and the alt-right. But 'white nationalist' is somewhat vague. It captures the idea of advocacy for a nation predominantly organized in terms of white identity or, in the extreme, creating an ethnostate. But the term locates the movement in nations, thereby obscuring the global scale and interconnections of the white power movement.

"As you can see," I continue, "there's disagreement. I tend to use the term 'white power,' which some scholars have argued is the best way to go.[9] If not perfect, this phrase has an openness that more easily captures how broad, multifaceted, and global white power is today.

"We can add 'extremist'—though it's also a complicated term[10]—to 'white power' and then speak of 'white power extremists' to capture some of the 'extreme' connotations of 'white supremacist,' such as a willingness to take aggressive, even violent, action to achieve a set of radical race-based goals, many of which are meant to perpetuate white supremacy."

"Like that guy Azzmador in the video," a student says. "He was talking about race war."

"And Cantwell was wearing a 'Radical Agenda' shirt," another student notes.

"That's the name of his talk radio show," I say. "But as you saw in the video and read in the Southern Poverty Law Center essay on Cantwell,[11] his views are right up there with Azzmador's in terms of white power extremism."

"Those two seem like white supremacists to me," a third student comments. "I still think white supremacist is the better term. 'White power' seems too vague and downplays the connections to the white suprema-cist system. I confront it every day."

"Many people would agree with you," I say. "The key thing is to think critically about whatever term we decide to use and to not let individu-alizing one-word explanations divert us from the longer histories and structures in which racism, hate, and white supremacy are embedded."

"What does all this tell us about Hovater?" a student asks. "If he's not a hater or a supremacist, where are the Rosebud reasons for his extremism?"

"Let's go back to Fausset's article," I suggest, "and consider the way it is framed and what this framing masks and reveals."

We revisit the headline, "A Voice of Hate," and the premise that there is a singular moment, such as an early childhood trauma, which turned this seemingly normal man into an extremist. This focus on the extraor-dinary diverts our attention from the ways in which Hovater's views are linked to structural violence and history.

Ohio, for example, is no stranger to racism and white power.[12] The Ku Klux Klan has long marched its streets; racial tensions remained after desegregation, inflamed in part by manufacturing decline, job loss, and addiction, including the opioid crisis.

Even as Hovater was being interviewed, Black supervisors were being harassed by resentful white employees at a GM factory.[13] They were called "boy" and "monkey," referred to as "nigger" and told to "go back to Africa." Other employees had swastika tattoos. Nooses were hung. Reference was made to the KKK. "Whites only" was graffitied on a bath-room wall. Employees at a Toledo UPS center lodged similar complaints. There are also a large number of hate groups that operate in Ohio, in-cluding branches of the Ku Klux Klan.[14] The Southern Poverty Law Cen-ter lists Ohio as the base of the *Daily Stormer*; it is also where publisher Andrew Anglin grew up.

While many people in Ohio are outraged by these sorts of actions, white power racism persists and is part of the milieu in which Hovater came to his views. His ideas are not exceptional. They emerge out of longer histories of systemic racism and structural violence in Ohio and the rest of the United States. For Hovater, Heimbach, and the Traditionalist Worker Party, economic decline and job losses are also key.

Fausset made a few references to these issues, mentioning Hovater's anger about affirmative action and the 2012 shooting of Trayvon Martin, a seventeen-year-old Black youth killed by a man on neighborhood watch patrol who some far-right extremists, invoking Jewish conspiracy and Black criminality tropes, argued had every right to open fire.[15] Hovater also mentioned books by people like Charles Murray (who links race and IQ) and Patrick Buchanan, who espouses a range of bigoted white power views. Unfortunately, Fausset did not probe such hints and pursue a historical and structural line of inquiry, instead focusing largely on the individual level of analysis.

"There's more to Hovater's story," I say at the end of class, "but acknowledging this backdrop is a first step toward understanding Hovater's 'fires.' The story turned him from a 'foot soldier' into a minor white-power-extremist star."

* * *

In February, my anthropology seminar shifts from the swastikas, torchlit marches, and chants of "blood and soil" at Charlottesville to an event they echo, Nazi Germany. Hitler's conflagration. We explore where scholars found explanations as they sought answers to the Nazi *why?*

At first, they saw the hater, Nazi sadists, monsters, and madmen. Nazi criminals were tested and analyzed. "Hermann Goering, Amiable Psychopath," read a 1948 article on Hitler's military commander. So, too, were the German people examined in a search for culture and personality clues. *The Authoritarian Personality* was published in this context.[16]

In the 1960s, with the rise of social psychology and as psychoanalytic theory declined, explanations increasingly emphasized the power of situation, the interactions of people in groups. A landmark was Hannah Arendt's study of Adolf Eichmann, the notorious Nazi who oversaw the bureaucracy of mass murder. The title of her book, *The Banality of Evil*, became a refrain for what might happen to anyone placed in a similar situation.

Stanley Milgram operationalized and tested this obedience-to-authority explanation, finding that, when given commands in the name of science, most people were ready to shock and harm others, even to the point that they might die. The Stanford Prison Experiments seemed like icing on the cake of situationist explanation, as college-age students, when given "guard" authority in a prison-like situation, abused their randomly selected "prisoner" peers.[17]

By the 1990s, the "ordinary men" thesis held sway, encapsulated by Christopher Browning's classic study of the "ordinary men" of a Nazi police battalion. There were exceptions, but most of these perpetrators were "everyday Joes" responsive to peer pressure and other situational cues. "Ordinary men" were soon matched by "ordinary women" and then *Hitler's Furies*, as one book was titled. Some argued for interactionist perspectives, a mix of psyche and group situation.[18]

But the specter of the Hater remained, the shadow of "ordinary men" explanations and close companion of everyday understanding. Few people want to imagine that they share things in common with mass shooters and the Charlottesville marchers: better "the Hater" than "ordinary men."

Hitler looms large in our class discussions. So, too, does the issue of structure and agency. For some, Hitler stands as the archetypal Hater, an ideological zealot intent on mass murder from the start. Others say, "Not so fast," viewing the genocidal process as one of twists and turns, not something preordained. In Holocaust studies, these differing perspectives are sometimes referred to as the "Intentional-Functionalist" debate—the Holocaust as the product of intention (agency) versus the Holocaust as a function of factors like bureaucracy (structure) and a process of "cumulative radicalization."[19]

Some scholars seek middle ground. My students read one such attempt, a book by Doris Bergen that uses a fire metaphor to answer the question, *Why?*[20] For a house to burn, Bergen argues, three things are needed: dry timber, a spark, and favorable weather. The dry timber refers to the preconditions, including racism, a historical backdrop of imperialism and war, and antisemitism new and old.

My students read the *Protocols of the Elders of Zion*, a screed that pins the world's woes on an evil Jewish conspiracy. I pair the tract with a long chapter from *Mein Kampf*, in which Hitler links blood and soil to an imagined Aryan purity that demands living space and the eradication of contaminating groups like Jews. He claims to distinguish the "racial characteristics" of Jews, whom Hitler describes as a "maggot in a rotting body," "filth," "poison," "sponger," "Christ-killers," "moral stain," "parasite," and so forth. The list is long. Hitler's ideas directly inform white power actors like Hovater today.

Hitler, Bergen continues, was the "match that set the house on fire" as he drove the process along.[21] To turn Hitler's fire into a genocidal conflagration, however, the "weather" conditions had to be just right, including the consolidation of Nazi power and World War II. Bergen calls her perspective a "modified intentionalist position."

My students study these arguments and theories, take up their own search for answers. By March, each has selected a person who set fires of violence and hate: Hitler, Stalin, the Unabomber, Castro, al-Baghdadi, Bashir, General von Trotha, Pinochet, Chemical Ali.

Meanwhile, our readings range far and wide. After Charlottesville and the Holocaust, we examine lynching, Christian militias, Mai Lai, ISIS, and Rwanda. The Hater remains close at hand, appearing in the news as the course proceeds: al-Assad's gassings in Syria, the desperate plight of the Rohingya in Myanmar, shootings at Stoneman Douglas High School in Parkland, Florida.

The accusations against President Trump also keep coming from commentators: "racist," "misogynist," "unstable" and even, mental health experts warn, a dangerous "malignant narcissist." Trump responds by labeling himself "a very stable genius."[22]

* * *

APRIL 3, 2018, RUTGERS UNIVERSITY, NEWARK, NJ

For two weeks in April, my class turns to the Khmer Rouge fires of violence and hate. We start with Nuon Chea, taking a deep dive into his path to revolution and the story of a moral compass gone wrong.

If he discussed parts of this story in court, Nuon Chea had been discussing it for years with a Cambodian journalist and genocide survivor, Thet Sambath. My class watches Sambath's 2008 film, *Enemies of the People*, in which Nuon Chea speaks of how he saw the truth and set out to right a host of wrongs. We read Sambath's coauthored book, *Behind the Killing Fields*, which fills in details, offering clues as we consider what made Nuon Chea "start fires" of violence and hate.

Nuon Chea's story emerges in bits and pieces.[23] Born in 1926 in rural Battambang. A child of poverty. His mother's favorite. Stand-out student. Few friends. Not close to his siblings. Allowed to study instead of toiling in the rice paddies.

Initial clues are revealed. French colonial oppression: taxes and forced labor. Nuon Chea also observed the devastation caused by moneylenders, his family's massive debt. He observed how the rich and powerful humiliated and maltreated Cambodia's poor. He himself was beaten by students from town, looked down upon, and scorned.

My students spot "the Hater," zero in on an intentionalist explanation: Nuon Chea's childhood rage. They cite Nuon Chea's words as proof: "The French treated Cambodians very badly, so [my] feelings of hatred and revenge started then."[24] Nuon Chea set fires because he experienced violence and oppression as a child, some claim.

"But what about Thailand?" I ask, complicating their explanation. We revisit *Behind the Killing Fields*, consider the twists and turns of Nuon Chea's life. World War II. The Franco-Thai war. Thailand seizes Battambang province, Nuon Chea's home. A path opens. He finishes high school in Bangkok, where he lives with monks.

Nuon Chea studied hard. Avoided girls. Passed his exams. Gained admission to the University of Moral Science and Politics, later Thammasat University, on a road to study law. Politics soon entered his life.

The Thai nationalist struggle. Thammasat, a hotbed of activism and dissent. Books and new ideas. Progressive friends. Nuon Chea read Thai communist newspapers, participated in political meetings and debates. He gave speeches on French colonial oppression even as the Cambodian independence movement back home was gaining momentum.

In 1950, Nuon Chea chose the path of revolution, joining the Thai Communist Party. Mao had just taken power in China; Ho Chi Minh would soon follow in North Vietnam. Cambodia's independence would come in 1953.

Nuon Chea returned to Cambodia in 1950 and began to build networks, as he would for years. To raise money for the movement, he worked for a Chinese businessman. He had to quit. The corruption was everywhere.

Morality: another source of Nuon Chea's fire.

"Why aren't we talking about Pol Pot?" a student asks during our discussion of Nuon Chea.

"Well, what does the book say?" I respond.

Pol Pot. Top five on lists of the world's most evil men. Born Saloth Sar in 1925, Pol Pot had a different trajectory, a path that crossed France.[25] A rural background, but wealthier than Nuon Chea. Pol Pot spent time in a Phnom Penh pagoda and attended good schools.

In 1949, as Nuon Chea protested at rallies, Pol Pot left on a scholarship for Paris, where he performed poorly in school but joined the French communist party. He returned to Cambodia in 1953 just as independence was won.

Pol Pot began to teach, foment revolution. He soon met Nuon Chea, a trusted comrade from the start. According to Nuon Chea, he and Pol Pot shared similar flames, hatred of the greed and corruption of the rich and powerful, outrage at the abuse of the poor. "Pol Pot hated the feudalist regime more than colonialism," Nuon Chea recalled, "because there was no democracy" and because Pol Pot himself had been "treated badly."[26]

Together, Nuon Chea and Pol Pot plotted revolution. But their successes were limited. And so, in the late 1950s, the Cambodian revolutionaries sought to "analyze . . . the real nature of Kampuchea society" and formulate a corresponding set of guiding principles for the movement.[27] They read books, studied the history of Cambodia and other revolutions, and gathered facts.

While Pol Pot and Nuon Chea would later point to a number of important moments in their accounts of the Khmer Rouge rise to power, both highlight September 30, 1960, as a key juncture in the revolutionary struggle—not a "smoking gun" but an event that helped cock the trigger—one that Pol Pot would say gave the revolutionaries "clear sight." On this date, a small group of revolutionaries made several key decisions, including finalizing the movement's Party Line.

Later, Pol Pot would tell the story in a 1977 speech marking the seventeenth anniversary of the founding of the Communist Party of Kampuchea and commemorating this moment when the revolutionaries established the group's political platform and leadership.[28] Only after extensive Marxist-Leninist "scientific analysis," Pol Pot proclaimed to the nation, did the revolutionaries see that there were two main "contradictions" in Cambodian society.

The first contradiction was with foreign imperialism, including Cambodia's state of military, economic, cultural, and social "semicolonialism," especially in relationship to US imperialism. The second and more primary "antagonistic contradiction" was class based, involving the oppression of the poor by the rich and powerful, especially the capitalists and landlords who exploited peasants, comprising 85 percent of the population.

This "life and death" contradiction, Pol Pot stated, generated hatred that historically had been "buried," in part due to Buddhism. To rectify this situation, the revolutionaries needed "to arouse the peasants," especially the lower-middle-class and poor peasants, "so that they saw [the contradictions], burned with class hatred and took up the struggle."[29] Khmer Rouge cadre began to build their base of support, especially in the countryside, where they lived with the poor and taught them about their Party Line.

More broadly, the Khmer Rouge often described the Party Line in terms of politics, organization, and consciousness. *"Politics"* referred to revolutionary ideology and corresponding propaganda, ranging from slogans to formal education. These ideas were operationalized through proper *organization*, including management structure, following the chain of command, institutional practices, and the revolutionary transformation of the means, relations, and forces of production from capitalist to socialist. *Consciousness*, in turn, involved the constant struggle to "forge" a proper revolutionary subjectivity, often expressed through the metaphor of "stance."

"Our line was right," Pol Pot stated in his 1977 speech, "and we applied it correctly" as they began to foment revolution following the 1960 meeting.[30] As a result, by 1967, when the first armed insurrection took place, the "situation in the countryside had reached a new height, like dry straw in the rice fields," needing only "a small spark to set it on fire."[31] *What makes a man start fires?* Pol Pot provided his answer.

Although it offers insight into the Khmer Rouge rise to power, Pol Pot's speech gives a partial account, a teleological narrative painting a picture of inevitable success, a revolution guaranteed to be victorious given the "all-seeing" Party Line.

The reality was more complicated. At first, the revolutionaries had modest success building their revolutionary forces.[32] A more immediate spark was provided by the Vietnam War, with the carpet bombing that devastated parts of the countryside, the arrival of foreign troops on Cambodian soil, and the degradation of the Cambodian economy.

The 1970 coup that led to the overthrow of Cambodia's long-time leader, Prince Sihanouk, was a second big spark. Sihanouk responded by joining the Khmer Rouge in a united front, which greatly increased the revolutionary ranks after Sihanouk called for his rural "children" to fight the new Khmer Republic (1970–75).

In 1970 and 1971, North Vietnamese troops took the lead in destroying the best units of the Cambodian army. By 1973, the Khmer Rouge controlled almost all of the country with the exception of the urban centers. With US support, the Khmer Republic was able to hold onto power until April 17, 1975, when the Khmer Rouge seized control.

The violence that ensued did not follow directly from the Party Line to the killing fields, but the potential was there in the regime's Manichean vision, moralism, and homogenizing impulse to create a singular society consisting only of pure revolutionaries. An initial phase of violence took place immediately after the revolution as the entire urban population was sent into the countryside and the Khmer Rouge purged military and civilian officials as well as monks and former political leaders. Ethnic Vietnamese were also targeted during this phase.

There was a lull in the killings. Then a much more violent phase commenced in early 1976, signified in part by the increased flow of prisoners to S-21 prison, which was charged with ferreting out "hidden enemies burrowing from within" who were said to be plotting coups and subverting the revolution. Muslim Chams also began to be targeted at this time after some localized 1975 rebellions in response to policy changes that conflicted with their traditions.

Pol Pot's speech was given in late 1977 as this massive spike in violence was abating somewhat following the destruction of large numbers of alleged "enemy agents, who belong to the various spy networks of the imperialists . . . and who secretly implant themselves to carry out subversive activities against our revolution." Nevertheless, some "reactionary elements" remained, perhaps "one to two percent of the population" who "camouflage themselves."[33]

The violence continued. When open war with Vietnam broke out in 1978, there was another spike as suspected pro-Vietnam elements were targeted. By the time the Khmer Rouge's Democratic Kampuchea (DK) regime was toppled in early 1979 by a small force of Cambodians—many of them former Khmer Rouge who had fled the purges—backed by roughly 150,000 Vietnamese troops, roughly a quarter of the population was dead.

* * *

APRIL 10, 2018, RUTGERS UNIVERSITY, NEWARK, NJ

"What made Nuon Chea start fires of genocide and hate?"

For today's assignment, my students have to answer this question.

Some students remain convinced Nuon Chea is a Hater, a twisted, evil man; others say he is a zealot, an unwavering fanatic committed to his cause. A number of students invoke the power of situation: peer pressure, obedience to authority, the power of roles, institutional constraints.

"It sounds like we're back to the intentionalist-structuralist debate," a student says. "Maybe we need some middle ground."

"What about Bergen's model?" another suggests.

"That's an interesting connection," I say. "Can you apply her Holocaust 'fires' model here?"

"I sort of did that for my paper," a third student interjects. "I tried to connect Nuon Chea and the Khmer Rouge to the Nazis and Hitler."

"How did you link them?" I ask.

"Bergen talks about dry tinder, the preconditions. That's like the civil war in Cambodia, colonialism, and communist ideology. She also talks about favorable weather. The civil war provided it. And then there was the conflict with Vietnam. The spark, that's harder, but I connected it to Pol Pot and Nuon Chea's fanaticism. Maybe I lean toward intentionalism in the end—or at least 'modified intentionalism' to use Bergen's phrase."

"You made some nice connections," I say. "What about 'cumulative radicalization'? Did you talk about that as well?"

"What's cumulative radicalization?" another student asks. "I can't remember with all the readings."

"It's a structuralist idea," I reply. "It suggests that, as opposed to being the outcome of predetermined intention, genocide emerges in fits and starts. The idea is that, instead of Hitler having a plan to annihilate Jews and other groups that can be directly traced back to things like the *Mein Kampf* chapter you read earlier, the 'final solution' emerged only after a series of events like the Nazis' early euthanasia program and the twists and turns of World War II."

"So the idea is that we can't just blame Marxist ideology for the Khmer Rouge killings," a student comments, "but need to focus on historical events as well."

"That's the basic idea," I say. "Structuralists also look at the pressure of institutions and social structures and how policy shifts and radicalizes as events unfold. I actually talked about intentionalism and cumulative radicalization when I testified at Nuon Chea's trial at the tribunal in Cambodia."

"You did?" a student says. "What happened?"

"I suggested that the idea of cumulative radicalization was a better way to look at the targeting of Muslim Chams, which proceeded in a less straightforward manner than the attacks on ethnic Vietnamese."

"Did you talk about what led Nuon Chea to start fires, Professor?" a student asks.

"That's your question to answer today," I reply. "But when I gave testimony at the tribunal, I offered an explanation and even had an exchange with Nuon Chea. The video is still on the Internet."

"Can we see it?" they ask.

I cue up the footage on the classroom computer, press "Play," and travel back in time to 2016. I appear on the screen, dressed in a suit and tie. We watch a clip from Day 1, when the prosecution questioned me about the genocidal process, then jump to my final exchange with Nuon Chea, where I responded, in part, to the defense denials based on attacking what they called the "Standard Total View."

"So that's what I told the court about the Cambodian genocide," I tell the students as I flip on the classroom light. The student clap. Then one shouts, "Mr. Expert Witness." My new nickname draws laughs.

"What's a Standard Total View?" a student asks.

"That was a critical part of Nuon Chea's defense," I explain. "His lawyers contended that there was a false dominant narrative that blinded everyone to the truth about DK. Oddly, that's the same sort of language white power actors use today when they claim that 'cultural Marxists,'

led by Jews, have brainwashed everyone and imposed a system of political correctness. Hovater thinks like that as well.

"But that's a long story to be discussed on another day," I continue. "I
turned the tables and stated in court that it was actually Nuon Chea's defense that was giving a 'Standard Total View' by trying to pin the blame
on others, especially Vietnam. Instead, I told the court that genocide
was a process involving factors like 'manufacturing difference,' which I
talked about in the first clip you watched."

"Can you explain that?" a student asks.

"It's from a book I wrote, *Why Did They Kill?*, which is based on my
dissertation fieldwork," I reply. "I argue that genocide is a process that
emerges from a historical backdrop and unfolds over time. It usually
is set against a more immediate context of upheaval and involves a set
of dynamics that include—especially in the case of what some scholars
call 'ideological genocides'—a vision for remaking society. Such visions
are premised on the reworking of identity categories of 'us' and 'them'
so that the outgroup is scapegoated, typecast, devalued, dehumanized,
regulated, and confined.

"This creates a dangerous situation," I continue, "one that, as Pol Pot
said, only needed a spark to 'light the flames' and, to use Bergen's phrase,
'favorable weather' that can lead to conflagration. The weather metaphor
captures part of the idea of genocide as process and cumulative radicalization in the sense that weather shifts and changes."

"What about agency or intention?" a student says. "How do we explain what motivates a person to 'start fires'?"

"We could use the macro-micro idea we read about,"[34] another student suggests. "That's one way to approach it: micro for the individual,
macro for the state."

"The meso level's also key," a third student comments. "You have to
take account of the group as well. Peer pressure, obedience—those sorts
of things."

"That's certainly one useful way to approach the structure-agency
problem," I agree. "It's important to remember that scholars sometimes

use those terms in different ways. The micro level deals with individual-level factors like human personality and motivation but is also used to speak about the immediate situation in which a perpetrator acts, which is also influenced by meso-level factors, like group pressure, rules, and midlevel decision making, and the macro-level factors like state power and organization, history, and ideology. Sometimes people also think of the meso level as midlevel decision makers and the macro level as the top leaders, but this can also individualize analysis and deflect from structural considerations."

"It's hard to escape the structure-agency problem," the first student notes.

"And to explain the fires," a student adds.

"It is," I agree. "To understand 'fires,' you have to consider all three of these levels since they are interrelated—as are structure and agency. For example, even if a perpetrator has sociopathic tendencies, their actions will still be influenced and constrained by group and state-level factors. In my book that was discussed at the tribunal, I also talk about the 'bodily inscription of difference,' which considers perpetration in terms of individual-level factors like projection and existential anxiety in micro-level contexts like the torture chamber. But even these individual-level dynamics are partly informed by the larger process of manufacturing difference as well as state ideology and power. It's a bit complicated."

"It's easy to see the fires," a student says, "but not to explain them. Rosebud explanations are hard to find."

"Let's pull together some of the threads from our discussion," I suggest. "First, it appears we need to be wary of anyone who claims they have *the* answer about 'what makes a man start fires.' There is no single 'Rosebud' answer. Genocide is a process, a flowing river that has cross-currents and is fed by tributaries and streams.

"Second," I add, "it's important to pause and interrogate what's being asked. For each question is a directive, a demand for a particular sort of answer.

"Consider the question 'what makes a man start fires?'" I continue. "It commands our gaze, demands we give answers about the true believer, the sadist, the Hater, and the fanatic. It directs us to focus on individual intention and look away from the structures that mediate human agency, including the forces of power and history.

"What makes a Nuon Chea or Tony Hovater start fires?" I go on. "Hate's too simple of an answer; the 'racist' label is, too. It's easy to get stuck in the 'fires' query, but there are also paths out. One's offered by the Khmer Rouge—by the way they explained their revolutionary fires.

"Remember their Party Line, the triad of politics, organization, and consciousness," I continue, "each geared to demarcate right from wrong, us from them, those who do and do not belong, purity and contamination. We often find this sort of moralism in genocide, sometimes passionate, in other situations more strategic. It was certainly a strong current in Khmer Rouge ideology.

"Why don't we use a 'fires' metaphor to say this another way," I suggest, "one that may help with your final papers. Imagine a campfire, then enclose it in a triangle, each side an element needed to start the flame.

"*Politics* (ideology and discourse) is the tinder," I begin, "*Organization* (structure) the overarching kindling, *consciousness* (subjectivity, identity, and personal investment) the branches topping it off. The sides are triangulated to enact a political and moral vision of how things should be, who belongs, who is fully human. The three sides press on one another, signifying the potential force, even violence.

"Still, to burn," I say, "the fire needs a spark, then wood, oxygen, and wind to fuel the flame. That spark is *circumstance*, the deep histories that inform the moment, the sudden upheavals that give it shape. The Cambodian genocide, as we have seen, was inflected by deep histories of colonialism, imperialism, and social structure, including distributions of wealth, status, and power. Prior to DK, we have more immediate factors—the spark that lights the fire—the Indochina War, a coup, US bombing. Together, these 'sparks' helped light the Khmer Rouge fire and then fan the flames, which roared, subsided, then roared again as events during DK unfolded—part of the process of cumulative radicalization—killing many of the people caught in the Khmer Rouge conflagration."

"How does this connect back to Hovater and the supremacists?" a student asks. "Why do they start fires? And can we compare a white power dude from Ohio to Nuon Chea?"

"Great questions," I respond. "It can seem like a long way from Cambodia's killing fields to Charlottesville. Anyone have a suggestion?"

"Nuon Chea and Hovater are both political," another student says. "So we can compare them in terms of Khmer Rouge 'politics,' like looking at ideology. And maybe 'organization' and 'consciousness,' too—the fire triangle."

"Don't forget 'circumstance,'" a student adds. "That influences how big a fire gets going."

"That's one way to proceed," I respond. "And the Khmer Rouge started out as a social movement and white power could be looked at as one, too. How, then, could we examine white power extremists like Hovater using this Khmer Rouge 'fires' triangle model?"

"That's not easy to figure out," a third students says.

"You're all anthro majors," I say. "How do you think we might begin to do research on white power extremism?"

"Interviewing," a student suggests. "But no way as a person of color I'm talking to a supremacist. That'd be dangerous. Participant observation is out, too."

"It's tricky, for sure," I respond. "That's probably part of the reason there's so little ethnographic research on white power extremists.[35] It's also difficult to build trust. Another way to proceed is through discourse analysis, or unpacking language and text. Or you could look at performance and symbolism. Each method has strengths and weaknesses, filters what's seen and obscured.

"One way to start searching for answers," I continue, "is to examine what someone like Hovater says in public interviews, websites, Internet forums, or even Twitter. Since the *New York Times* story, Hovater's actually been talking about Fausset's article during white power podcasts.

We have a little time before the end of class, so why don't we listen to a clip? See what you can find out about Hovater's 'politics,' 'organization,' or 'consciousness.'"

~

We listen to part of a podcast on Nordic Frontier, an arm of the neo-Nazi group Nordic Resistance, whose revolutionary platform includes standard white power points: combating "the global Zionist elite," creating a national socialist Nordic state, and stopping "mass immigration," an issue that increased dramatically in salience following the European refugee crisis of 2015. Sweden, in particular, had taken in large numbers of refugees, leading to social tensions and a rise of the domestic white power movement.[36]

In another part of the podcast, Andreas Johansson, the Swedish podcast host, jokes about race war and Trump's "shithole countries" remark, made days before. Johansson himself has come to white power after a self-described life of decadence and then enlightenment when, he says, he understood that the Holocaust is a hoax and that Jews are responsible for white genocide.[37] Johansson introduces his show to listeners as "the final solution to your podcast problems." His interview banter with Hovater is full of such antisemitic quips.

Hovater recounts how he helped start the Traditionalist Worker Party (TWP) in 2015 after meeting Matthew Heimbach—the group's leader, who was a featured speaker at Unite the Right and appeared in the VICE documentary—at a conservative convention. Heimbach was moving nearby in Ohio, so the two joined forces. They began postering and did protest work, including an early demonstration at a Tyson Chicken plant in Kentucky that was replacing local workers with Somali immigrants for less pay.

Charlottesville marked a key moment for the TWP and the broader white power movement. Hovater noted, almost with awe, that they were the center of world attention for several days and had become part of history. "You know, the UN had to comment on it," Hovater told Johansson. Meanwhile, many new people were exposed to the white power movement cause, enabling its network to grow.

The downside of Charlottesville was "the great shutdown," as white power actors around the world were pushed off mainstream platforms, not just Facebook and Twitter but also financial services like PayPal, which created problems even if they could be overcome by switching to alternatives like cryptocurrency. "We're going to find ways to do what we've got to do," Hovater told Johansson. "We're big-brained white guys!"

The *Times* story also had a similar double-edged effect. It generated a "staggering" recruitment response for the TWP, Hovater claimed. Hovater said he was prepared for the public outcry at the article, including the "Twitter freak out," but was surprised, and a bit pleased, that even celebrities had condemned him—including Cher, he said with a laugh before he and Johansson mocked her.

Hovater also was aware that he challenged assumptions as a white power actor who everyone assumed would be like an "evil Nazi," skinhead, or a "1980s Klansman" instead of just a "normal guy." Even as he scoffed at such stereotypes, Hovater constantly labeled others: "libtard," "leftist rags," "faggots," or "shitlibs." The advantage of being viewed as "Nazi scum," Hovater noted, is that the establishment doesn't see how white power actors are networking and building social media connections and other sorts of "really big stuff. And if they want to disregard us and act as if we're idiots, that's like giving us cover. That's fine."

Hovater knew he would be exposed after the article. Almost immediately, a local Dayton group published his identifying information and the phone number of the restaurant where he, his wife, and his brother-in-law worked. They were fired. Hovater and his wife moved, staying afloat with the help of a "GoyFundMe" drive, an antisemitic play on "GoFundMe."

Johansson also asked Hovater about his path to white power, noting that Fausset's *New York Times* article had featured a photo of his bookshelf that included a text by Holocaust denier David Irving. "It's funny," Hovater replied. "[Fausset] could have taken a picture of basically any other shelf in my house and it would have been considerably more damning."

Hovater explained that, while reading history was important to his "entry into the movement," *Mein Kampf* was the book that had most influenced him in his path to National Socialism. Even as a youth, Hovater had questioned the Holocaust. "Why would you kill all those people," he said to Johansson, "if you had free labor." Invoking a Holocaust denial trope, Hovater said this was another example of "the big lie" that unthinking "normies" took for granted.

In contrast, Johansson and Hovater positioned themselves as the ones who are critical thinkers and see through the mystifications of Jewish media control. Having seen the truth of the situation, Hovater and Johansson had committed themselves to the National Socialist cause, turning from decadent pleasures and making sacrifices—like the one Hovater made by exposing himself.

The jokes drop away at this point, their conversation serious. "I value our message," Hovater says. "I value white people having an ethnostate over some job. That doesn't matter. Or my anonymity—that doesn't matter. A future for our white children is just vastly more important than any secrecy I could have maintained." If he doesn't act, his children are "guaranteed to grow up in a world where we [whites] are a minority and we'll be hated and we'll be history's villains forever."

"We're all going to die," Johansson replies. "Death is a real thing" that most people ignore as they engage in frivolous pursuits. What is important is to promote a "white future and a future for Nordic babies." Hovater agrees, "There are bigger things we're trying to work toward here." He adds, "When you're in your deathbed . . . what are you going to tell your kids?" They have arrived at a moment suggesting a Rosebud answer: their devotion to "the movement" is directly linked to securing a future for the white race.

They note difficulties their movement faces: a Jewish-controlled system, "slumbering" masses, "pathological altruism," and immigrant replacement. Hovater complains that white people are blamed for all social ills even as people are being "brought in to displace us" and given "our jobs, our homes, and our money."

The importance of this issue to Hovater is underscored by his Twitter account, which headlines in caps and boldface, "Repeal the 1965 Immigration Act" (which loosened immigration restrictions). Hovater's Gab social media account, in turn, features what appears to be a Nazi "total war" banner on the top and, below, a picture with Trump's head and the words "They Have to Go"—likely a reference to a 2015 remark Trump made about undocumented immigrants.[38]

~

"So do you see connections between Hovater and Nuon Chea?" I ask my students.

"It's odd. But they both claim to have joined their cause in the name of a good," a student replies.

"Both Nuon Chea and Hovater looked to the future," I say, "as they sought to create a better world in the name of righting wrongs. Both foregrounded grievance—class for Nuon Chea versus white race oppression for Hovater—while claiming to see the true state of things, a truth obscured. Once that truth was glimpsed, they sought to act and rectify the situation. They shared a common beginning in grievance leading to their different social movement extremist paths, each with reasons for turning to violence and hate."

"We're back to the issue of twisted morality," a student notes, then asks, "What about Nuon Chea and the Khmer Rouge Party Line? How does Hovater connect to 'the fires' model?"

"What did you get from the podcast?" I query.

"They have demonstrations, like in Charlottesville and that chicken plant in Kentucky," a student responds, "but the Internet seems key to their 'organization.' We listened to a supremacist podcast, after all. And they seem to like trolling. Poor Cher!"

"And the movement's global," another student notes. "The host's from Sweden."

"What about 'politics'?" I ask.

"They hate Jews!" a student answers. "They were talking about Jewish media control and called the Holocaust 'the Big Lie.' They seem to have their own language."

"Yeah," another student adds, "and they claim to be critical thinkers. They were even talking about death. Heavy. They aren't stupid, but they say bizarre stuff."

"Anything else?"

"White power!" a student says. "Hovater talks about white rights and seems to want a white homeland. He also said he worries about the future of white babies."

"Immigration's key, too," a third student points out. "He talks about the immigrants taking the white jobs."

"What about 'consciousness'?"

"He says he's always leaned pro-white," a student replies, "and he loves *Mein Kampf*. That's full of hate against Jews."

* * *

"Do you think you can use the Khmer Rouge 'fires' triangle in your final essays?" I ask as the class session draws to a close.

"It may be useful," a student replies, "but the terms are a bit abstract. I hope I can remember all of it."

"That's true," I agree. "Maybe we can take the Khmer Rouge 'fires' triangle and phrase it in a slightly different way. I'm actually using a related acronym as a mnemonic device in a lecture I'm giving to educators about the Khmer Rouge 'fires.' A fire needs fuel to stoke the flames, so I'm using the easy-to-remember acronym 'FUEL.' The four letters of 'FUEL' stand for 'Fiction,' 'Upheaval,' 'Establishment,' and 'BeLief,' which loosely overlap with the four dimensions of the Khmer Rouge 'fires' model we discussed—politics (fictions), circumstance (upheaval), organization (establishment), and consciousness (belief)."

I give a short lecture to finish class.

"'F' is for 'Fiction,'" I begin, "the narratives legitimating violence and hate. These fictions center around a vision, a notion of both what should be and what prevents it—an us and a them, the former pure, the latter devalued as contamination. The Khmer Rouge fiction was clear: a vision of a utopian society, one from which dangerous and corrupting 'elements' and 'contradictions' had been eliminated—leaving only pure revolutionaries with a proper revolutionary consciousness.

"'U' is for 'Upheaval,'" I continue, "the tumult that sets the stage, makes people more receptive to the narrative that promises a better future and scapegoats the 'others' who are supposedly to blame. If this upheaval comes in many forms—political change, social upheaval, economic crisis—it most often is linked to earlier violence and war. The Khmer Rouge rise to power provides an illustration of all of these types of upheaval, but the Vietnam conflict and Cambodian civil war loom particularly large.

"'E' is for 'Establishment,'" I go on, "the structures intended to make the fiction a reality. If Fiction overlaps with the politics (ideology and discourse) of the Khmer Rouge Party Line, Establishment is a more dynamic way to think of its formal and informal organization: the structures, routines, practices, and disciplines meant to actualize and enforce a new and exclusionary revolutionary way of being that is freed from 'contradictions.'

"'L' is for BeLief,'" I finish, "devotion to the movement and cause. Some believers are firm in their convictions, drivers of the enterprise. Some may have more pragmatic and instrumental goals. Belief helps propel the Establishment and enact its fiction-based goals, including genocidal exclusions. Belief is directly linked to Khmer Rouge consciousness, the idealized revolutionary subjectivity calibrated to accord with the politics/fiction and organization/establishment of the Khmer Rouge Party Line.

"So one way to think about 'what makes a man start fires,'" I recap, "is to consider the F-U-E-L that feeds the flames. But bear in mind that these fires are also continuously influenced by 'weather,' part of circumstances that heighten or dampen the flames, sometimes leading to pathways of cumulative radicalization. The inclusions and exclusions of Khmer Rouge ideology were present from the start, manifest in the talk of 'contradictions' and 'elements' in the 1960 formulation of the Party Line. They remained evident in Pol Pot's 1977 speech. But there is no straight path to genocide. The fires require fuel to get started, then favorable 'weather' to begin to blaze, winds to fan the flame, sometimes with gale force that catalyzes a genocidal conflagration.

"How does this connect to Hovater?" I continue. "His group has its National Socialist and white race plight Fictions. They blame Jews, immigrants, and people of color for their woes, seek to transform society. Hovater's also part of an Establishment, if a small one. The Traditionalist Worker Party is organized and seeks ways to fulfill its future-oriented goals. It lacks, however, larger access to the political system, though it has forged ties and made common cause with other white power groups and recognizes Trump as someone who is sympathetic to its fictions and goals. Hovater is also clearly a Believer, a devoted white power extremist ready to fight for his cause.

"They seek recruits," I note, "drawing on upheaval, displacement, and job loss, framing these issues in terms of immigration, desegregation, and the threat to white race survival. But, in the end, they lack access to the levers of power in the present even as they are loosely organized and ready to fight. And there are many more groups and actors like them. Unite the Right underscored the danger of such groups joining together as part of a larger white-power-extremist movement.

"In this regard," I conclude, "the white-power-extremist movement somewhat resembles the 1960s Khmer Rouge movement—both have a vision, decentralized organization, and believers. It took circumstance, the winds of change, to create a situation in which the Khmer Rouge could rise to power. As events unfold, each group and every person assess their moral compass, make decisions about how far they are willing to go in the name of their cause. Some take small steps, like participating in Charlottesville. Others, like Nuon Chea, are willing to take things to a much greater extreme in the name of an apocalyptic vision demanding victory over the impure and evil—to achieve what they perceive as an all-important good.

"We're out of time," I finish. "We can discuss this more in the next class if you'd like. In the meantime, good luck with finishing your 'fires' final essays!"

* * *

APRIL 24, 2018, RUTGERS UNIVERSITY, NEWARK, NJ

On the last day of class, my students present PechaKuchas—a six-minute, forty-second format originated by architects, which involves presenting twenty slides advancing on a twenty-second timer—on the perpetrators they have been studying all semester.

We dim the lights. "The Hater" appears on the screen. Hitler. Stalin. Castro. Pinochet. Even Kaczynski, the Unabomber. Drawing on the course readings, each student gives their answer to Fausset's question, "What makes a man start fires?"

Then we reach the last presentation of the class. A student takes the podium. She shouts, "There's an elephant in the room!"

A large elephant, crammed into a tiny green room, appears on the screen. The student pauses for effect, then says, "American genocide." Her next slide is an animated map showing the European colonial expansion since 1450. The screen rapidly fills with dots covering most of the globe. A statue of Columbus, hands blood red, appears next. Her "Hater" is Captain John Underhill. She tells about his role in the early-seventeenth-century Pequot War, a Massachusetts Bay genocide—one of the first among many "American fires," this one taking place before there even was a USA.

"Professor's asked us a trick question," she announces, then allows a long pause. The image of a man breathing fire appears on the screen.

"What makes a man set fires?" she says, then falls silent, her words hanging in the air. "The question is a misdirection!" she suddenly exclaims. "It focuses attention on the actions of a single individual. We need to account for structure." The student goes on to look at the pre-conditions of the Pequot genocide and the sparks that set the conflict aflame. She touches on ethnocentrism, dehumanization, social struc-ture, and the longer history of settler colonialism that laid the precondi-tions for the Pequot War.

The Hater. Interrogate the question. A lesson learned in Trump's USA.

~

"What are you going to do after graduation?" I ask. The presentations over, we sit around a seminar table eating slices of "Congratulations!" chocolate fudge cake.

"I'm going into the Air Force," says a student who had presented on the leader of ISIS. She explains, "It'll pay for grad school."

One wants to work at the United Nations. Another is starting an MA, hoping for a future in anthropology. "AmeriCorps," a student who had focused on Fidel Castro states. The others say "not sure" or "no idea."

"What about you, Professor?" a student asks, turning the question on me.

"I'm not certain," I reply. "But I'm thinking of writing a book on Nuon Chea and my experience testifying at the ECCC."

"Mr. Expert Witness!" she exclaims.

"If I do," I continue after the laughter subsides, "I'll also talk about President Trump, trace connections to our current historical moment."

Then I add, "I may write about the question we discussed in this course and the question you presented on today: 'What makes a man start fires?'"

"What's the title?" a student asks.

"I don't know—maybe I'll call it 'The Hater,'" I reply, then add, "but that might be too strong. I could just call it something like 'Against Hate.'

"Which one do you like best?" I ask.

"The Hater!" the students shout, giving this book a first title.

"What happened to Nuon Chea?" a student queries. "Was he convicted?"

"Nuon Chea's case is expected to be decided later this year," I reply. "We'll see if he's convicted of genocide."

"How will your book relate Cambodia to President Trump and Charlottesville?" another student asks.

"That's a good question," I reply. "In some of the ways we've discussed in class, no doubt. Maybe I'll use the 'fires' model and look at 'politics,' 'organization,' and 'consciousness.' The book will have to look at the longer history of white power and link it to the present, for sure. It will also need to examine social structure, ideology, and power, the things that 'Hater' discourse and an overemphasis on agency too readily obscure.

"As we saw when we analyzed Hovater's podcast," I go on, "there's a lot more to be unpacked about white power in today's USA—as well as possible connections to the Trump administration in terms of things like hate speech and immigration policy."

"Will you write about Charlottesville?" a student asks.

"For sure," I say. "And there may also another chapter to that story. One of the organizers is trying to get a permit to hold a one-year anniversary sequel, a 'Unite the Right' part two. If they do, I expect that a lot of what Hovater was talking about in the podcast will be on display. Maybe I'll attend and search for more answers to Fausset's 'what makes a man start fires' question about white power extremists like Hovater. As usual, though, I expect most commentators will still be spotlighting the Hater."

3

White Genocide

"Kessler, you racist motherfucker!" a man screams, red-faced. Hundreds of protesters add to the din. "Shame!" "Fascist scum!" "Creep!"

The expletives come fast as I watch Jason Kessler and a few dozen Unite the Right 2 demonstrators emerge from the depths of the Foggy Bottom Metro and begin their march down Pennsylvania Avenue in Washington, DC. Hundreds of people, cordoned off by the police, greet them with "the finger," shouts, and a hint of violence.

I had spent time with some of the counterprotesters in the days leading up to the march. After coming across an Internet announcement from the Shut It Down DC Coalition, composed of thirty-eight counter-protest groups, I attended a one-day "Free School" on "Resistance Training" at a DC Episcopal church.[1] When I arrived, I went to the wrong door. Two young men, dressed in black, were guarding and pointed me to a different entrance. Antifa.

Inside, hundreds of people were breaking into panels with titles like "How to Abolish White Supremacy, and Why," "Deescalation 101," and "Queer/Femme/Two-Spirit/Gender-Non-Conforming/Trans/Womxn/Disability Resistance." Some people wore Black Lives Matter shirts or dressed in Antifa black. Others, like me, did not belong to a particular group but were curious to learn more. Many of the attendees were the age of my students. Event promotional materials warned, "Keep This Space an Alt-Right, White Supremacist, Fascist Free Space."

I joined a session, "Resisting Anti-Semitism 101." A young gay man explained how antisemitism related to intersectionality and other forms of oppression, past and present. Next, I participated in "Security for Actions."

We stood and did safety exercises for when, we were told, we would be on the "front lines" facing "fascists." Our speaker warned, "Remember, you are dealing with two types of fascists. The supremacists and the police."

The last session, "Investigating White Supremacy Overview," was led by an African American activist and journalist who shared his years of experience attending white power rallies and doxing or exposing the participants. A young man in a black shirt that had two eyes above "Antifa" lettering asked very specific questions about databases. As the discussion proceeded, people began to refer to the Unite the Right marchers as "the Nazis." "Take photos of everything," our speaker suggested toward the end of the session. Then he added with a chuckle, "They will also be doing that to you."

The next evening I attended "A Mindful Response" at the Western Presbyterian Church, just a ten-minute walk from Foggy Bottom. A banner at the entrance read "Black Lives Matter" on the right, "'Love one another'—Jesus" on the left. This service, the first speaker told us, would differ from other counterprotests in its focus on loving the enemy and God's love of all. At one point, we were asked to sit in silence and meditate on oppression, othering, and oneness. "God is in you and me," a pastor said, then paused before finishing, "and in those [Unite the Right 2] marchers." Together, young and old, we walked to Foggy Bottom Metro to chalk "prayers of oneness" to greet them. "You are loved!" chalked a little girl. The cement filled with dozens of messages: "No White Supremacy," "Free Hugs," and "Hate Has No Home Here." An older man wrote, "Walk in Peace."

～

Now, their messages are being trampled underfoot by Kessler and his two dozen or so Unite the Right 2 demonstrators. They look at the screaming crowds, not the faded chalkings on the ground. The police direct the marchers along a secured corridor.

Carrying a US flag, Kessler smiles and chats with a colleague as his group begins marching toward Lafayette Square, located behind the

White House. Just a couple of days earlier, neo-Nazi Patrick Little, dressed in a dark suit, stood there holding a sign that read "Expel the Jews." Little was initially listed as one of Kessler's featured speakers.

The Unite the Right 2 protesters are protected by two rings of police—riding motorcycles on the outside, bicycles on the inside. Kessler's group videotapes the screaming counterprotesters, and vice versa, each side seeking to expose the other.

As the speaker noted at the "Resistance Training" workshop, doxing had been used to great effect after Charlottesville. Some Unite the Right marchers lost their jobs and were ostracized in their communities. Other white power groups and actors, including the *Daily Stormer*, were scrubbed from mainstream social media and Internet platforms—what Hovater and Johansson called "the great shutdown" during the Nordic Frontier podcast interview—forcing them to use alternative services like Gab.[2] Many claim their free speech rights are being violated, as had been the case in the shutdown of their Charlottesville rally. Social media providers and anti-hate groups, in turn, argue that there are limits to hate speech.

Some Unite the Right actors, including Kessler and Cantwell, have been sued or charged. Anti-hate groups such as the Southern Poverty Law Center have been using lawsuits since the 1980s, sometimes winning damages that brought down major white power organizations—or at least held them accountable in situations where criminal justice failed.

On October 12, 2017, ten Virginia residents who had been injured at Charlottesville filed a major lawsuit against a range of white power actors, including Kessler, Cantwell, Spencer, James Fields (whose car struck and killed Heather Heyer), Azzmador and Anglin from *Daily Stormer*, Matthew Heimbach and his Traditionalist Worker Party, Vanguard America, and different branches of the KKK.[3] Kessler, in turn, sued the city of Charlottesville for its failure to stop the violence and protect the marchers' freedom of speech. The litigation would continue throughout Trump's presidency.

These stressors contributed to ruptures within the white power movement, historically loosely organized given the wide range of groups, actors, and interests. These fissures are manifest at Unite the Right 2. Many key Charlottesville actors have refused to attend. Cantwell posted, "Follow Kessler at Your Peril." On the *Daily Stormer*, Anglin warned his followers that they would "look like ruffians" and be blamed.[4] Kessler's initial rally permit application listed David Duke, Patrick Little, and others who did not attend. For many of these actors, the potential cost of participating was too high. Charlottesville had also underscored the importance of good optics as critical to achieving the long-term goal of mainstreaming white power.

As a result, Kessler moved center stage ahead of the rally.[5] He was everywhere in the news. The day before Unite the Right 2, the *Washington Post* ran a feature on him, "Inside Jason Kessler's Hate-Fueled Rise." The story traced Kessler's bumpy path from the Left (Obama supporter and Occupy Wall Street participant) to the far Right (interacting with a host of white power "stars" and leading the Charlottesville charge against the removal of the Lee statue). Kessler now positions himself as a victim, someone who has been ostracized by his local community and unfairly turned into the face of white hate.

On the drive to Washington, DC, I had listened to a National Public Radio interview with Kessler. Kessler sought to distance himself from extremists while situating himself as a white civil rights actor. "I'm not a white supremacist," he stated. "I'm not even a white nationalist. I consider myself a civil and human rights advocate focusing on the underrepresented Caucasian demographic." Later he would emphasize that neo-Nazis were not welcome at Unite the Right 2. Just as the Lee statue was a pretext to promote white power at Charlottesville, so too are white civil rights now a cover to espouse extreme views at Unite the Right 2.

When pressed in the interview, Kessler's white power views came into focus. At one point, Kessler invoked a debunked theory about racial differences in IQ that places Blacks at the bottom of a hierarchical order.

"Just as a matter of science," Kessler contended. "IQ testing is pretty clear." The racist pseudoscience my students had read about during our Charlottesville Teach-In was on display. A quick perusal of Kessler's social media posts and podcast interviews reveals his more extremist leanings, including claims about Jewish conspiracy, immigrant menace, and white peril.[6] And then there is his key role in Charlottesville.

Kessler's claims are also belied by the two dozen or so protesters who march with him from Foggy Bottom Metro to Lafayette Square—a minuscule showing for which Kessler will be later mocked by the Left and the Right even as he complains that the DC police had forced his group onto trains ahead of schedule and left many marchers behind. Some of those who walk with him now have masked their faces, around which some wrap scarves imprinted with the US flag. A few wear MAGA caps.

The marchers and counterprotesters engage in banter. But the DC police, better prepared than those in Charlottesville the year before, keep a distance between the groups. There will be no violence today. I watch the Unite the Right 2 protesters disappear into the blocked-off Lafayette Square, where they will hold their small rally far from the counterprotesting crowds that vastly outnumber them. Antifa, Black Lives Matter, and many other groups keep watch on all sides of the park, awaiting the marchers' return.

Unite the Right 2's Charlottesville echoes are soon on display. Close-ups of the protesters belie Kessler's promise that white supremacists and neo-Nazis are not welcome at the rally. A masked and gloved man holds a sign reading, "Wake Up White Men! You are a minority by 2042. Don't let OUR nation turn into the slums of India, Mexico, or Africa." Another placard reads, "White Lives Matter. It's not racist to love your own people. Take a stand—Being White is still right." At the bottom, the sign gives an e-mail address: "wlm1488ny@gmail.com."

Others have hate symbols stained on their skin. The number "1488" is tattooed on the forearm of a dark-haired woman with glasses, her face covered by a black scarf. A nearby man, goggles across his forehead and a flag draped across his shoulders, has "14" tattooed on his forehead and "white power" across his neck amidst a sea of Aryan symbols.

"1488." White supremacist code.

~

"I wonder when they'll come back out," I say to another anthropologist I had run into at the Unite the Right 2 rally. We both have been furiously taking notes and snapshots.

"Hopefully they won't sneak out the back," he replies.

We stand near a police barricade blocking the hundreds of protesters who would like to confront Kessler's group in Lafayette Square. The protesters stretch in all directions, young and old, religious and radical, rich and poor, straight and queer. Many hold signs: "My Grandfather Fought Nazis So I Wouldn't Have To!" "From Charlottesville to the White House: Shut Down White Supremacy!" "'Nothing in the World Is More Dangerous Than Sincere Ignorance and Conscientious Stupidity'—Martin Luther King, Jr." The White House looms in the background.

Dozens of Antifa mill about. They dress completely in black, hoodie tops and black scarves obscuring their faces. I observe an Antifa couple holding hands—love amid the hate and forged by shared cause—and think of the "Resistance Training" workshop. I wonder how many of the young attendees are among the masked Antifa crowds. Some Antifa also hold signs. One reads "BASH FASCism," with a baseball bat beating "ism" into lowercase lettering.

There is a sense of expectation in the crowd, the memory of Charlottesville still fresh. At one point, the police put on gas masks. Another time, they rev their motorcycle engines as if something is about to happen. Meanwhile, Antifa press against the barricade, ready for Kessler's return. I notice an Antifa counterprotester carrying a pail of paintballs. Later someone will throw Roman candles at the police. The police and Antifa engage in cat-and-mouse chases as we wait.

"Let's check out Kessler's Twitter to see if we can figure out what's happening," I suggest to my colleague. Kessler's account is running footage that pans the angry crowds.

"Doesn't it look like the footage being shot from around here?" I ask. We do some quick sleuthing.

"There it is," my colleague says. "See the camera by the hot dog stand?" He points to a cameraman accompanied by a taller man.

"Let's go talk to them," I say. "Maybe he's with Kessler and we can ask some questions."

We thread our way across the street, still packed tight, and approach the two-man crew.

"Are you filming for Kessler?" I ask.

"No, we're from a TV agency in Berlin," the taller man replies with a slight European accent.

"Well, your video is being live-streamed by Kessler."

"Who is Kessler?" the shorter cameraman asks in heavily accented English. He shows us his media pass and shakes our hand.

"The guy who organized the rally," the taller man tells him as his cameraman stops filming. "Ugh, let's go. We could get killed. They must be streaming from our YouTube channel. Anyone can do it."

I glance at the teeming crowds of Antifa and realize he is right. Many of the counterprotesters are frustrated. Some came expecting confrontation. When I turn around, the tall man has already disappeared into the crowd.

At bit of research reveals that their media outlet, Ruptly, is part of the RT network, a Russian news agency that many allege is a Kremlin propaganda tool.[7] Ruptly's feature story for the day headlines, "USA Far-Right Rally Organizer Kessler Warns against 'Making White People an Oppressed Minority,'" and includes an interview with Kessler.

Amid the circulating claims of Russian interference in US politics, the connection is notable. Putin and Russia are also valorized in white power circles. Might RT be trying to promote their cause and inflame already high political tensions in the United States?

"Do you think there's a connection?" I ask my anthropology colleague.

"It's quite a coincidence," he says. "But there's no way to know."

The police announce that the Unite the Right 2 marchers have left DC. The crowds begin to disperse. It starts to rain. Before too long, white power extremism will again be headlining the news.

* * *

OCTOBER 28, 2018, PITTSBURGH, PENNSYLVANIA

"HIAS likes to bring invaders in that kill our people," the post warns. "I can't sit by and watch my people get slaughtered. Screw your optics, I'm going in."

On October 28, 2018, Robert Bowers writes these words before massacring eleven worshippers at Tree of Life synagogue in Pittsburgh. While shooting, he shouts, "All Jews must die!" His social media account on the far-right platform Gab, which is quickly taken down, is filled with antisemitic and white power images, including this one about the Hebrew Immigrant Aid Society (HIAS), which has assisted immigrants and refugees for over a hundred years. An earlier Bowers post reads, "Open your Eyes! It's the filthy EVIL jews Bringing filthy EVIL Muslims into the Country!"[8]

People search for answers. "What makes a man start fires?" "Why?"

Trump offers an answer. He spotlights Bowers as the Hater, a man of "twisted malice" and "cruel hate." Trump pinpoints the source of Bowers's "evil" act: the "vile, hate-filled poison of anti-Semitism."[9]

His response wins praise in some quarters. Supporters argue that Trump's remarks illustrate the absurdity of Trump-Hitler comparisons and the idea that Trump supports neo-Nazis. They note Trump's strong support of Israel and the fact that his daughter and son-in-law are observant Jews. "Synagogue Shooter Hated Donald Trump and Shows What Real Hatred, Anti-semitism Looks Like," headlines a *USA Today* op-ed.[10] The author points to Bowers's antisemitic social media posts, including suggestions that Trump is a pawn in the hands of "globalist"

Jews and critique of Trump for betraying the far right with his condemnation after Charlottesville.

Others say not so fast. They make connections between Trump's incitement past and present and blame him for acting like an inciter-in-chief. Charlottesville looms in the background. The head of the only synagogue in Charlottesville, who had watched the Unite the Right marchers pass by with swastika flags and "Heil Hitler" shouts, contends that there is a "straight line" from Charlottesville to Tree of Life, one that made Tree of Life "an inevitable tragedy."[11] Trump's incitement, ranging from his "very fine people on both sides" remark to his recent demonization of (Jewish) "globalists" like George Soros, provides the connection.

Trump critics add detail to this line of thought. Some underscore Trump's long history of incitement, including his stoking of the flames of the Central Park 5 case—when five Black youths were jailed and later exonerated for assaulting and raping a white jogger—and then the Obama "birther" conspiracy. Trump invoked both issues again during his presidency, including a Charlottesville echo that "you had people on both sides of" the Central Park 5 case.[12] Others point to how Trump encouraged his supporters to attack protesters at his rallies.

Some focus on the more immediate context in which Trump made his remarks about Tree of Life, noting that Trump had been fanning the flames of hate for months. In the days before the Unite the Right 2 rally, for example, Trump insulted the intelligence of several African Americans, including CNN host Don Lemon, basketball star LeBron James, and Congresswoman Maxine Waters. He also called his former aide Omarosa Manigault Newmann a "dog" and a "crazed, crying low-life."[13] On the anniversary of Charlottesville, Trump provoked still more controversy by failing to condemn white power violence, generically denouncing instead "all types of violence."[14]

Trump's white fear discourse took on a new urgency in the months after Unite the Right 2 as, with the November 6, 2018, midterm elections approaching, he began to relentlessly talk about an "onslaught of illegal aliens" invading across the southern border. To underscore his point, Trump warned of the looming threat posed by an approaching "caravan" filled with "criminals" and other supposedly dangerous types. At times, his language took on almost apocalyptic tones, which were echoed by some Republicans and conservative media outlets.

White nationalists cheered. Sometimes they took action. In the days before Tree of Life, the nation was stunned by a series of pipe bombs sent to prominent Democrats and Trump critics, including Hillary Clinton, former president Obama, George Soros, Maxine Waters, and CNN, a Trump favorite for the charge of "fake news."

On October 26, a Trump fanatic, Cesar Sayoc Jr., was arrested. Images of the muscled Sayoc, wearing a "Make America Great Again" hat and holding anti-CNN signs at Trump rallies, began to circulate in the media. So too did images of Sayoc's white van, covered with images of Trump and his enemies. One, titled "The Swamp," featured many of the people targeted by Sayoc's failed bombs. In another, Hillary Clinton's head was placed in gun site crosshairs. Sayoc would later liken Trump rallies to "a new found drug."[15]

It was in this late October 2018 context that Bowers launched his Tree of Life attack. Bowers named immigrant invasion, facilitated by Jews, as his motive, invoking fear of a "great replacement" and antisemitic conspiracy theory. "Jews are the children of satan," Bowers's Gab social media account claimed, invoking a Christian Identity trope. Elsewhere Bowers used another code word for Jews, demonizing "globalists" like George Soros.

Undeterred, Trump condemned Bowers but was soon back on message, ramping up his white-fear rhetoric even more. The situation was so bad that, Trump informed the nation, he was sending troops to the border. "Many Gang Members and some very bad people are mixed into the Caravan heading to our Southern Border," Trump warned, adding, "This is an invasion of our Country and our Military is waiting for you!" Meanwhile, his campaign began playing a commercial so tinged with racist hate that networks pulled it from the air.

In interviews, Trump made it clear that he knew what he was doing and that he could "tone it up" even more. Even as he did so, he continued to blame "fake news" for the hate. Around the same time, the Anti-Defamation League reported that antisemitic hate chatter was increasing and antisemitic hate crimes had risen 57 percent the year before.[16] It was in this charged context that Bowers attacked Tree of Life.

* * *

NOVEMBER 6, 2018, RUTGERS UNIVERSITY, NEWARK, NJ

Now, like everyone else, my students are searching for answers—just as they were after Charlottesville. In response to Tree of Life, I revise my syllabus once again. On November 6, my afternoon undergraduate class on human rights holds a Tree of Life Teach-In. It focuses on white-power-extremist history and ideology as we seek to unpack the motivations behind Bowers's shooting.

Bowers's social media posts provide a trail of clues. For his profile picture, Bowers had posted a photo of a radar gun flashing four numbers: "1488." The same numbers tattooed on the Unite the Right 2's marcher's face. The same numbers Dylann Roof, the white power extremist who broke into a Charleston church and killed nine African Americans in 2015, carved into the sand of a beach before posting a photograph of the image on his website. Roof appears to have used "AyranBlood1488" as his handle on Anglin and Azzmador's extremist website, the *Daily Stormer*.[17] In white-power-extremist circles, "1488" is everywhere.

"1488." A mystery. Another clue to the Charlottesville question, "Why?" Today, my students will learn to break this white power code.

∼

"Why do you think Bowers attacked Tree of Life?"

I ask this question at the start of our Tree of Life Teach-In, which falls on the day of the midterm elections.

"Trump!" a student quickly suggests, then adds, "All he's been talking about recently is Black and Brown invasion!"

"Some people are suggesting that," I say. "And they said similar things after Charlottesville. And inflammatory language is certainly a facilitator. The problem is that it makes it seem like white power extremism is primarily due to President Trump. But white supremacy has been around a long time. If we view events like Tree of Life and Charlottesville as exceptional, we lose sight of how they are connected to the longer history of white supremacy in the US. Maybe the Holocaust adage, 'never forget,' applies to white power as well to remind us that such violence doesn't appear out of the blue.

"So even if there is a connection between President Trump and white power," I go on, "it's necessary to carefully consider the evidence to make such a claim. And it's all the more important to do this given how charged political discussions are today. There needs to be room for different perspectives. Otherwise, we'll simply be making statements based on opinion, not analysis and facts.

"Why else do you think Bowers might have attacked?"

"Because he's a supremacist and antisemite," another student suggests, offering the sort of "hater" answer that has been dominating news coverage of the Bowers attack.

"Let's start with your first term," I respond. "What do you mean by 'white supremacist'?"

"White race rule," another student says. "It was there at the start of this country. It's here today. Just look at the manifesto we read for class." The student is referring to a tract written by the neo-Nazi David Eden Lane.

"That's a good start," I say. "But perhaps we need to start making some distinctions. Is white supremacy today the same as it was back in 1619 when Jamestown was founded or 1776 when the Declaration of Independence was proclaimed?"

"A lot of stuff happened between those dates," a third student notes. "The Civil War. Martin Luther King. Civil rights. But white supremacy is alive and well today. And it's not just Charlottesville or Tree of Life. It's around us every day."

"Those are good points, and they suggest we need to start with some historical distinctions," I say. "How might white supremacy have changed through time?"

"The civil rights movement is huge," a student offers. "Suddenly Black and Brown people had far more rights. The same is true about the Civil War."

"Until Jim Crow," another student notes.

"That's certainly true," I reply. "And you indirectly raise a critical reminder. There are different ways to analytically parse the past, and the choices we make inflect our analysis. For example, if we select the civil rights movement as a moment that marks a 'before and after,' we also fold white supremacy into a continuous stream.

"Some people have graphically represented white power this way," I continue, "denoting enslavement by a red bar that runs from 1619 to the Civil War, then segregation in blue from 1865 until the 1964 Civil Rights Act, and finally 'free' denoted by a green bar from 1964 into the present. As you can imagine, the red and blue bars dwarf the green, underscoring how long white supremacy was overtly institutionalized in the US."

"Things now don't seem so free to me," a student cuts in. "What about the mass imprisonment of people of color? And now we have ICE, DACA kids, border detentions, and the Charlottesville crowd."

"Those are good points," I note. "And they suggest one of the dangers of such historical markers. They lead us to think of the 'before and after' in uniform ways when more complicated historical dynamics are in motion. They direct us away from process and change. To say enslavement started in 1619, for example, obscures how it developed more gradually, becoming more systemic and codified by law by the end of the century in places like Virginia.

"And," I go on, "a singular focus on enslavement, important as it is, diverts us from how white supremacy impacted other people of color, such as Native Americans and immigrants. The system of racial hierarchy that undergirded enslavement emerged in part out of early encounters with

Native American 'savages,' who were the first victims of settler-colonial genocide and atrocity crimes in what would become the United States."

Systemic White Supremacy

To deal with such issues, some scholars argue that white supremacy should be viewed as a system premised on notions of hierarchy and difference that varies across time and place.[18] This perspective is partly a response to scholarship that individualizes racism as learned prejudice, thereby directing attention away from how it is embedded in longer histories and broader social structures.

For such scholars, then, contemporary racism must be understood as part of a global white-supremacist system that emerged with European colonial explorations of the New World, the slave trade, and capitalist expansion. This perspective dovetails with strands of research on colonialism, especially work on settler colonialism in North America and Australia.

If some colonial regimes were more focused on resource extraction, settler colonialism was also centered on territoriality. In British North America, colonial encounters with Indigenous peoples proceeded in varying and more or less violent ways focused on the appropriation of land.

Patrick Wolfe has argued that this settler-colonial process was characterized by a "logic of elimination."[19] Drawing in part on the work of Raphael Lemkin, who coined the term "genocide," Wolfe argues that settler colonialism operates through a two-part process involving both the destruction of the Indigenous group and the imposition of a new society echoing the colonizers' country of origin. As opposed to being a genocidal "event," Wolfe argues, the destruction of Indigenous peoples often takes place over long periods of time and is structural.

These structures encompass a range of ideas, institutions, laws, and practices. When first encountering Indigenous peoples in the New World, Europeans often viewed them through a religious, patriarchal, and proto-racial lens.[20] This lens was hierarchical and stigmatizing as Indigenous peoples were seen as "beasts," "savages," and "devils" subordinate to Christians, and especially Christian men, in God's "great chain of being." A range of debates arose concerning the degree of Indigenous humanity and their right to land, which was appropriated on pretexts ranging from Lockean concepts of property to Puritan notions of exceptionalism.

Such views, later reinforced by notions of race, extinction, and Manifest Destiny, were paired with institutions and practices that legitimated taking land and diminishing the claims of Indigenous peoples. This process, facilitated by the disruptions and devastation of disease, was at times highly coercive and violent (war, massacres, enslavement, forced relocations, the reservation system) and in other situations more indirect (boarding schools, treaties, and laws regarding property, citizenship, and rights). If events unfolded in different ways across time and place, the end result was often the same: Indigenous erasure through death, social destruction, and assimilation[21]—what Wolfe calls "structural genocide."

This process of Indigenous destruction and land appropriation helped lay the groundwork for enslavement, which was at the heart of the white-supremacist system that emerged in the North American colonies. While some white settlers were contractually bound as indentured servants in early colonial history, enslaved Africans increasingly performed the hard labor necessary to work the appropriated Indigenous lands to produce crops like tobacco for trade—just as they did on sugar plantations in places like Brazil and the Caribbean Islands. The collapse of the tobacco market in the 1660s increased this need for cheap labor further.

By the end of the seventeenth century, a system of white supremacy was largely in place in British North America. Ideologically, enslaved Africans were initially often viewed through the same religious and great-chain-of-being lens as Native Americans (for example, as "savages," "uncivilized," animalistic, and devilish). The permanence of their enslavement, however, had to be justified in new ways. The idea of race, which was emerging as Enlightenment thinkers sought to classify human difference, was critical in this regard. Hierarchical typologies linking physical characteristics to cultural and mental traits could be used to assert that race was immutable.

In British North America, this idea was increasingly filtered through a stark white-Black binary, with other races, such as "redskin" Native Americans, inflected in somewhat different ways, such as through extinction discourses that dovetailed with the eliminationist logic of settler colonialism.[22] From this racial vantage, then, black skin was tied to a Black "nature" legitimating enslavement—ignorance, animality, criminality, hypersexuality, immorality, deceitfulness, laziness, bad smell, savagery, and inferiority. Many of these racial caricatures persist into the present.

This ideology of white supremacy was reinforced by related institutions and practices.[23] In the second half of the seventeenth century, for example, Virginia had passed laws forbidding miscegenation and affirming the status of Blacks as property and the right of their owners to treat them accordingly and with brutality and violence if deemed necessary. Such laws continued to be developed into the eighteenth century and were reinforced by the Constitution and the organization of political power after the creation of the United States by white elites, many of whom owned slaves and held white-supremacist views. The boundary between Blacks and whites was policed and regulated, with status, rights, property, and privileges invested in those who satisfied the formal and informal "one drop" hypodescent rule—a situation that differed somewhat from the treatment of Native Americans, which was aimed more toward elimination by destruction or assimilation.

By this time, the key elements of systemic white power were fully operational: white dominance and Black servitude legally sanctioned, politically legitimized, ingrained in everyday practice, violently enforced, and ideologically naturalized.[24] This racial system did not just deprive Blacks of basic rights but was designed to make their servitude perpetual even as the abolitionist movement and North-South tensions would erode it over time. If the Civil War disrupted this system, it continued in modified form through segregation and Jim Crow and was reinforced by new notions of scientific racism and Social Darwinism.

As the United States expanded and new waves of immigration took place, this system of white supremacy was transposed onto other groups.[25] In the mid-nineteenth century, for example, the US frontier shifted westward, a move justified in part by the doctrine of Manifest Destiny and enabled by conquest, including the southwestern territories won by the 1846–48 Mexican-American War. Mexicans living in the new territories were depicted through racial stereotypes, ranging from weakness and laziness to female hypersexuality, and were dispossessed, segregated, and disempowered by social practices, politics, and law.

A convergence of race and gender, characteristic of systemic white supremacy from the start, was also extended to Chinese laborers who began arriving in the United States in the middle of the nineteenth century. They were stigmatized, segregated, and attacked, particularly during moments when "yellow peril" racial fears were spiking.[26] This animus helped fuel passage of the 1882 Chinese Exclusion Act, which severely restricted immigration from China.

If European immigrants were also disempowered by the white-supremacist system and sometimes viewed as a lesser race, most were more quickly assimilated as white—in contrast to Latinx and Asian immigrants, who remained marked and continue to face discrimination in the present. Indeed, even after the civil rights movement, systemic white supremacism endures—both in the United States and globally—albeit in modified, contextually variable, and more covert forms.[27] From this perspective, then, an event like Charlottesville or Tree of Life is an expression of this underlying structural system as opposed to being exceptional.

* * *

"So what, exactly," a student asks, "does this have to do with Bowers? He was attacking Jews, not Blacks. And he doesn't exactly seem like part of 'the system.' He was a lone wolf shooter."

"He's modern-day KKK," another student responds.

"But the KKK lynched Blacks," a third student says.

"They hate Jews, too," the second student says. "Remember the chants of 'Jews will not replace us' at Charlottesville. And weren't Jews sometimes lynched, too?"

"How is that part of a white supremacist 'system'?" the first student responds.

"Well, the police stood by and didn't do anything at Charlottesville," the second student replies.

"But one of the articles we read mentioned that some of the extremists were sued," the first student notes.

"Those are interesting points," I say. "And they speak to a key issue related to white power—the relationship of violence, law, control, and order. If a sociopolitical order is organized informally by traditions, norms, and practices, it is also regulated formally by law. Laws provide guidance and legitimate certain actions and behaviors. But sometimes law has to be 'enforced' by violence or at least the threat of it. That's when the police and courts step in. But there are also informal means of enforcing order, such as the violence of paramilitaries or vigilantes. So if we're talking about systemic white supremacy, then, what is this system seeking to order and control?"

"Black slaves," student replies.

"And other nonwhites," a second student adds. "Don't forget about groups like the Native Americans."

"While recognizing that there were important variations across time and place," I say, "how then was this white-supremacist order enforced prior to the Civil War?"

"With the whip," a student says. "There were a bunch of laws as well. An owner could do whatever they wanted to a slave. But they got worried after Nat Turner's rebellion. They started up slave patrols that did brutal stuff. I read about that in a class I took on race."

"Good points," I state. "So we can say that, prior to the Civil War, a system of white supremacy, which had been established by the late 1600s, was institutionalized and in place, especially in the South, where it was a backbone of the economy and often enforced by fear, violence, terror, and the law—and by both formal and informal means, like the night riders.

"The Civil War," I continue, "severely disrupted this system. It persisted in a modified form, however, through segregation and Jim Crow. New laws were enacted to restrict nonwhite rights. If the police and courts helped enforce this white-supremacist order, so too did vigilante groups like the KKK, which first emerged after the Civil War. In fact, scholars sometimes talk about the 'three waves' of the KKK, which provide a sort of snapshot of how systemic white supremacy changed and continued to use formal and informal mechanisms to enforce this order."

The Three Waves of the Ku Klux Klan

Our Tree of Life Teach-In turns to a discussion of these three waves.[28] As I had noted to the class, the Ku Klux Klan emerged shortly after the Civil War in response to Black empowerment and a system of Reconstruction meant to usher along the racial transformation of the South. While short-lived and largely based in the South, this first wave of the KKK helped subvert early Reconstruction efforts and undermine new rights gained by Blacks, including the right to vote. This first wave of the KKK often did so through vigilante violence, intimidation, and terror. It was aimed at helping to perpetuate white supremacy through continuing segregation and what would become the related laws and practices of Jim Crow.

Roughly fifty years later and on the heels of the tumult of World War I and the 1918 Spanish Flu pandemic, the KKK reemerged, in part as a response to socioeconomic anxieties and immigration fears. In contrast to the first wave, this second wave was much larger and was nationwide as opposed to being centered largely in the South. By the 1920s, the KKK's membership reached into the low millions—and enjoyed the support of millions more, including local officials and even national political figures like future Supreme Court justice Hugo Black. Women were also active in the second wave of the KKK, underscoring the point that, if such groups are typically male dominated and valorize Aryan hypermasculinity, women have also played an important role in the white-power-extremist movement, past and present.[29] At one point in 1925, a KKK march in DC drew tens of thousands of people, many in KKK regalia.

Mainstream, reformist, nativist, puritan, and white Protestant, the second wave of the KKK targeted a broad range of groups—not just Blacks but Catholics, Jews, Asians, non-Protestant immigrants, and Latinos. If this second wave would begin to taper off by the late 1920s, in part because of corruption, it marked the bigotry, racial animus, and anti-immigrant sentiment of the moment, which included the 1924 Immigration Act that dramatically curtailed immigration and more or less banned it from Asia, in part due to continuing "yellow peril" fears. During this period, antimiscegenation laws were passed and large numbers of Confederate monuments built, including Charlottesville's Robert E. Lee statue.

Like the first wave, the second wave of the KKK arose during a time of upheaval, socioeconomic stress, and perceived moral decline and challenges to white supremacy. The first and second waves of the KKK involved vigilante violence and terror, including lynchings and shootings, to help maintain white-supremacist rule. As suggested above, however, the second wave was more widespread, mainstream, nationwide, and broad based in its racial animus—and more directly, openly, and formally aligned with levers of US government power.

In this regard, the second wave echoes the contemporary white power movement. Indeed, though there are important differences, the second wave of the KKK shares many features with contemporary white power.[30] It directed its animus against a wide range of nonwhites, was xenophobic and anti-immigration, had sympathizers and even advocates in the corridors of power, enjoyed broad-based popular support, was fueled in part by socioeconomic stress, was hypermasculine and idealized white femininity even as some women were involved, and relied on pseudoscientific race theory and replacement fears, including ideas of eugenics and "race suicide." The 1920s also marked the emergence of a preoccupation with "illegal aliens" on the southern border. The period further underscores the fluidity of racial identity as groups considered white today, such as Italians, were stigmatized and viewed as nonwhite.[31]

Meanwhile, antisemitism was rising,[32] a point punctuated by an infamous 1915 lynching of a Jewish businessman and Henry Ford's 1920s publication of antisemitic material in the *Dearborn Independent*—including text echoing the infamous Jewish world conspiracy tract, *Protocols of the Elders of Zion*. It was at this time that Jews were first targeted by the KKK and then, in the 1930s, subject to antisemitic animus from Nazi sympathizers ranging from the widely popular Catholic radio host, Father Coughlin, to William Pelley's Silver Shirt movement. Both were inspirations for Sinclair Lewis's *It Can't Happen Here*. A more contemporary novel, Philip Roth's *Plot against America*, begins in 1940—the year after more than twenty thousand Nazi supporters packed Madison Square Garden and antisemitism was widespread—and imagines the rise of another notorious antisemite and xenophobe, the aviator-hero Charles Lindbergh.[33]

The third wave of the KKK emerged the following decade in response to the civil rights movement, which is sometimes temporally bookended by the Supreme Court's 1954 *Brown v. Board of Education* decision ending segregation in schools and the 1965 Voting Rights Act. In contrast to the second wave, the third wave of the KKK's membership was much smaller (perhaps fifteen thousand to thirty-five thousand people) and splintered, a trend that continues into the present.[34] And like the first wave, the third wave involved widespread vigilante violence and a focus on maintaining white supremacy in the face of newly gained Black rights, especially in the South—even as its animus was at times directed against other groups ranging from Jews to Communists. When people think of the KKK, they sometimes think of the murders, bombings, burnings, and other forms of violence committed by the KKK during this third wave.

While the third wave began tapering off by the late 1960s, KKK groups continued to operate and included well-known figures like Don Black and David Duke, who is college educated, dresses nicely, is articulate, and gained considerable support while running for political office.[35] Some refer to this 1970s "professionalization" of the KKK as a "fourth wave," though it remains relatively small and highly factionalized.

Meanwhile, the white power movement had broadened significantly. If Christian Identity groups have long operated in the United States, other white-power-extremist groups have emerged, including neo-Nazis, skinheads, neo-Confederates, and, most recently, the alt-right. Members of many of these groups marched at Charlottesville. Some openly backed President Trump, David Duke among them. Indeed, President Trump was heavily criticized when he was slow to disavow Duke's endorsement. Duke nevertheless continued to make fawning statements about President Trump, whom he saw as helping to "take our country back."[36]

Three Phases of Contemporary White Power

"While bearing in mind that the history of white supremacy is complicated and changes over time as our discussion of the three waves of the KKK illustrates," I say to the class, "we can, for the purpose of today's teach-in, use the civil rights movement as a 'before and after' moment that looks back on a US system of white supremacy that had operated, especially though not just in the South, for hundreds of years.

"But what then," I ask, "happened to white supremacy after the civil rights movement? If white supremacy persists, as some of you contend, how has it changed? And how does all of this relate to '1488,' the number posted on Bowers's webpage?"

"It's no longer just the KKK," a student offers. "Now we've got the alt-right and the other Charlottesville supremacists."

"So one question," I say, "is if and how groups like the KKK and the alt-right are related—and how we get from the civil rights movement to Charlottesville and Tree of Life. While there are different ways to analyze and order this historical background, as was the case with white supremacy and the KKK, one way of considering them is in terms of three key phases we can refer to for our purposes today as 'new world order' (white power as resistance), 'Fourteen Words' (white victimization and legitimated forceful response), and '#white genocide' (white power extremism in the social media age)."

"New world order," a student says. "Isn't that a political phrase?"

"That's right," I respond. "It was used by President G. W. Bush to characterize radical change and new possibilities for peace and democracy that would follow from the end of the Cold War. But the term has also long been used by conspiracy theorists to refer to plots to take over the US government and destroy the foundations of US society. The imagined plotters have included 'globalists,' the UN, cultural Marxists, and, in keeping with the long history of antisemitism, Jews.[37]

"What links these varying uses of the phrase 'new world order,' which is widely used by white power extremists new and old," I continue, "is the idea of radical change that is perpetrated by devious actors and threatens to upend traditional ways of life. So it is a useful expression to characterize a shift in the white power movement from a concern with maintaining a long-standing white-supremacist order to one that seeks to resist and reverse perceived radical changes that seem to be upending it.

"Such perceptions of the emergence of a corrupt new world order are linked not just to the civil rights movement and desegregation, critical as they were, but to events such as 'Red Scare' fears of communism, the Vietnam War, the hippie movement, and the 1965 Immigration and Nationality Act, which reversed earlier immigration restrictions. In fact, an interesting book has just come out that traces some of these shifts, particularly those related to the Vietnam War and the white power radicalization of some vets who began to view the US government as the enemy and used their military skills to 'bring the war home,' as the author titles her book.[38] This is a very different situation than earlier periods when vigilante violence was used to support the white-supremacist governmental order."

"The fears of foreign control of the new world order sound a lot like the Lane reading we did for today," a student notes, referring to a famous 1980s white power tract I assigned for our Tree of Life Teach-In.

"It does," I reply. "That brings us to a second key development in the post–civil rights white power movement, what we can call the 'Fourteen Words' phase. It is at this time that the white power movement increasingly adopts discourses of white victimization and the idea emerges that whites have the right to forcefully and even violently respond to the threat of what begins to be called 'white genocide.' Some white power extremists even declared war on the US government during this phase. Meanwhile, long-term economic changes, including manufacturing decline and growing stress in rural communities, including a 1980s farming crisis, were underway, a process of impoverishment that made these white power discourses of victimization more resonant for some—as would, in 2016, President Trump's 'Make America Great Again' populist message.[39] It's a bit of a long story, but the background is important to understanding Bowers and Tree of Life.

"It's also critical," I go on, "to understanding the alt-right and the current third phase I mentioned, what we might call '#white genocide,' or white power extremism in the social media age. Socioeconomic factors, ranging from reverberations of the 2008 financial crisis to continuing impoverishment and the opioid crisis, remain important, but white power extremists are now able to communicate much more readily in forums like podcast interviews, platforms ranging from Twitter to the Gab site where Bowers posted his messages before Tree of Life, and discussion boards such as 8chan.

"White power groups like the alt-right," I add, "also view themselves as engaged in online warfare, including trolling, in an attempt to combat the dominance of what they call Jewish-led cultural Marxists, who, through multiculturalism, media control, and political correctness, are fueling white genocide. Sometimes they say their goal is to change 'the narrative' and shift the 'Overton window,' or the boundaries of acceptable speech and, by extension, public policy. They want to make it okay to talk about white rights, Jewish conspiracy, racial difference, and even the need for a white ethnostate—which sounds a bit like the Nazis, who sought Aryan 'living space.'"

"Sounds a bit like Trump, as well!" a student notes. "He says things that sound like that."

"White power actors are very aware that President Trump does this," I reply. "But they themselves actively seek to shift the Overton window through things like social media trolling and the use of satire. They even make Holocaust jokes about the gassing of Jews."[40]

"That's awful," another student comments.

"It is," I agree. "But they are willing to do whatever it takes to stop what they see as white genocide—which brings us back to Bowers. But we've jumped to the end of the story. Let's go back in time and discuss the origins of this idea of white genocide, which is the focus of the Lane manifesto you read for today. It's also key to breaking the '1488' white power code."

* * *

"Who is this Lane guy?" a student asks. "He thought up some wild stuff. What exactly is a 'ZOG' and why would anyone write a 'White Genocide Manifesto'? It was a really strange reading. And scary."

"Lane was a famous white power extremist who emerged in what we're calling the 'Fourteen Words' second phase of the contemporary white power movement," I respond. "In the early 1980s he was part of a group called 'The Order' that committed a bunch of crimes, including robbing banks, counterfeiting, and killing a Jewish radio host. Later he was arrested and went to prison, where he wrote the manifesto and a bunch of other stuff on white power. He even claimed to invent his own neopagan religion he called Wotanism."

"Did he invent the idea of white genocide?" another student asks.

"That's a great question," I respond. "Not exactly. You might say he crystallized an idea that was already circulating."

"Who invented it, then?" the student follows up.

"In one sense," I reply, "the idea has a long history. It echoes earlier tropes of racial threat, some of which still circulate in the US today: the Indian savage, the Black brute and rapist, and the Asian peril and other feared immigrant invasions.

"The idea of white genocide began to take on its more modern form in the age of scientific racism and eugenics," I go on, "when early-twentieth-century authors like Madison Grant and Lothrop Stoddard warned of 'race suicide' and wrote books with titles like *The Passing of the Great Race* (1916) and *The Rising Tide of Color against White World-Supremacy* (1920), ones regarded as classics by white power actors today. The idea of 'race suicide,' like white genocide, drew on earlier extinction discourses that had been used to describe Native Americans and legitimate their settler-colonial erasure—except now the concept was reversed to warn against the extinction of whites.[41]

"Another strand of white genocide is related to German notions of *völk* spirit," I continue, "which assert connections to land and threat from outside forces. Jewish menace, exemplified by antisemitic tracts like *Protocols of the Elders of Zion*, the one that Henry Ford pushed in the 1920s, was regarded as a key threat. Hitler and the Nazis took these notions to the extreme. In fact, many people don't know that the Nazis were aware of and partly inspired by the history of white supremacy in the US. In fact, a book just came out called *Hitler's American Model*.[42] But that's a story for a different day. What's important to note for the purposes of today's teach-in is that the idea of white genocide emerged from this background even as it crystallized in the US."

"When?" a student asks.

"After the civil rights movement," I say. "It was in part a response to the shattering of the old system of white supremacy and 'the new world order' that followed. So we might say the idea of white genocide emerged in what we called the first phase of contemporary, post–civil right white power extremism ('new world order') and crystallized in a second ('Fourteen Words'). Lane's manifesto marks the second moment."

"Who marks the first?" a student asks. "Did Lane have a teacher?"

"Not exactly," I say. "But one of his influences was an important first-phase extremist, a professor turned neo-Nazi named William Pierce. He wrote a book that has been called the 'white supremacist bible' that is all about white genocide. Maybe it would be good for me to tell you in detail about Pierce and his book, *The Turner Diaries*, since they are important to the emergence of the idea of white genocide and laid the ground for Lane's manifesto."

William Pierce and *The Turner Diaries*

Pierce marks 1963 as the year of his political awakening, a moment when he grew dissatisfied with liberal arguments about race and noticed media bias and Jewish influence in the civil rights movement.[43] He sought explanations in the library, where Pierce read Hitler's *Mein Kampf* and his views on racial difference solidified.

By 1965, Pierce was convinced "there was a massive, well-organized effort afoot to bring about profound and irreversible changes in the racial character of the American population." He believed Jews were behind this racial attack. Radical measures were required to address the dire situation. Pierce sought to mobilize people around the fundamental insight that was the basis of his radicalization: "What *must* be saved is the gene pool of our race." White genocide.

Pierce joined several extremist groups in the 1960s, first the John Birch Society—a far-right conspiracist group to which a number of white power extremists, including Lane, belonged—and then the American Nazi Party and Youth for Wallace, which supported Alabama governor George Wallace's pro-segregation presidential bid.[44] In 1970, Pierce transformed Youth for Wallace into the National Youth Alliance and then, in 1974, the National Alliance.

Pierce's vision for the National Alliance had developed partly in response to his early engagement with George Lincoln Rockwell's American Nazi Party (1959–67). He first met Rockwell—who often dressed in Nazi garb and traveled with his "storm troopers" on a "hate bus"—in 1964 and later edited the group's *National Socialist World* magazine. By the time Pierce left the group in 1970, he had learned that, to reach a broader audience, he needed to avoid the sorts of "losers," "degenerates," and "crackpots" who had surrounded Rockwell.[45] Later white powers actors would follow this strategy, sometimes, like Pierce, donning jackets and ties.

In response, the National Alliance developed strict by-laws, including the requirement that members be of "good character"—as well as heterosexual, non-Jewish, and "of wholly European ancestry."[46] The National Alliance would come to include publication, radio, and hate-music arms located at first in Arlington, Virginia, and then on a West Virginia compound.

It was in this context that Pierce wrote *The Turner Diaries* in serial form before publishing it as a book in 1978. His dystopian novel embodied his white genocide ideas and provided a blueprint for race war and extermination that would influence white power extremists for years.[47]

The text begins on September 16, 1991, with "the System," the Zionist-controlled US government, in the midst of banning gun possession and implementing policies that place minorities in positions of power in the name of equality. In response, the protagonist, Earl Turner, joins a clandestine movement seeking to overthrow what it views as an oppressive and illegitimate government. The revolutionaries carry out operations large and small, including counterfeiting, robberies, assassinations, and bombings.

After bombing an FBI headquarters, Turner is inducted into "The Order," the inner circle of the revolutionary movement. The remainder of the book follows Turner as he helps the organization topple "the System" before his last "martyrdom" mission. Among the events detailed in the book, which is filled with hate language, is the "Day of the Rope," when tens of thousands of white "race traitors," ranging from liberal intellectuals to those engaging in miscegenation, are hung en masse. Using nuclear weapons and warfare, the revolutionaries seize control of the United States and destroy Israel. Eventually they overrun the entire world, which they "purify" by massacring all nonwhites in fulfillment of, as the book's epilogue states in its penultimate paragraph, "the dream of a white world."

White genocide victimization, then, orchestrated by Jews and advanced in the name of multiculturalism and civil rights, leads the victims (whites) to launch a race war and eliminate the threat to their existence by committing a genocide of their own against nonwhites. This idea, which is at the heart of *The Turner Diaries*, gained popularity and inspired action that was the stuff of Pierce's dreams.

Pierce believed the masses needed to be guided to revolution. In messianic terms, he offered a vision that would lead whites to prevent their extinction and emerge victorious from an inevitable race war. *The Turner Diaries* condensed his ideas in easy-to-read form. The National Alliance provided organizational structure, including publication arms that released the text. Indeed, hundreds of thousands of copies of *The Turner Diaries* have been sold, and the book has been read online by legions more.

By the late 1990s, the Anti-Defamation League would call the National Alliance "the single most dangerous organized hate group in the United States today,"[48] with dramatic growth, sixteen cells across the country, a well-oiled propaganda apparatus, and the widespread influence of *The Turner Diaries*. While it is important not to overstate the importance of the National Alliance, which rapidly declined after Pierce's 2002 death, it was among the most dynamic white power organizations that emerged during the critical "new world order" juncture in the white power movement.[49]

While previously aimed at upholding a system of white supremacy, white power actors increasingly saw themselves as victims disempowered and threatened by radical change, which many believed was orchestrated by Jews. New civil rights laws, desegregation and the end of Jim Crow, and affirmative action arrived at roughly the same time as the Vietnam War and hippie movement.[50] These trends dovetailed with a recession and manufacturing decline that further inflamed a sense of white grievance and victimization, a notion that was gaining increasing prominence after the Holocaust and with the rise of trauma discourses.

If the white power movement had been long dominated by the KKK and Christian Identity groups, a plethora of new groups, ranging from neo-Nazis to skinheads, emerged at this time. They were largely splintered due to a lack of organization and divergent orientations, a situation that led some to seek common ground.

The Turner Diaries and its idea of white genocide would prove instrumental. On the one hand, the book provided a model and a hero narrative for aspiring Earl Turner–like revolutionaries. Yet, *The Turner Diaries* also offered an ideology, cause, and blueprint for white-power-extremist revolution, race war, and genocide—a genocide of nonwhites legitimated by the imagined genocidal threat to white race survival (white genocide).

Bob Mathews and The Order

The Turner Diaries and its message of white genocide had an almost immediate impact. The text served as inspiration for The Order, a domestic terrorist group that operated in the United States in the early 1980s and whose name was taken from the revolutionary leadership in Pierce's novel.[51]

This group was led by Robert Jay Mathews, a National Alliance member who was strongly influenced by *The Turner Diaries* and determined "to create an Order of his own . . . and start a revolution."[52] Born in Texas in 1953, Mathews joined the John Birch Society in his youth and became increasingly strong in his pro-white, antitax, and antigovernment beliefs. In 1980, Mathews joined the National Alliance, giving a speech at its 1983 convention where he spoke of how he was recruiting new members, many of whom, including truckers and farmers, were suffering from economic distress.[53]

Around this time, Mathews made contact with Aryan Nations, led by Richard Butler and based on an Idaho compound that served as a meeting point for white power extremists. Butler, a nautical engineer who became a Christian Identity minister, had been influenced by Wesley Swift, known for his Holocaust denial and preaching the Christian Identity "two seedlines" thesis. This doctrine claimed that whites of European descent were the true descendants of the "lost tribes" of Israel instead of Jews, who were in reality the Satanic offspring of Eve and the Serpent[54]—an idea that may have inspired Bowers's "jews are the children of satan" post. Nonwhites, in turn, were dehumanized as pre-Adamic "mudpeople."

If espoused in Christian Identity churches, these beliefs circulated and influenced a wide range of white power extremists, including those who began gathering at the annual Aryan Nations World Congress. The 1983 congress, which Mathews likely attended, was particularly significant since it is thought to have included a secret meeting where white power actors agreed to wage war against the government using decentralized cells that could not be traced back to the movement's senior figures.[55] These ideas echoed Pierce's views and the way "the Organization" worked in *The Turner Diaries*.

On September 22, 1983, Mathews invited eight men, most members of Aryan Nations or National Alliance, to join him in waging war against the government. Their initial goal was to create a white ethnic homeland.[56] To this end, The Order undertook a variety of actions echoing *The Turner Diaries*: bank and pornography-shop robberies, counterfeiting, arson, bombing, and assassination, including the 1984 shooting of Jewish radio show host Alan Berg. At one point, The Order robbed a Brinks armored car, netting over three million dollars that it then distributed to white power groups around the country, including National Alliance.[57]

The group sought to expand. The FBI, however, launched Operation Clean Sweep, a massive effort to take down this growing domestic terrorism threat. The FBI set out to arrest Mathews, who issued a proclamation of war against the US government while on the run. The FBI tracked Mathews to a house on Whidbey Island near Seattle where, after a standoff, Mathews died in a fire. Mathews's death would serve as a white power rallying point, providing the movement with a martyr and an example of perceived US government corruption and excess. This show of government force also encouraged some, like former KKK member Louis Beam, to advocate for a "leaderless resistance" strategy, an idea that still circulates in white power circles.[58]

David Lane and the "White Genocide Manifesto"

Other arrests soon followed, including that of David Eden Lane in 1985. Lane, born in 1938, claims to have had an early interest in the Nazis and later, due to his poverty and working-class roots, became "disenchanted with Capitalism."[59] In an autobiography, Lane wrote of a dissatisfying early involvement in the John Birch Society, followed by an "awakening" that came after reading a "Pamphlet detailing Jewish control of the media." His research convinced him that "Western nations were ruled by a Zionist conspiracy . . . [that] wants to exterminate the White Aryan race."[60] By 1979, he had joined the Denver branch of the Knights of the Ku Klux Klan, established by David Duke a few years earlier.[61] He also began to distribute a pamphlet he had penned, "The Death of the White Race." In 1983, Lane visited the Idaho compound of Aryan Nations, where he met Mathews and attended the annual Congress.

Less than two years later, Lane was arrested in North Carolina. He spent the rest of his life in prison, where he wrote extensively and distilled the idea of white genocide that undergirds *The Turner Diaries* in his 1988 tract, "White Genocide Manifesto."[62] If *The Turner Diaries* is an implicit call to action in response to impending race extinction at the hands of Jews, the "White Genocide Manifesto" is explicitly so.

The tract begins with excoriation, lamenting a Zionist-controlled "power system" that manufactures false consciousness as white people remain unaware that the survival of their race is in imminent jeopardy—in contravention of the "first and highest Law of Nature," the "preservation of one's own kind." After this preamble, the "White Genocide Manifesto" seeks to reveal this true state of affairs in fourteen points that lead to the concluding "Fourteen Words" mantra.

The first six points focus on the problem of white genocide, which the manifesto asserts is caused by the lack of racially pure living space, integration and miscegenation, the repression of resistance, the small number of pure white women of child-bearing age, and the permanence of race extinction even in the face of the white male "instinct" for race survival. In this vision, Aryan hypermasculinity is juxtaposed to the softness, beauty, vulnerability, and potential victimization of goddess-like white women whose role in racial reproduction must be protected from nonwhite sexual predators. Such gender norms echo a patriarchal dimension of systemic white supremacy that dates back to early settler colonialism in North America and remains a key element of white power today.[63]

Having foregrounded the problem, Lane's manifesto turns to its root cause: "a Zionist conspiracy to mix, overrun and exterminate the White race." In the United States, the "Zionist occupied government" controls the levers of state power and the media, using this power to hide the truth, implement policies like integration and abortion, and promote multiculturalism, homosexuality, and race mixing.

Lane concludes with a call to action, demanding a response to these "innumerable crimes against the collective white race . . . [including] the policy of genocide." The manifesto calls for the creation of a white homeland. If denied, the tract threatens, "we will seek redress in whatever measures are necessary." In boldface, the manifesto highlights "our goal, expressed in the FOURTEEN WORDS: 'We must secure the existence of our people and a future for White children.'"

These two phrases—"white genocide" and the "Fourteen Words"— and the ideas they connote provided a key connecting thread for the white-power-extremist movement. Whatever their views and ideological emphases, many skinheads, neo-Nazis, Christian Identity adherents, KKK members, and other white power extremists could broadly agree that the white race was threatened and a strong response was needed— including, in the extreme, apocalyptic and revolutionary change involving genocide against nonwhites threatening the survival of the white race. The sense of urgency and moral righteousness was amplified by the invocation of genocide, one of the most charged and ontologically resonant words of our times—even if the term was being misappropriated.[64]

Lane's manifesto, then, serves as a marker for a second "Fourteen Words" phase in contemporary white power extremism, as the idea of white genocide emerged as a key conceptual frame providing a shared cause for otherwise fragmented and ideologically diverse white power groups. The white genocide frame's abstractness and emphasis on victimization at the hands of diabolical forces and a corrupt government sometimes also appeal to groups with interests not necessarily or primarily focused on race, such as gun rights groups, militias, heritage associations, and antitaxers. Indeed, in The Turner Diaries, Earl Turner initially joins the resistance in response to new gun restrictions.

The white genocide frame thus has potentially broad appeal that can extend beyond overt discourses about white power and race. Its lens of white victimization and legitimate response has the flexibility to be easily intertwined with a host of current issues, including group and individual rights, ecological destruction, gun control, job loss, overpopulation, race, and national space, borders, and belonging.

If white power groups and actors selectively draw upon a range of frames, white genocide is one of the most central ones to the broader white power movement today and critical to understand given the way it may be used to legitimate violence, race war, and even the genocide of nonwhites. And, as we shall see in the next chapter, the white genocide frame informed Trump's immigration discourse and policy, creating a dangerous situation.

Timothy McVeigh and 1990s Extremism

Despite the FBI clampdown, the white power movement persevered, taking on new ideological and organizational forms—for which *The Turner Diaries* often continued to be a source of inspiration—that were sometimes met by FBI force. If Mathews and Whidbey Island were a rallying cry of the 1980s, Ruby Ridge and Waco, high-profile situations in which massive federal force was used against armed far-right extremist resisters, served as further reminders of supposed government oppression in the 1990s.[65]

Timothy McVeigh's April 19, 1995, bombing of the Oklahoma City Federal Building was one violent response, resulting in the deaths of 168 people and over 500 wounded. McVeigh, a former soldier, was directly inspired by *The Turner Diaries*, which he sold at gun shows and which includes a scene in which an FBI building is truck-bombed using ammonium nitrate—the same substance used by McVeigh.[66] McVeigh had extensive contacts with the larger white power movement, including the KKK and the patriot militia movement that had proliferated after Waco and Ruby Ridge.[67]

Other domestic terror attacks also took place during the 1990s, some inspired by *The Turner Diaries*. For example, the Aryan Republican Army, a sort of second coming of "The Order," carried out a series of robberies and for a time took refuge in Elohim City, a Christian Identity compound where *The Turner Diaries* was required reading for the guards.[68]

Meanwhile, the National Alliance and other white power groups were making transnational white power connections. The National Alliance's membership supposedly included Europeans. Pierce traveled to Europe to speak and, in turn, invited European radicals to speak at National Alliance meetings.[69] At this time, Europe's far-right extremist movement, which included neo-Nazis and other white power elements, was experiencing a post–Cold War resurgence, in part due to economic issues and immigration. These trends would continue, punctuated by Anders Breivik's July 2011 shooting of seventy-seven people in Norway—which, along with Breivik's fifteen-hundred-page white power manifesto, inspired later white power extremists[70]—and the 2015 immigration crisis.

Such connections among US, European, South African, and other white power extremists were facilitated by the Internet. Indeed, white power extremists were early users of the Internet as they sought to promote their cause. Pierce and the National Alliance were particularly active in this regard, developing a website that posted its white power tracts and radio broadcasts and that included links to European far-right parties.[71] In 1995, former KKK leader Don Black established the online message board Stormfront, which would grow to be one of the most popular and extensive white power platforms.[72] Such early use of the Internet was a precursor of the third key phase of contemporary white power extremism in the social media age—the one in which Bowers carried out his attack.

* * *

"So, can you break the 1488 code that Bowers used on his radar gun?" I ask the class.

"The fourteen must come from the Fourteen Words in Lane's manifesto," a student answers. "But what about the 88? I didn't see anything about that in the reading."

"Lane also wrote a tract called the '88 Precepts,'"[73] I say. "I'll give you a hint. 'H' is the eighth letter of the alphabet and Lane was a neo-Nazi. And who do neo-Nazis worship?"

"Hitler?" a student answers. "But why would there be a double 'H'? 'Hitler Hitler'?"

"Heil Hitler, maybe?" another student suggests. "The Fourteen Words plus Heil Hitler."

"That's it," I confirm. "Bowers was flashing code for white genocide at the hands of Jews. A lot of white power extremists use 1488 or sometimes just 14 to signal white genocide. Some tattoo it on their skin."

"That's wild," a student says. "I'm going to start looking more carefully at tattoos! I thought white supremacists just had swastikas."

"Some have those, as well," I note. "But remember that Pierce and other contemporary white power actors have traded in their robes and stormtrooper uniforms for dress jackets. They want to go mainstream and shift the Overton window, as we discussed before."

"I thought you said that's part of the third phase of white power after the civil rights movement," a student notes.

"And how do we get from Pierce and Lane's Fourteen Words to Charlottesville, Bowers, and the alt-right?" another student asks.

"That's a key question," I reply. "There were major twists and turns, including 9/11, the election of Obama, and now President Trump. But we can see several trends, already evident in the National Alliance and other white-power-extremist organizations in the 1990s, which have directly shaped the movement's form today.

"First and as we just discussed," I continue, "a wide range of white power extremists from different ideological positions have been able to unite around the white genocide conceptual frame, which broadens the movement by creating common cause in the imperative of white race survival in a situation of extinction threat. Second, the white power movement, while always manifesting in local forms, is global, with members around the world frequently corresponding, networking, and exchanging ideas.

"And third," I say, "such white power communication and messaging, both domestically and abroad, has been facilitated by new media technologies, including dark web spaces where white power advocates dialogue out of public view.[74] After the mid-2000s, and especially during the last decade, these new media spaces, ranging from Facebook and Twitter to 8chan, have facilitated white power extremist community and radicalization in new ways. This is the third and most recent phase of post–civil rights white power extremism in the social media age.

"Earlier," I note, "I referred to this phase by the handle '#WhiteGenocide' since contemporary white power extremism is often centered around the white genocide conceptual frame. In fact, a few days ago Facebook got into trouble when it was revealed that, even after Tree of Life, it still permitted advertisers to target people using the phrase 'white genocide.' Apparently, 168,000 of their users had shown interest in white genocide. After the story broke, Facebook changed their policy."[75]

"That's hard to believe," a student says. "But don't social media bans raise free speech issues?"

"That's long been a big issue about white power extremism," I comment, "but especially after Charlottesville, when white power groups and actors, including those belonging to the alt-right, were deplatformed and removed from sites like Facebook, Twitter, and PayPal."

"And what exactly is a 'frame'?" another student asks. "You mentioned the 'white genocide frame.' And we read about human rights frames earlier in the semester."[76]

"Major theorists have taken up that question," I reply.[77] "Some define a frame as an interpretive structure that organizes experience. That's a bit abstract, I know. So for our purposes today, you can just think of it as a lens, or a bundle of understandings that lead the looker to view the world in a particular way—a perspective or 'framework' for understanding, if you will. More concretely, think of a picture frame. It encloses and foregrounds an image (the picture) while backgrounding whatever is outside of the frame. In other words, a frame is a lens that gives meaning to our experience by providing a way of looking at reality.

"A scholar named Joe Feagin," I say, "has used this idea to examine white supremacy, arguing that this system is undergirded by a framing cluster of ideas, narratives, stereotypes, and beliefs.[78] This 'white racial frame' plays on emotion and is often gendered, as illustrated by stereo-types of Black and Brown criminality or hypersexuality.

"Feagin contends," I continue, "that this frame emerged in the seventeenth century and, while changing through time, supports white supremacist institutions, practices, and discourses in today's USA, even if it is often masked, naturalized, or expressed in less overt forms. This sort of white racial frame, Feagin and other scholars who focus on systemic racism contend, continues to inform contemporary US society and politics. From their perspective President Trump—and Charlottesville—are not exceptional but instead just a more recent manifestation of a long-standing system of white supremacy that continues to operate in the US and globally.

"So by referring to white genocide as a 'frame,' I'm referring to a white power 'lens' that draws on elements of the larger 'white racial frame' and provides white power extremists with a way of interpreting their experience and acting in the world. Some scholars also use the idea of framing to analyze how social movements, including far-right extremism, give meaning to their members and motivate them to act, in part by playing upon grievance. This white genocide frame, which is also centered around grievance and victimization, fits nicely with this perspective as well.[79]

"Circling back to our discussion of the three recent trends that inform contemporary white power extremism," I add, "we can examine how the white genocide frame informs groups like the alt-right, including their extensive use of social media. So it might be useful to discuss the alt-right in more detail. They actually recently released a 'manifesto' of a sort called *A Fair Hearing: The Alt-Right in the Words of Its Members and Leaders*. It foregrounds white genocide."

The Alt-Right, Social Media, and White Genocide

In the introduction of *A Fair Hearing*, editor George Shaw states that the alt-right centers on white "group interests," an issue he says is distilled by the "14 Words."[80] Those identifying as alt-right, Shaw continues, share three related convictions: "demography is destiny" (fixed traits exist and the white race is diminished by diversity); "the Jewish question is valid" (since Jews seek white race decline); and "white genocide is underway" (due to this Jewish plot, immigration, and policy).

Discussion of these issues, Shaw contends, is banished by "political correctness" and the ideology behind it, "cultural Marxism." For the alt-right, then, the front lines of the fight for white survival lie in combating cultural Marxism. This idea is forcefully argued in an essay, titled "Metapolitics," by Daniel Friberg—a Swedish far-right leader who collaborates with alt-right leader Richard Spencer, attended Charlottesville, and runs the Budapest-based, white power publisher Arktos, which released *A Fair Hearing*.[81] The inclusion of one of Europe's leading alt-right figures underscores the global interconnections of white power extremism today.

European heritage, Friberg warns, is "being replaced by such things as 'human rights,' 'tolerance' and liberal democracy." "Metapolitics," Friberg explains, refers to a "battle for hearts and minds" that is part of a "war of social transformation" being waged by the alt-right against these "cultural Marxist party" views that, other contributors suggest, are fomented by a Jewish-controlled media and political machine.

The goal of metapolitics, Friberg contends, is to influence both the masses and public "influencers," especially those who are already somewhat sympathetic to alt-right views such as "moderate right-wingers" and libertarians. "Through a process of relentless idea-seeding by alt-righters," Friberg says, "this person has slowly softened to our views" about white race interests.

Friberg names conservative commentator Ann Coulter as a person who "red-pilled" in this manner, writing her anti-immigration tract, *Adios, America*, after seeing the "forbidden Truth" revealed by alt-right ideology. The idea of "red-pilling," frequently discussed among white power extremists, comes from the movie *The Matrix*, when the protagonist, Neo, is given a choice between taking a blue pill of comfortable delusion or a red pill of revelation that unmasks the truth of a dire situation.

Coulter's book, Friberg claims, then influenced Trump, including Trump's "Mexican rapist" statements. This connection provides one illustration of the link between Trump—a president who was willing to fight for white interests and attacked political correctness—and the alt-right, a point many essays in *A Fair Hearing* underscore. One contributor notes the parallels between Trump's views and those of the far-right politicians who preceded him, such as Patrick Buchanan, a failed presidential candidate and author of *The Death of the West*, a book popular among white power extremists.

To wage this "metapolitical warfare," Friberg goes on, the alt-right uses social media weapons to "dissipate the politically correct haze" of cultural Marxism. Friberg claims the mantle of critical thinking, arguing that alt-right metapolitics is a project that seeks to "undermine and deconstruct" even as it inspires and "illuminates." Among the alt-right's social media tools, Friberg lists "memes, podcasts, blogs, books, alternative media outlets, [and] 'trolling.'" Another essay in the volume, titled "The Art of the Troll," asserts that such trolling centers on deploying the Socratic method to show the flimsy foundations of cultural Marxist views.

The alt-right does so in part through language. George Shaw's contribution emphasizes the importance of undermining the "Newspeak" of the "Marxist social engineers," which the alt-right does in part by reappropriating language and creating neologisms like "Cuckservative," "Counter-Semite," and "shitlib," a term that refers to pseudo-intellectual liberal "wearers of pussy hats" who are "slovenly, perverted, mongrelized, devious, tantrum-prone buffoons and lunatics."[82]

Shaw also discusses the term "Cargo Cult," an anthropological concept that the alt-right uses to refer to nonwhites who take on the airs of white knowledge and status, ranging from doctoral degrees to political titles, while lacking true understanding and making little contribution to the white society created by European settlers, whom the alt-right sometimes refers to as "Amerikaners."

Anthropologists are a particular academic target of alt-right ire given their contributions to the understanding that race is a social construct. In his introduction, Shaw derides these "anthropological theories that place absurd amounts of emphasis on nurture, or environment, and completely overlook heredity,"[83] an argument that is picked up by other contributors to *A Fair Hearing*, including Richard Spencer, who contributed an essay arguing for the reality of race.

The essays in *A Fair Hearing* are bound by a conviction that the existence of the white race is threatened and that action is urgently required to prevent genocide and revitalize the white society—even if this project of social engineering and renewal requires radical, violent, and apocalyptic measures. The first essay, by the "revered" alt-right writer Gregory Hood, underscores this victim-centered discourse as he likens the white race to the kulak class enemies targeted for elimination by the Soviet Union. The very word "white," Hood contends, has become a slur. In "Physical Removal: More Than a Meme," Augustus Invictus, a featured speaker at Charlottesville, warns that "civil war is already upon us." This battle, he contends, legitimates "legal and moral" action, including internment and physical removal.

Such apocalyptic *Turner Diaries*–like language also emerges at the end of a contribution by Spencer's deputy, Evan McLaren, who recounts their experience of "Ground Zero at Charlottesville." McLaren claims the alt-right marchers were "set up" by local officials and the police, who failed to intervene and protect their free speech rights.

McLaren confirms that, as opposed to Trump's backlighting focus on the Lee monument, the Unite the Right rally was primarily about bringing together the alt-right and the more moderate "alt-lite" to create a unified "youthful, energized Trumpian right." When alt-lite participants like Gavin McInnes (founder of the Proud Boys) pulled out, however, the alt-right was left to unite with white power groups lying "in the op-

posite direction," such as the League of the South and the Traditionalist Worker Party to which Hovater and Heimbach belonged. "We came
to Charlottesville to ignite a new consciousness," McLaren concludes.
"What we found there was a challenge, a test of our willingness to be
seen as villains for the stand we had taken, that we one day might inherit
a new world as its heroes."[84]

A number of the contributors make statements that would seem outrageous to many readers unfamiliar with alt-right tactics. But such remarks are part of a strategy of provocation, as highlighted by Invictus's
essay, which semi-jokes about "throwing commies from a helicopter"—a
notorious practice under Pinochet in Chile that has become an alt-right
meme. The alt-right contributors to A Fair Hearing are not simply a
bunch of moronic racist "haters" or "crazies." They use the tools of de-
construction and critique. Their ideas, if flawed, often have depth and
are strategically deployed in a battle waged on multiple fronts ranging
from "metapolitics" to action in the streets.

A number of the authors note with derision how they are dismissed
as "haters." The alt-right, Shaw states in his introduction, does not consist of "simple minded 'racists' and 'bigots'" or the "inbred bumpkins and
psychotic skinheads of Hollywood lore. The alt-right is made up primarily of eminently sane and intelligent white men who have woken up to
find themselves marked for elimination in their own civilization."[85] As
Hovater stressed during his Nordic Frontier podcast and as other contributors to A Fair Hearing note, such caricatures provide white power
actors with an advantage since the stereotypes enable them to organize
out of view.

Of course, not all white power actors have formulated their views
to this extent. The alt-right contributors to A Fair Hearing are well-
educated; several have advanced degrees from top schools. Spencer,
Friberg, and others are part of the white power movement's ideological
leadership, distilling a platform and organizing accordingly.

McLaren's distinction between the alt-lite, alt-right, and what I earlier
referred to as the "hard far Right" (McLaren's reference to groups lying

"in the other [furthest right] direction") provides one way of subdividing the white power movement, even though these groups contain subgroupings, overlap, and have varying degrees of radicalness. McLaren places Heimbach's and Hovater's Traditionalist Worker Party (TWP) on the hard far Right, though the TWP was more moderate than some in this cluster.

Matthew Heimbach, the Traditionalist Worker Party, and White Genocide

If Kessler, Spencer, and other alt-right leaders sought to "unite the right" at Charlottesville, so too did Heimbach, who had been working separately, and with some success, to bring together a range of white power actors, including neo-Nazis, KKK members, and skinheads. Like Pierce and other contemporary white power actors, Heimbach believed that the white power movement needed to professionalize and minimize inflammatory racist language while focusing on their common cause of white empowerment and on addressing the white socioeconomic distresses he saw close to home in Ohio and Appalachia.[86]

Heimbach's outlook was influenced by Patrick Buchanan's *Death of the West* as well as alt-right forums like the white power website VDARE. Heimbach also affiliated with the neo-Confederate League of the South at one point, part of his broad vision for the white power movement,[87] which he also saw as coalescing in Charlottesville.

Journalist Vegas Tenold followed Heimbach for years as Heimbach made contact with these and other white power extremists, including Spencer, for whom Heimbach, Hovater, and other members of the Traditionalist Worker Party (TWP) even provided security at an Auburn University speaking event.[88] Heimbach's organizational successes and rising stature were underscored by his invitation to be a featured speaker at Unite the Right.

The TWP had emerged out of the Traditionalist Youth Network, established in 2013 by Heimbach and Matthew Parrott, who would become Heimbach's father-in-law. In 2015, the TWP was created as the network's political arm and soon had an active website and social media presence. Like other contemporary white power groups, the TWP made extensive use of new media technologies to connect to white power activists across the globe. And indeed, the TWP was also inspired by European Identitarianism.[89]

In 2015, Heimbach also began campaigning for Trump, who was, Heimbach wrote in a blog, "blowing the dog whistle for White racial interests harder than any other candidate" and threatening Jewish control.[90] Indeed, it was Heimbach who, heeding Trump's call to "get 'em out of here" at a March 1, 2016, campaign rally in Louisville, shoved and allegedly shouted racial slurs at a Black twenty-one-year-old protester. Heimbach was wearing a red MAGA cap and black TWP t-shirt.

Heimbach's and the TWP's star would fall as quickly as it had risen. In March 2018, Heimbach was arrested for choking unconscious his TWP cofounder and stepfather-in-law, Matthew Parrott.[91] He was also accused of assaulting his wife during the incident. Parrott quit the TWP and the organization soon disbanded.

This bizarre ending aside, it is important to recognize that, while neither Heimbach nor fellow TWP member Hovater had an advanced degree from a prestigious university (though Heimbach was college educated), both had given their views thought. They articulated their ideas, often in the guise of critical thinking, in podcasts like the one Hovater did with Nordic Resistance.

While it touched on many important aspects of Hovater's background and general neo-Nazi orientation, Fausset's *New York Times* profile piece never delved deeply into the ideological underpinnings of Hovater and the TWP. If he had, Fausset would have found part of the answer that eluded him. White genocide was one of the key factors that motivated Hovater to "start fires."

Much of what Hovater said during his *Nordic Resistance* interview with Johansson, including his references to the future of the white race, was directly reflected in the TWP's platform. While espousing a range of positions, ranging from being anti-abortion to being anticapitalist and pro-environment, the TWP was neo-Nazi in orientation, as suggested by the group's twenty-five points, an echo of Hitler's Nazi Party twenty-five-point manifesto.[92]

The preamble to the TWP's 25 Points states that its "guiding principle" is to fight for white rights and that "the Fourteen Words . . . best exemplifies the mission of our movement." Point 1 is to fight for an "independent White ethno-state in North America" and to stop being "slaves to the wishes of the globalists and Wall Street." The second point expands on this issue, calling for "a Nationalist Socialist government" that will stop the exploitation of "the Jewish and their capitalist running dogs." Point 22 directly invokes white "genocide," a topic Heimbach also invoked during podcasts and speeches. Similar neo-Nazi language appears in the social media posts of Bowers.

* * *

"So, with these post–civil rights transformations of the white power movement in mind," I ask my students as our "Tree of Life Teach-in" concludes, "how does Bowers's shooting, or the actions of the Charlottesville marchers for that matter, look different? Can we explain their actions by calling them 'racists,' 'haters,' and 'supremacists'?"

"I think 'supremacist' captures something important," a student replies. "I see racism and supremacy every day."

"We still need to take account of history," says another. "Otherwise it sounds like they are all the same."

"I wonder if Bowers read Lane's manifesto," a third student says. "His post about Jews, invaders, and white people getting 'slaughtered' sounds like it comes straight from the white genocide playbook."

"And remember the 1488 radar gun," a student adds.

"He also allegedly told a police officer," I comment, "that 'they're committing genocide to my people. I just want to kill Jews.' He mentioned genocide repeatedly. He had social media posts that mentioned white genocide and even retweeted a post referring to the early neo-Nazi Rockwell and William Pierce."[93]

"He may also have been listening to Trump on the campaign trail," a fifth student comments. "Trump can't stop talking about 'invaders' during the midterms."

"That's possible," I say. "But Bowers also claims to have had issues with President Trump, whom he called a 'globalist,' a term that's often used to refer to Jews. Bowers also posted, 'There is no #MAGA as long as there is a kike infestation.'

"Some white power extremists like Bowers," I continue, "are wary about President Trump's support of Israel and family ties since his daughter converted and married a Jew. Bowers also shared an image on social media that depicts an orthodox Jew towering over President Trump saying, 'Your character will appear to the public as a white racist. It's how we control Whites.' Trump replies, 'Yes sir.' But Bowers's social media posts most often mention his hatred of Jews, immigration, multiculturalism, and white genocide.

"Of course," I go on, "many white power extremists remain strong backers of President Trump. That includes members of a New Jersey group that participated in Unite the Right 2, this summer's follow-up to Charlottesville."

"What!" a student exclaims, then pauses before adding, "I'm surprised, but I guess not that surprised. White supremacy is part of the system. Here, too."

"We don't need a Jersey Bowers!" another student complains. "That's creepy."

"Actually," I say, "New Jersey has a troubled history in terms of white power extremism. At times, it has been ranked near the top of the list of states with the most hate groups. That includes the KKK. It's worth noting, though, that there are also Black power extremist groups who have been active as well. Some of them also hate Jews. So Jews face threats from different directions, though most of all from white power extremism. Antisemitism has dramatically increased over the past couple of years."[94]

"Who is the Jersey group you mentioned?" a student asks.

"They call themselves the New Jersey European Heritage Association," I reply. "They seem to be based down in central Jersey near Princeton. It's a new group that only appears to have been established this past year. The leader was recently exposed on the Internet."

Indeed, even before Unite the Right 2 had ended, images of the protesters began to circulate as the doxing began.[95] Two participants were linked to the radio arm of Stormfront, the extremist website founded by Don Black in 1995. Jovanni Valle, a former Proud Boy who spoke at the rally while wearing a black MAGA cap, was also named. Someone reported on Twitter that the man with white genocide tattoos was "Rich" from New York.

At the Unite the Right 2 march, I had noticed several marchers wearing khakis and dress shirts, their faces obscured by tinted sunglasses and US flag scarves. Each wore a black hat featuring a Roman soldier with a helmet, shield, and raised spear. One made a "Heil Hitler" salute while he marched. At the rally site, they held up posters. One, featuring a white mother and her infant, was captioned, "Protect the Endangered Species: Stop White Genocide."

Later, I was surprised to discover that they were from the New Jersey European Heritage Association (NJEHA).[96] The NJEHA's website explains that the organization seeks to "wake up" people to the threats they face so that "swift and immediate action can be taken against the people who are destroying our race and civilization." It does not name these enemies directly, but flyers and posters warning of the danger of Jews, Communists, and immigrants provide clues. The group's "creed," the website states, is the Fourteen Words.

The NJEHA put up white genocide and anti-immigrant posters in central New Jersey, including Princeton, which caused an outcry. Several months after the Unite the Right 2 rally, "AntiFash Gordon," an antifascist Twitter handle, claimed to have identified the group's leader, "Titus D'Andrea," as a New Jersey man who worked in a newspaper printing shop.[97] The Twitter handle included a post about the NJEHA's white genocide platform, noting that their website includes a video interview with William Pierce.

As is often the case with doxing, "AntiFash Gordon" provided "D'Andrea's" work phone number and encouraged the handle's thousands of followers, "Give them a call and tell them to fire white nationalist [D'Andrea]." Just a week before Tree of Life, "AntiFash Gordon" posted that "D'Andrea" had confirmed in a podcast that he lost his job "and was destitute after being doxxed in October." The Twitter handle finishes with an expletive and a warning, "Hate has consequences."

4

Could It Happen Here?

NOVEMBER 6, 2018, RUTGERS UNIVERSITY, NEWARK, NJ
"Do you think it could actually happen in the US?"

A student asks this question halfway through my evening graduate class, where I am also holding a "Tree of Life Teach-in." During the first part of the three-hour seminar, we have, like the undergraduates, been discussing white genocide. The graduate class now turns in a different direction.

"Have any of you heard of *The Turner Diaries*?" I had just asked. Only a couple of students had raised their hands.

"It's a troubling book," I continued, "filled with racist language and hate. It concludes with a revolutionary white power movement taking control of the US and 'exterminating' Jews, nonwhites, and 'race traitors' in the name of saving the white race."

The ending of *The Turner Diaries*, seemingly so outlandish, had prompted the student's question in light of the Tree of Life attack, Charlottesville, and the resurgence of white power in Trump's USA. Could something like this happen in the United States?

It is not the first time this sort of issue has come up in class. The graduate course, Atrocity Prevention and the International Human Rights Regime, is directly focused on prevention, part of my continuing commitment to teach about violence and hate after Charlottesville. Among other things, this class considers how the lessons of past violence can help us assess risk in the present. The students have been examining human rights prevention infrastructures, from the grassroots to the global, meant to assist in the task of prevention. They are studying cases past and present as they consider interventions made before, during, and after atrocity crimes.

The students have directly grappled with the issue of predicting mass human rights violations. Atrocity-prevention websites often note risk with "heat maps," the "at-risk" countries glowing more or less red. Each student has been tasked with monitoring a current hot spot and writing a policy brief that includes recommendations. They chose crises new and old, incipient and acute, chronic and just hitting the news. Syria. Yemen. Burundi. Central African Republic. South Sudan. Myanmar. Gaza. Cameroon.

"What about the US?" a student had asked early in the semester as we discussed heat maps. "Why isn't it on the maps? Why isn't anyone talking about the dangers here? And what about Charlottesville?"

We have returned to the question, now inflected by Tree of Life.

～

"What exactly do you mean by 'it'?" I ask the student. "Every question is also a directive. So we need to clarify the terms and consider what it masks and reveals before we move forward. This sort of question has an interesting history. People asked it in the US in the 1930s when fascism was on the rise in Europe. The novelist Sinclair Lewis invoked it in the title of his 1935 best-seller, *It Can't Happen Here*. Copies of the book flew off the bookstore shelves after President Trump's election.

"Many people are asking the same sorts of questions now," I add. "Earlier this year, former secretary of state Madeline Albright published a book titled *Fascism: A Warning*. And another book by a group of public intellectuals is called, echoing Lewis, *Can It Happen Here?* The subtitle specified that they were talking about *Authoritarianism in America*, though the contributors also used terms like 'fascism' and 'tyranny.'"[1]

"What did they decide?" a student asks.

"Their answers vary," I reply. "Some see authoritarianism as a distinct possibility under President Trump. Others see it as possible but unlikely. A few said there is little or no chance of 'it' happening here at all."

"What sorts of factors did they look at?" another student queries.

"This varies depending on the scholar's definition and analytical approach," I answer. "There's a large literature on fascism, of course, so people have looked at things like authoritarian populism, ethnonationalism, propaganda, the erosion of law, power consolidation, nostalgia for a glorious past, victim and savior discourses, and so forth. A former Rutgers professor just published a book on 'how fascism works' and argued that there are troubling resonances with what's going on in the US today.[2]

"Others have focused on President Trump himself, contending that he is a Hitler-like fascist or manifests authoritarian or fascistic personality traits, including a lack of empathy, sense of grandiosity, and extreme narcissism.[3] Some people have even invoked rumors that President Trump slept with copies of a Hitler speech by his bed. If some dismiss such claims as exaggerated and outlandish, the Trump-Hitler comparison has been made since the beginning of his presidential campaign.

"So, what do you want us to discuss?" I ask the first student. "What did you mean by 'it'?"

"Those are all important issues," the student says, "and they relate to what I was talking about in my question—genocide. Could white supremacists commit a genocide in the US? Maybe not the *Turner Diaries* version, but genocide along the lines of what we've been talking about in this class? And, if so, how do we prevent it?"

"That's a great question," I reply. "And one people have largely ignored. But to answer we still need to ask another question: what exactly is genocide? The way we define 'genocide' will inform our answer."

A brief discussion of genocide ensues. Some of the students favor a broad definition like Raphael Lemkin's, which focuses on multifaceted group destruction and includes cultural destruction.

"Lemkin's definition is powerful," a student counters, "but it doesn't have legal force. We need to stick to the law and use the UN definition." Several other students concur.

∾

The product of intense political negotiation and compromise, the United Nations Convention on the Prevention and Punishment of Genocide was passed on December 9, 1948, the day before the Universal Declaration of Human Rights. Both documents were responses to Nazi atrocities, including the death camps discovered at the end of World War II.

The UN Genocide Convention definition requires proof of intent and restricts the purview to ethnic, racial, national, and religious groups. Political groups are excluded. So, too, is cultural genocide. While having the force of international law and including the words "prevention" and "punishment," the UN Genocide Convention lacks strong powers of enforcement.

For various reasons, ranging from conservative worry about the diminishment of sovereignty to concerns, especially by representatives from the South, that the United States would be accused of genocide and mass human rights violations for slavery and Jim Crow, the United States did not ratify the convention until 1988.

Ironically, white power extremists now invoke the UN Genocide Convention—and a few, like Norway shooter Anders Breivik, Lemkin's definition—to support their genocide claims. Just two months before Charlottesville, Jason Kessler wrote an essay titled "Yes, Virginia (Dare), There Is Such a Thing as White Genocide" for a white power website, VDare, which is named after the first English child born in British North America and which frequently publishes essays related to demographic replacement.[4] Kessler's invocation of the UN Genocide Convention, like that of most white power extremists, showed little understanding of the nuances of the genocide concept or the related legal and academic scholarship.

White power extremists often invoke subclauses of the UN Convention—especially one stating that, in addition to killing, genocide includes "deliberately inflicting on the group conditions of life calculated to bring about its physical destruction in whole or in part"—to argue that demographic replacement constitutes genocide. To support such claims, they draw on anecdotal evidence or conspiracy theories, especially about Jewish plots, contending that things like desegregation, multiculturalism, assimilation, and immigration are coordinated, systematic, and intentional efforts to commit white genocide.[5]

Kessler's essay argues along these lines. After quoting the UN Genocide Convention, Kessler complains about the demographic decline of whites in the name of "diversity" before stating that the only question "is whether this is a deliberate effort or not. Even a casual glance suggests it is." He proceeds to list a rambling string of anecdotes, statistics, and assertions before suddenly concluding that "governments of the West are waging a campaign of slow extermination against their own core populations. It *is* white genocide."

Like many other white power extremists, Kessler uses the genocide concept in a confused manner and with mistaken assumptions. He falsely equates race and space (epitomized by the neo-Nazi "blood and soil" chants in Charlottesville), ignores the fluidity and social construction of identity, confuses demographic trends with genocide, fails to prove intent, and overlooks settler colonialism and the history of systemic white supremacy, including its contemporary manifestations. This latter issue of contemporary white supremacy, which undercuts the white genocide argument, necessitates white power recourse to conspiracy theories.

Risk Assessment

"What about prediction?" a student asks. "It's not just about definition. To answer the question, we also need to assess the likelihood of genocide happening."

"How should we do that?" I counter. "We've read a lot about this during the semester."

"Why don't we use the criteria from the 'Framework of Analysis' booklet that we're using for our case studies?" a student suggests. "We can just use its definitions and assessment tools to consider atrocity crimes."

"That's a great idea," another student says. Others agree. Our criteria are set.

~

The "Framework of Analysis for Atrocity Crimes: A Tool for Prevention," is a thirty-four-page booklet developed by the Office of the Special Adviser of the Secretary-General on the Prevention of Genocide established in 2004 as part of UN Secretary-General Kofi Annan's attempt to foreground prevention—partly in response to the failure of the UN to prevent genocide in Rwanda in 1994 despite warning signs and having troops on the ground.[6] In 2018, it was headed by Adama Dieng, a Senegalese lawyer who had served as registrar at the international court established to try crimes committed during the Rwandan genocide.

Dieng's office, which is among the key global actors and the primary UN office devoted to atrocity crimes prevention, has figured prominently in my students' work. Indeed, just last month, my students visited his office at the UN.

After it was established, Dieng's office began developing a set of predictors, which my graduate students are using for their policy briefs. Their office also confronted the challenge of defining terms and developing corresponding risk-assessment categories. The "Framework of Analysis for Atrocity Crimes" lists eight shared and two distinct risk factors for each of the three atrocity crimes banned by international law: genocide (targeted attacks on national, racial, ethnic, and religious groups), crimes against humanity ("a widespread or systematic attack" against civilians), and war crimes (attacks on combatants and noncombatants during armed conflict). While it is not a specific crime in international law, the office also monitors ethnic cleansing or removing populations from an area to make it homogenous—an idea that also appears in white power discourse.

At times, the "Framework of Analysis" is a dense read, with long checklists that must be considered in tandem to assess risk. When a situation becomes "hot," Dieng's office issues warnings, such as one it had recently issued in September 2018 about civilian vulnerability in Idlib, Syria.[7]

My graduate class has recast the "Framework of Analysis" risk factors in somewhat more user-friendly terms. The eight common factors include *Instability* (especially armed conflict); *Past Violence* (histories of violence, impunity, and human rights violations); *Lack of Safeguards* (judicial, security, and human rights infrastructures); *Motivation* (ranging from economic incentives to ideology); *Capacity* (resources, actors, and organization); *Weak Buffering* (ranging from civil society to media); an *Enabling Environment* (for example, emergency laws, militias, and hate speech); and *Triggers* (including troop deployments, power transfers, and incitement).

The two specific risk factors for genocide include identity-based *Discrimination* and signs of *Intent* to destroy groups because of their identity. This intent distinguishes genocide from crimes against humanity, which involves *Widespread Attack* but does not require the intent to destroy a group as does the UN Genocide Convention. Hate speech and incitement appear in a number of the risk factors, serving both as a warning sign and a trigger of atrocity crimes.

Not all factors, the "Framework of Analysis" notes, need to be present for atrocity crimes to take place. Each situation is fluid and involves a constellation of factors and a degree of danger that spikes, ebbs, and flows. In the end, analysts must use qualitative and quantitative information to make assessments while bearing in mind that information is imperfect and that the analytical categories and indicators have strengths and weaknesses.[8]

This is the task my students have undertaken for their policy briefs on at-risk situations. Now, in the wake of Tree of Life and Charlottesville, they apply this knowledge to Trump's USA.

A History of Genocide and Atrocity Crimes

"Which risk factor," I ask, "do you want to look at first?"

"For starters," a student replies, "it has happened here. So we can check 'Past Violence' off the list."

"Can you be more specific?" I say. "Which historical moment are you talking about and why does it fit the definition of genocide?"

"Slavery. Jim Crow. Lynching. The contemporary mass incarceration of Blacks," the student answers. "Take your pick. Blacks were targeted and died in huge numbers."

"And don't forget about Native Americans," another student adds.

"That's a long list, so let's start with the historical treatment of Blacks and African Americans." I suggest.

"In fact, just a couple of years after the UN Genocide Convention was passed," I go on, "a group of African Americans wrote a petition arguing that the US had committed and was continuing to commit genocide against its Black population. A famous Rutgers alumnus, the African American sports star and singer Paul Robeson, delivered the petition to the UN office in New York in 1951."

~

The petition, *We Charge Genocide: The Crime of the Government against the Negro People*, was part of an effort by Black activist groups to use the UN and its new human rights norms to spotlight racism in the United States. A few years earlier, for example, W. E. B. Du Bois had helped draft an NAACP petition that was delivered to the UN Commission on Human Rights.[9]

In the first line of the petition, *We Charge Genocide* claims that the United States had violated the UN Genocide Convention: "Out of the inhuman Black ghettos of American cities, out of the cotton plantations of the South," it begins, "comes this record of mass slayings on the basis of race, of lives deliberately warped and distorted by the willful creation of conditions making for premature death, poverty and disease."

This history of "institutionalized oppression and persistent slaughter," *We Charge Genocide* continues, was based on race, had been going on for three hundred years, and was "the result of the consistent, conscious, unified policies of every branch of government." Accordingly, the petitioners were warranted to be "the first in history to charge the government of the United States of America with the crime of genocide."

The petition likens this crime to that of "the monstrous Nazi beast," contending that, like the Nazis', the US genocide posed a global threat as illustrated by the fact that "the genocidal doctrines and actions of the American white supremacists have already been exported to the colored people of Asia." It continues, "White Supremacy at home makes for colored massacres abroad. . . . The lyncher and the atom bomber are related."[10]

To make this argument, the petition describes the history and structure of white supremacy in the United States. Historically, this genocide had its origins in enslavement and its post–Civil War iteration in segregation and Jim Crow. Structurally, this system of white supremacy has been imposed by law and discriminatory practices and enforced by a system of terror employing tactics ranging from lynching to police murders and the violence of the KKK.

If more pronounced in the South, the system permeated almost every dimension of life for the fifteen million Blacks in the United States at the time of the petition: racist law and politics; racist education, employment, and health care practices; ghettoized housing; voter suppression; sharecropping; racist language; racist law enforcement; and so forth. The system was largely centered around profit, extracted first from the labor of the enslaved and then from that of sharecroppers and menial laborers. This system of white supremacy, the petition alleges, has resulted in a genocide that is both physical, including over ten thousand recent deaths, and psychological. To prove this point, *We Charge Genocide* links evidence from the postwar period (1945–51) to specific criminal acts included in the Genocide Convention.

❧

"So what happened after the petition was delivered?" a student asks.

"What often happens after atrocity crimes," I reply. "Denial—which is arguably another risk factor."

"The petition," I continue, "just like the NAACP one focused on human rights, was suppressed, discredited, and ignored. In fact, very few people remember it today. It was more or less erased from consideration. This had ramifications for how we now look at genocide since most people immediately think of it in terms of dramatic and seemingly exceptional moments like the Holocaust, not settler colonialism and the long-term and often slow destruction of Indigenous communities—or enslavement and Jim Crow."

"I'm not sure I totally buy it," a student says. "Slavery was horrific, but it wasn't genocide. They wanted slaves to work the fields, not die. The point was to get free labor, not kill them."

"People have made that argument," I reply, "including Raphael Lemkin, the person who coined the term 'genocide.' However, some critics view his response as a stain on his legacy."

~

In the midst of Cold War politics, Lemkin contended that the petitioners, many of whom were aligned with the communist movement, were attempting to divert attention from Soviet atrocities. He argued that, while discrimination was unfortunate, Blacks in the United States were not facing "annihilation and destruction," but instead a situation in which there was evidence of their growing "prosperity and progress."[11] He added, "Can one be guilty of genocide when one frightens a Negro? Obviously not."

While Lemkin may have had strategic reasons for making this argument, including worries that such allegations of US genocide would greatly diminish the chances that the country would ratify the UN Genocide Convention, his response failed to fully consider the arguments made in *We Charge Genocide*.

Indeed, when Lemkin coined the term "genocide" in 1944, he defined it as a "coordinated plan of different actions aiming at the destruction of essential foundations of the life of national groups, with the aim of annihilating the groups themselves."[12] As discussed in the last chapter in relation to settler colonialism, Lemkin argued that annihilation was not simply physical destruction but involved political, social, economic, biological, physical, religious, and moral "techniques" mobilized to destroy a group's spirit while imposing "the national pattern of the oppressor."

Transatlantic slavery arguably fits this definition. In his unpublished notes, Lemkin includes "slavery—exposure to death" as a physical technique of genocide along with "separation of families," which was also common with enslaved peoples. For Lemkin, influenced in part by German philosophy, the key element was the destruction of the "spirit" of a people.[13] Forcibly removing people from Africa and placing them in a situation in which they were racially codified, regulated, and dehumanized as "Blacks" (and other slurs) would seem to meet Lemkin's criteria for genocide.

From this perspective, the plight of Blacks in the United States at the time of the *We Charge Genocide* petition, particularly in the Jim Crow South, could arguably be viewed as part of a long-term genocidal process—one that also involved crimes against humanity. While Lemkin did consider the destruction of Indigenous people as genocide, he also failed to mention Native Americans in the context of the *We Charge Genocide* debate. Instead, and continuing a pattern that has persisted into the present, Lemkin helped sweep consideration of the legacy of genocide and atrocity crimes in the United States under the rug.

∼

"So at a minimum," a student states, "atrocity crimes against Blacks took place in the US."

"It would appear so," I say. "And there is a consensus that many Native American groups were victims of genocide, though when most people think of genocide they think of slaughter and so overlook other issues like forcing Indigenous children to attend boarding schools so they could be 'civilized.' The conditions in these schools were often horrible. Many Native Americans suffered greatly and lost touch with their cultural roots. Many also died. The US, however, seems a long way from any sort of accountability process for past atrocity crimes."[14]

"Why?" a student asks.

"I'm actually going to take up these issues in a class I'm teaching next semester on The Anthropology of White Supremacy," I reply. "We'll read *We Charge Genocide* and look at Native American experience as well as issues such as immigration and today's controversies about the southern border and President Trump's wall. The class will also examine notions like Manifest Destiny and American exceptionalism, which assert that the US occupies a unique moral position in the world as a bastion of human rights and democracy."

"Yeah, right," a student exclaims. "Did they forget about things like Japanese internment, Guantanamo, drone strikes, and southern border camps?"

"And what about the US bombing of Cambodia?" a student adds, perhaps thinking of our earlier discussions of my testimony at Nuon Chea's trial.

"I'm sure we'll consider several of those issues in the class," I say. "But, with regard to your first question, one reason nobody wants to take up issues like the genocide of Native Americans or historical treatment of African Americans and Blacks—or other groups like Asian Americans who were targeted because of 'Yellow Peril' fears—is this idea of 'exceptionalism,' which suggests that horrible things like genocide can't occur in the US. Instead, they only happen in more 'savage' places like Nazi Germany or Cambodia. And then, of course, there are potentially massive economic stakes to acknowledgment."

"We need to consider this history, especially since past genocide is a risk factor," a student notes. "But how exactly does this relate to Bowers's antisemitic attack at Tree of Life?"

"1488," another student answers. "Tree of Life was an attack on nonwhites made in the name of genocide."

"Aren't Jews white?" a third student asks.

"That's an important question," I respond. "Many white power ex-tremists believe Jews are a different race that is trying to destroy the white race. There are even far-right religious groups who believe that Jews are from a Satanic racial 'seedline.' But these sorts of racial identi-ties are socially constructed. So the categorization of many groups has been fluid and historically marked as both as 'white' and 'nonwhite.' It's not just the Jews. For example, Irish were once considered to be a differ-ent race and viewed as 'savages.'

"On the other hand," I continue, "different groups have more or less access to the category of 'whiteness,' as a comparison of the Irish versus Blacks underscores. Irish became 'white' while Blacks were prevented from doing so in a variety of ways, including 'one drop' and antimiscege-nation rules. So it might be better to say that racial identities are socially constructed and regulated by power.

"This brings us back to the first question," I say. "Can you expand on how *We Charge Genocide* is connected to 1488 and white power extrem-ism today?"

"White genocide is a justification for twenty-first-century white su-premacy," the second student says. "They want to bring back white race rule."

"It never left," another student comments. "The KKK just dresses more nicely. Look at David Duke."

"But the KKK didn't shut down the *We Charge Genocide* petition," I note. "Politicians did. The same was true of the NAACP petition regard-ing human rights. That suggests something systemic."

∿

At the time, both petitions had generated concern that they would undercut US support for the new human rights infrastructures that were emerging after World War II. Southern politicians were at the fore-front of efforts to sabotage robust human rights safeguards that might be directed back at the United States, particularly the Genocide Conven-tion. Some were members of US delegations to the UN that helped craft the language of the new human rights norms. Others openly stated that they would oppose domestic human rights legislation that threated the ability of southerners to maintain white supremacy. As a result of such efforts, the international human rights norms, laws, and institutions that undergird global governance have a blind spot—some would say intentional disregard—for the issue of race and the history of colonial inequities to which it is linked.[15]

These tensions would continue to play out in the United States and later find expression in the civil rights movement, which marked a second major transformation in the US system of white supremacy. The first was the Civil War and Reconstruction, which catalyzed a shift from a racial ordering characterized by settler-colonial conquest, genocide, and an almost totalitarian domination of Native Americans and Blacks to one marked by segregation, Jim Crow, vigilante violence, and animus directed against a broadening range of immigrant and nonwhite groups. The *We Charge Genocide* petition was delivered on the cusp of the "second Reconstruction," the post–World War II civil rights movement, which was echoed by anticolonial struggles against racial regimes in other parts of the globe.

If, like the post–Civil War Reconstruction, the "second reconstruction" was marked by sociopolitical change and laws that dismantled parts of the white-supremacist system, this system persisted after the civil rights movement in a modified, somewhat diminished, and largely masked form.[16] Some scholars refer to this new third phase of white supremacy as the "new racism," which contrasts with the overtness of the "old racism" that preceded it.[17] If it had been previously acceptable to express white-supremacist views in public and even on the floors of Congress, then, these discourses were increasingly coded in the sorts of racial dog whistles Trump uses.

This reworking of white-supremacist rhetoric, policy, and power began to emerge toward the end of the 1960s—at roughly the same time as the "new world order" phase of contemporary white power extremism was getting underway. Emerging in the backdrop of the 1964 Goldwater and 1968 Wallace campaigns, the "new right" movement helped reart-iculate systemic white supremacy, in part through the coded language central to the "southern strategy" that Nixon, and later Reagan, used to appeal to white voters, especially former Dixiecrats.[18] Republican con-sultant Lee Atwater infamously explained how this strategy played on race: "You start out in 1954 by saying, 'Nigger, nigger, nigger.' By 1968 you can't say 'nigger'—that hurts you, backfires. So you say stuff like, uh, forced busing, states' rights, and all that stuff, and you're getting . . . a hell of a lot more abstract than 'nigger, nigger.'"[19]

Such coded racial language helped obscure the systemic white su-premacy that was manifest in many of the same domains *We Charge Genocide* discusses: inequity and discrimination in education, housing, mass incarceration, health care, immigration, socioeconomic mobility, policing, access to jobs, criminal justice, income levels, mortality rates, and political rights, including new techniques of disenfranchisement and voter suppression.[20] Beyond racist dog whistles, such policies were masked by assertions that the United States had reached a "color-blind" or "postracial" phase. Some even argued that race-related reforms had gone so far that "reverse racism" was taking place, a line of thinking that dovetails with the victimization and white-rights concerns of white power extremists and the white genocide frame.

This systemic white supremacy perspective on contemporary US politics and society, one that Du Bois helped pioneer and that was manifest in *We Charge Genocide*, dovetails with the point made ear-lier in this book: seemingly "exceptional" moments like Charlottesville and Tree of Life are more like ruptures, when something present but pushed just out of sight suddenly bursts forth.[21] This dehiscence is not a pathological aberration of individualizing "racists" or "haters," but a symptom of an underlying reality of structural racism and white su-premacy that is supported and naturalized by a "white racial frame," to return to Feagin's term.[22]

Likewise, if often ostentatious, Trump's racially inflected dog whistles and positions on issues like immigration reflected this underlying reality as opposed to being an aberration in an otherwise "color-blind" or "postracial" society. Trump followed in a long line of post–civil rights, "southern strategy," dog-whistle politicians—not just populists and nativists like George Wallace and Patrick Buchanan, but mainstream presidents like Nixon and Reagan, both of whom used racist language out of public view. Post-Charlottesville controversies about contemporary Democratic and Republican politicians who had used blackface suggests how pervasive and taken-for-granted systemic white supremacy remained, a point the public focus on "exceptional" moments of racism further underscored.[23]

This perspective on contemporary systemic white supremacy suggests that Blacks in the United States continue to be subject to atrocity crimes. While far from the center of genocide studies scholarship, which has largely overlooked such considerations, some academics have argued the strongest case: that the allegations made in *We Charge Genocide* largely apply to the situation of Blacks in the United States today.[24] In making this case, such scholars draw on sources ranging from Orlando Patterson's notion of "social death," which dovetails in interesting ways with Lemkin's idea of the destruction of the "spirit" of a people, to Wolfe's arguments about the settler-colonial "logic of elimination," to contend that, as is the case with Native Americans, the genocide against Blacks is part of a long-term process linked to global capitalism, enslavement, and systemic white supremacy. From this perspective, the question is not "can it happen here?" but a recognition of what this question, which suggests exceptionality, obscures—that it has happened and still is happening here.

Enabling Environment of Hate Speech and Incitement

"It sounds like you all agree that *Past Violence* has taken place in the US," I say to the class, "though some of you disagree about particular instances. So, besides *Past Violence*, do other risk factors in the 'Framework of Analysis' suggest the US is 'at risk' for atrocity crimes?"

"Trump's inciting violence," one of the graduate students contends. "He's been engaging in hate speech since day one. And hate and incitement create an *Enabling Environment* and can also *Trigger* violence. Both of those are key risk factors."

"We thought Charlottesville was bad," another student comments. "Look at Tree of Life and all the talk about alien 'Caravan' invaders— Trump keeps beating the hate drum and inciting people."

"Is there a difference between incitement and hate speech?" I ask.

"The Special Advisor's office distinguishes between the two," a student replies, referencing another reading for the day.[25] "They define hate speech as 'any kind of communication in speech, writing or behavior, that denigrates a person or a group on the basis of who they are.' But they also say that 'not all hate speech constitutes incitement.'"

"What about incitement?" I ask.

"They note," the student answers, "that 'incitement to violence' is prohibited in international law and can 'include any communication that encourages violence against a group or individual.' This can involve anything from a speech to social media posts. So Trump may be in trouble!"

"Convicting someone's a different matter," another student remarks. "If we go with their definition, incitement seems to be a subset of hate speech. Trump engages in hate speech all the time. What would it take to convict him?"

The second student again refers us to the text: "The text says that to prove incitement to violence you need a bunch of things, 'including a context conducive to violence, an influential speaker, a speech act that is widely disseminated, a receptive audience and a target.' And you need intent. That's the trickiest part."

"So did President Trump incite Sayoc to send the bombs?" I ask. "And what about Bowers and Tree of Life?"

Another student answers, "He might have incited Sayoc. But it would be really hard to prove intent. Bowers is a different matter since he was ambivalent about Trump."

"Based on the UN definition," the second student adds, "Trump's engaging in hate speech all the time. He's creating a climate of violence. Rising hate crimes stats support that case. No doubt his hate speech influenced Sayoc and Bowers. But incitement is a different matter. Legally, it's really hard to prove. Nothing happened after those pre-election rallies where Trump encouraged crowds to attack protesters."

"Actually," I say, "President Trump was sued for incitement when, after protesters interrupted one of his campaign rally speeches in 2016, he encouraged the crowd to 'get 'em out of here.' A few protesters got roughed up by members of the crowd that included white power extremists and sued. But the suit was eventually dismissed."

Motivation

"Let's move on and look at some other risk factors," I suggest.

"How about *Motive*?" a student offers. "That's a key factor in the 'Framework of Analysis.'"

"*Motive* is important, for sure," I say. "Is there any connection between President Trump and white power actors and ideology? Is President Trump, for example, actively playing on the idea of white genocide? And if so, what are his motives, and could they lead to atrocity crimes?"

"That's a tough question," a student replies. "Like incitement, it's hard to prove."

"It has to be inferred," another student notes. "For that matter, has Trump ever directly spoken about white genocide?"

"Actually, he has," I reply. "In early 2016, President Trump retweeted a post from the handle 'WhiteGenocideTM' that included a photo of the infamous neo-Nazi, George Rockwell."[26]

Less than two weeks after Unite the Right 2 and following related comments made on Fox News, Trump also tweeted that he had asked Secretary of State Pompeo to examine the "large-scale" seizure of land from and killings of white South African farmers, a situation the alt-right and other white power extremists refer to as an illustration of "white genocide." The *Daily Stormer*, Anglin and Azzmadore's white power extremist website that had endorsed Trump, headlined "IT'S HAPPENING: Trump Tweets about WHITE GENOCIDE in South Africa . . . This is a significant step in the right direction."[27]

At other points, Trump's invocations of white genocide were more indirect, but still interpreted by white power extremists as racial dog whistles nevertheless. Indeed, one of Trump's central motifs, immigration, played on white genocide fears of invasion and replacement. These ideas were foregrounded in messaging from the start of Trump's political campaign, beginning with his stoking of the Obama birther conspiracy and warnings about Muslim and Latino invaders.

They were also clearly manifest in his campaign rally readings of "The Snake," which Trump also read at the 2018 meeting of the Conservative Political Action Conference (CPAC). After touching on many of his usual issues, ranging from boasts about the greatness of his presidency to complaints about the "fake news," Trump began talking about the dangers of immigration, including "criminal aliens" and the "savage" and "animal killers" of the MS-13 gang. "Think of it in terms of immigration," Trump told the crowd. Just before he started reading, Trump repeated, "Immigration."

Given Trump's framing, "The Snake" serves as a parable of white genocide. Most abstractly, the "vicious" snake signifies the dangerous nonwhite outsider who lurks without (on the other side of the border) and within (inside the country). If this idea is epitomized by "criminal aliens" and the MS-13 gang, Trump applied it much more broadly in his rhetoric, including his 2018 midterm election depictions of immigrants as an "infestation" and his later description of predominantly Black Baltimore as "rat-infested."

The dangerous "snake" is counterposed to the innocence of the "tender-hearted woman" who kindly gives the treacherous and ungrateful snake shelter before being killed by its deadly bite. Most obviously, the woman represents the United States, with its femininity historically depicted through images like Columbia and Lady Liberty. In this regard, the woman is a source of fertility, beauty, and the reproduction of the nation, which is violated and endangered by the snake. It crosses the threshold of the woman's home (the border), thereby violating and contaminating the sanctity of this sacred space (the nation).

This imagery plays directly into the white genocide idea that the future of the white race is endangered and thus that people must act in accordance with the Fourteen Words imperative, "We must secure the existence of our people and a future for White children." Along these lines, the sexual undertones of Trump's rendition of "The Snake" (giving it "milk," clutching it "to her bosom," and stroking the snake, which she kisses and holds tight) are also suggestive of the white genocide focus on race mixing and miscegenation.

By extension, the moral imperative of the situation depicted in "The Snake" is to prevent this violation and threat of racial extinction at the hands of dangerous nonwhite others. Trump situated himself as the savior who would prevent white genocide by his Muslim "travel ban," cutting off the immigrant caravan "invasion," preventing "infestation," and building "the wall." The desperate situation, "The Snake" story suggests, justifies extreme measures: deportations, incarceration, detention, and potentially even mass violence.

Bowers legitimated his Tree of Life attack in terms of such "invasion" language, targeting Jews who, in a long-standing antisemitic trope, have been depicted as dangerous snakes. Hitler and the Nazis also used this metaphor, even publishing a version of the Aesop fable that inspired "the Snake" with an annotation noting that the viper represented Jews who, like a poisonous snake, needed to be eradicated.[28]

Ideology, Incentives, and State Power

"Even if we're agreed that President Trump plays on white power themes, including white genocide," I say, "is there evidence that he has white power actors in his administration and, if so, that they carry out policies based on this ideology?"

"Bannon," a student immediately replies, naming Trump's controversial campaign advisor and political strategist. "He's an alt-right bigshot and headed *Breitbart*."

"But he's out," another student notes, referring to Bannon's White House exit shortly after Charlottesville.

"Anyone else?" I ask.

The class is silent.

"It's hard to know," I continue, "though many people jump to the conclusion that President Trump's administration is alt-right. We don't really know how deeply or effectively white power actors have penetrated the Trump administration beyond well-known appointments like Bannon, Sebastian Gorka, Michael Flynn, and Stephen Miller. But other hints have emerged."

The "POTUS & Political Warfare" Memo

One of them was a May 2017 white paper titled "POTUS & Political Warfare." Written by Richard Higgens, a high-ranking member of the National Security Council linked to Flynn and Bannon, the tract echoes alt-right ideology.[29] The white paper warns that the "hard Left" (ranging from Antifa to the American Civil Liberties Union and the UN) is aligned with Islamists in seeking to delegitimize and topple Trump, who threatens the ascendancy of the cultural Marxist narratives they seek to advance. These narratives include political-correctness "memes" related to hate speech, racism, tolerance, human rights, multiculturalism, and diversity that threaten the country and, by implication, white group identity. "America is at risk and is slipping away," Higgens warns.

The forces that support cultural Marxism run deep, Higgens contends, encompassing the media, academia, deep state actors, globalists, Democrats, and even Republican leaders—who are included among the mainstream "cuckservatives" the alt-right so despises. To combat Trump, these opposition forces "seamlessly interoperate through coordinated synchronized interactive [cultural Marxist] narratives," ones that draw on Maoist insurgency–like "political warfare" tactics operating on the "strategic, operational, or tactical levels." Their goal is to maintain the dominant systems of cultural (Marxist) "conditioning" of the masses, which Trump threatens. While he uses somewhat different language, Higgens echoes Friberg's discussion of metapolitics, emphasizing the urgent need to reveal what is mystified amid a "battle for hearts and minds."

The tract includes a "primer" on cultural Marxism, the perceived source of "political correctness" memes and a favorite target of the alt-right and white power extremists like Anders Breivik, the Norwegian mass shooter who extensively discussed cultural Marxism in his manifesto. More recently, the link between cultural Marxism and political correctness has been elaborated by William Lind, who argues that cultural Marxism was formulated by the Frankfurt School, which sought to advance Marxism through cultural domination, including control of the media.[30] Contemporary notions of political correctness, Lind argues, are part of this long-standing communist plot to undermine Western Christian (capitalist) society.

Many members of the Frankfurt School were Jewish, a point the alt-right underscores, sometimes by using coded language—as Higgens does through his references to "globalists" or unspecified forces controlling the media. Higgens uses the work of a Jewish member of the Frankfurt School, philosopher Herbert Marcuse, to support his contentions, arguing that Marcuse's work on tolerance demanded the intolerance of racism and discrimination. Today, Higgens states, such cultural Marxist ideas are manifest in the anti-hate and political-correctness narratives promoted domestically and abroad by a host of actors ranging from the UN to Islamist organizations.

Higgens, like many on the alt-right, depicts Trump as an enlightened hero confronting these diabolical cultural Marxist forces, a point Higgens underscores by quoting a 2016 Trump remark. "The establishment and their media enablers," Trump stated, exert "control over *this* nation through means that are very well known. Anyone who challenges their control is deemed a sexist, a racist, a xenophobe, and morally deformed."[31] Despite such obstacles, Higgens contends, Trump must continue to valiantly fight for "the vision of America that led to his election," one cultural Marxists and the Islamist opposition seek to destroy.

The memo apparently circulated through the White House and was read by Trump's son, who passed it on to his father. Trump is said to have "gushed over" the memo.[32] When it became public, however, the memo sparked controversy and Higgens was forced to resign. Some dismissed the Higgens memo as crazy, failing to consider that the white paper suggested how deeply alt-right ideology had penetrated the Trump administration and informed Trump's vision, in part through the influence of people like Bannon and Flynn. Indeed, at the time, General McMaster, who had replaced Flynn, was trying to purge the National Security Council of Flynn and Bannon loyalists, some of whom, like Higgens, had alt-right views and were suspected of leaking information to an alt-lite social media personality, Mike Cernovich.

Trump apparently was "furious" at the firing.[33] Given this response and his other statements that dovetail with the Higgens memo, Trump's tirades against the "fake news," the "Deep State," and "political correctness" may be viewed as less the statements of the crazed "Hater" than those of an advocate of white power positions that had been well articulated by the alt-right at the time even as they have a long genealogy in US history and are intertwined with the white genocide frame.

Stephen Miller and the Great Replacement

If other more minor Trump administration officials, including a White House speechwriter and a Homeland Security analyst, would also be found to have white-power-extremist sympathies, perhaps the most direct evidence of alt-right influence emerged in November 2019 when a story broke about Trump's senior advisor and immigration policy strategist, Stephen Miller.[34]

At this time, the Southern Poverty Law Center (SPLC) announced that it had obtained hundreds of e-mails Miller exchanged with Katie McHugh, a *Breitbart* editor who leaked the e-mails after renouncing her extremist views.[35] Bannon was included on some of the e-mails—as was another *Breitbart* editor, Julia Hahn, who like Miller would work in the White House.

The 2015–16 e-mails, sent amid the presidential campaign, reflect a variety of white power concerns, including Confederate symbols, race, immigration, crime, and terrorism. Miller offers suggestions for stories and at times is directly involved in shaping content that eventually appears in *Breitbart* articles, including ones invoking white genocide themes.

At one point, Miller recommends an anti-immigration article on the white power website VDare, which published Unite the Right organizer Jason Kessler's essay "Yes, Virginia (Dare), There Is Such a Thing as White Genocide." Another time, Miller refers McHugh to *American Renaissance*, a far-right website founded by Jared Taylor, a white power extremist who contributed an essay to *A Fair Hearing* titled "Race Realism" (arguing that, to prevent "the great replacement" and "disappearance of whites," it is first necessary to recognize that race is a biological reality as opposed to a social construct).

On September 6, 2015, Miller—then working with Senator Jeff Sessions, Trump's future staunch anti-immigration attorney general—suggested that *Breitbart* produce a story on *The Camp of the Saints*, an anti-immigrant novel that occupies a status in Europe similar to that of *The Turner Diaries* in the United States. Responding to Pope Francis's 2015 call for the United States to accept more refugees, Miller wrote to McHugh, "You see the Pope saying west must, in effect, get rid of borders. Someone should point out the parallels to Camp of the Saints."[36]

Written in 1973, *Camp of the Saints* begins with the arrival of a flotilla of a million refugees from India on the shores of France. Near death, the refugees, led by the "turd eater," are allowed in and quickly overrun France and beyond, leading to the demise of white civilization. The book, filled with racist stereotypes and dehumanizing language and imagery, was an inspiration for "The Great Replacement" theory and gained new popularity amid the 2015 European immigration crisis.[37]

Two weeks after Miller's e-mail, *Breitbart* published an article, written by Julia Hahn, titled "'Camp of the Saints' Seen Mirrored in Pope's Message." It summarized the book's plot and directly linked it to the dangers of mass immigration in the present. This was not an isolated incident: other members of the far right, ranging from Bannon and Patrick Buchanan to French far-right leader Marine Le Pen, have praised the novel's supposed prescience about the dangers of immigration.

The Miller-*Breitbart* e-mails suggest that what was long rumored about Stephen Miller, that he has strong white power and alt-right sympathies, is accurate. Previously, his white power leanings had been inferred in part from his past anti-immigrant statements.[38] Some commentators also noted that, while at Duke, Miller co-organized an event with Richard Spencer that brought Peter Brimelow, the founder of VDare, to speak on campus. They both belonged to the Duke Conservative Union, and Spencer claims they "knew each other quite well."[39]

If Miller, who is Jewish, likely does not subscribe to the extreme antisemitic aspects of the white-power-extremist movement, his views align with alt-right ideas about white genocide and immigration and, through him, directly impacted White House policy. McHugh made this point in an interview after the release of the e-mails, stating, "Miller is the most prominent architect of immigration policy within the White House and it's easy to draw a clear line from the white supremacist website where he is getting his ideas to current immigration policy."[40] Interestingly, Miller joined the Trump campaign in January 2016, just as Trump was beginning to use "The Snake" at his rallies. While it is impossible to know if there is a direct connection, there is a convergence in white power orientation at a minimum.

When interviewed on CNN after the Southern Poverty Law Center broke the story about the Miller e-mails, Katie McHugh stated that she would "absolutely call him a white supremacist" driven by an ideology of "white supremacy and anti-immigration especially."[41] She added that she knew because she had been one as well—as illustrated both by her professional life at *Breitbart* and by her personal life, which included hanging out with white power extremists at a home they called "the house of hate." Given these white power sympathies, a number of Democrats and social justice groups called for Miller's resignation. It was not forthcoming. Miller eventually responded by suggesting that he was the victim of an antisemitic smear campaign.[42]

White Power in the Mainstream

If perhaps the most notorious, *Breitbart* is not the only media source that promotes white power ideas, including white genocide and great replacement narratives. A range of conservative commentators have done so, Fox News personalities among them.[43] Just days before Unite the Right 2, for example, Fox host Laura Ingraham claimed on air that "the America we know and love doesn't exist anymore. Massive demographic changes have been foisted upon the American people."[44] Her remark, which was later disavowed, won the praise of David Duke and others who similarly lament "the browning of America" and future minority status of whites.

White power extremists have made laudatory remarks about other Fox hosts, including Tucker Carlson, who commented on South African white genocide and is a favorite of white power extremists, including the neo-Nazi Andrew Anglin, who has said Carlson is "literally our greatest ally."[45] Carlson's top writer had to resign after it was revealed that he was posting anonymous racist screeds under a pseudonym. Peter Hegseth, in turn, inveighs against "globalism" and "political correctness," longstanding white power dog whistles.

These sorts of invocations of white power tropes, including white genocide, have been mainstreamed on Fox, a point noted by a number of commentators and underscored by a *Salon* headline, "The Alt-Right Isn't Dead: It Was Just Taken Over by Fox News." And Fox, it is important to remember, is the number one rated cable news network; Carlson and Ingraham are among the most watched shows, with millions of viewers.[46] The Fox push to promote white power views is part of a larger Fox ownership effort that panders to nativist impulses in the United States and abroad.[47] One employee claimed that Fox had "created a white supremacist cell inside the top cable network in America."

Trump has long had a close relationship with Fox, one that continued through his presidency. He watched and sometimes responded to Fox broadcasts about white power themes, as illustrated by Trump's tweet about white genocide. But Trump remained attuned to the broader far-right social media ecosystem promoting white power views that extends from Fox and *Breitbart* to more extreme social media personalities who push white power views, including white genocide. Some were even invited to White House press briefings and a White House "social media summit."[48] This synergy among Trump, Fox, and far-right extremists led to more overt expression and mainstreaming of white power extremist views—exactly as the alt-right and other far-right actors have sought to do through metapolitics and shifting the Overton window of what is acceptable to say and do.

There is a reason why Trump and Fox have invoked white power themes, just as there was for Republicans to implement the southern strategy. There is an audience for it. This audience does not just consist of hard far-right extremists like Anglin and Duke, even as their numbers may be larger than many realize.[49] Millions of people in the United States hold white power views, and many more have white power sympathies and the sense of victimization upon which the white genocide frame plays.

Shortly after Charlottesville, for example, a 2016 poll found that roughly 6 percent of non-Hispanic whites—eleven million people—held strong white power sentiments.[50] The statistic was likely an undercount since the investigator required positive answers to three questions about white identity, solidarity, and victimization, whereas the numbers for each individual question were much higher, ranging from 27 to 38 percent. A 2017 poll discovered similar trends, with 10 percent, over twenty million people, indicating their support of the alt-right and 9 percent saying it was okay to have white-supremacist or neo-Nazi views.[51]

It is important to recognize that these statistics are not an anomaly. If stoked by Trump, Fox News personalities, *Breitbart*, and the alt-right, among others, white power views are rooted in systemic white supremacy dating back to the origins of the United States. Contemporary white power has just been enabled in new ways by social media and, during the Trump presidency, by an administration that often aligned with white power in its rhetoric and policy. This situation was all the more dangerous given that white power attitudes extend into key institutional levers of power in the United States, including law enforcement and the military, both of which have a history of white power extremism and white-supremacist violence.[52]

Buffers and Safeguards

"The more we talk about it," a student says, "the more dicey the situation seems. A genocidal past. Hate speech. Armed white supremacists. And Trump. Still, we haven't discussed buffers."

"That's certainly a key factor in assessing risk and for prevention," I reply.

"Trump has been weakening these as well," another student states.

"Which ones and how?" I ask. "And which ones does the 'Framework of Analysis' highlight?"

The students begin to name them.

"Judicial independence and the rule of law."

"Free speech."

"Civilian control of the military."

"Accountability."

"Democratic checks and balances."

"Civil society."

"Media independence."

"The Constitution."

"Which ones has President Trump weakened?" I query.

"The 'fake news'!" a student offers, referring to Trump's continuing assaults on media outlets. "And remember Flake's warning about 'enemies
of the people' language. It's the language of authoritarians and genocidal
regimes."

"A number of commentators—from academics to journalists—have
been looking at President Trump's attack on the sorts of buffers you
named," I tell the class, "though many of them focus on authoritarianism and fascism.

"In *Can It Happen Here?*, the recently published book I mentioned
earlier," I go on, "the contributors all note that President Trump has
eroded democratic safeguards and checks and balances. But they disagree about the extent of the danger. Some think we're just a step away
from authoritarianism. Others see it on the horizon, distant but in view.
A few argue that the danger is remote."

"Many discuss President Trump's attacks on the media and the courts
as well as his assault on the truth," I continue. "They discuss the importance of civil society, bureaucratic structures including 'the Deep State,'
as well as the checks and balances of other branches of government.
Some note the ascendency of authoritarian populists in other parts of
the world—Putin in Russia, Turkey's Erdogan, and the leaders of Poland and Hungary—and how they have undermined different state and
nonstate structures that serve as buffers. The contributors to the *Can It
Happen Here?* volume also discuss attacks on the rule of law."

"Like obstruction of justice," a student states.

"At least we have 'Anonymous,'" a second student comments, referring to a September 2018 essay written by someone inside the Trump
administration who claimed that he was part of "the Resistance" that
was trying to curb Trump's worst tendencies.[53]

"That's a good example of a bureaucratic check that may be working,"
I say.

"And we have the Mueller investigation," the second student adds. "This sort of oversight is a check on Trump. Impeachment would be, too."

"Yeah, but he keeps trying to influence Mueller's investigation and dismisses it as a 'hoax' and 'witch hunt,'" a third student points out. "And look at what's taking place on the southern border. He's separating mothers and children."

"They did that during slavery," a last student adds. "And remember the Japanese internment camps right here in the United States during World War II."

Triggers and Instability

"This brings us to the *Triggers* of atrocity crimes," I say. "Even if state structures have been weakened, there are often events that further amplify risk or even spark the violence."

"Like Trump's election," a student suggests.

"Or Charlottesville," another student adds.

"Yes, but no genocide took place after those events," a third student notes.

"What does the 'Framework of Analysis' suggest?" I ask.

"Elections, regime change, and hate speech are all listed," the first student notes. "It also lists the mobilization of security forces and economic problems."

"For those who agree that there is a chance that 'it can happen here,' can you imagine a scenario in which genocide or atrocity crimes could be triggered in the US?"

"They already have been on the southern border," a student states.

"That's bad, maybe crimes against humanity, but not genocide," another student says. "For genocide, there has to be intent to destroy a group as opposed to a more general attack on them. Trump hasn't gone anywhere near that far."

"The Bowerses of the world are ready for that, if Trump asks," another student says, returning us to our Tree of Life Teach-In theme. "He has a ready army of genociders."

"Your remarks raise a key question," I note. "Could white power extremists ever be more fully empowered under President Trump, so much so that they could seek to carry out a race war—or, in a less extreme scenario, strongly influence US government policy that does this in a less obvious manner?"

"Like the border camps," a student finishes.

"What if Trump gets impeached or loses the next election?" a student answers. "Things could get bad. Before he was elected, he said he might not accept the results. What would he do now—call on the Bowerses of the world to fight? There are a lot of extremist militias and they have guns, lots of them."

~

Indeed, commentators have increasingly grown concerned about the possibility of civil war under Trump. If these sorts of questions began to be asked when Trump said he might not respect the results if Hillary Clinton defeated him in the 2016 presidential election, they were asked more frequently after Charlottesville.[54] Some wondered if Trump, who constantly spoke of "witch hunts," "hoaxes," "coups," and voter fraud, would willingly leave office if impeached or not reelected—including his former lawyer Michael Cohen, who told Congress, "Given my experience working for Mr. Trump, I fear that if he loses the election in 2020 there will never be a peaceful transition of power."[55]

When one of the governmental checks and balances on the president, impeachment proceedings, was activated, Trump himself began to invoke such language directly. On September 29, 2019, Trump tweeted a quotation from a Fox News commentator who stated that impeachment would "cause a Civil War–like fracture in this Nation from which our Country will never heal."[56] Trump followed it up with another tweet that claimed the impeachment proceedings were an attempt at a "COUP."

The far-right Oath Keepers militia responded to Trump's civil war tweet by affirming that the country was "on the verge of a HOT civil war" and suggesting they were ready to act in the event of Trump's removal from office, a sentiment that other armed Trump supporters, including white power extremists, shared. Such an event could have created the sort of *Instability* that often accompanies atrocity crimes.

~

"It was this sort of conjunction between extremist militias and a populist leader," I tell the class, "that Sinclair Lewis, the author of *It Can't Happen Here*, was so wary of in the mid-1930s USA.

"Indeed," I continue, "Lewis was aware of the Brownshirts paramilitaries who had supported Hitler's rise to power. His wife was a well-known journalist who had interviewed Hitler in 1931 and was later kicked out of Germany for her reporting. Lewis knew about Mussolini and his Black Shirts supporters. And the US had the KKK as well as Silver Shirts fascist extremists and other Nazi supporters. Meanwhile, a left-wing populist demagogue from Louisiana, Huey Long, was planning to run for president before being assassinated.

"Lewis looked around and—like the protagonist in his novel who observes a dangerous populist president rising to power and supported by paramilitary forces—saw people in the US saying that, despite the danger signs, 'it can't happen here.' His book took aim at this naivety."

"American exceptionalism," a student states.

"People always think 'it can't happen here,'" another student says. "But, as we were talking about earlier, it has happened here. Look at US history. Look at the southern border now. Look at Charlottesville and extremists like Bowers."

Several other students nod their heads.

"Perhaps you have come up with another 'risk factor' to add to the 'Framework of Analysis,'" I respond. "We can call it 'Denial,' 'Naivety,' or a 'Failure of Moral Imagination'—the unwillingness or inability to seriously consider seemingly remote or uncomfortable possibilities.

"Can you think of any other scenarios that could trigger atrocity crimes in the US?"

"War," a student replies.

"Like Pearl Harbor and Japanese internment," I add. "Or war crimes committed during the War on Terror. Torture at Guantanamo."

"What about mass incarceration in the US today?" another student asks.

"That's an interesting point," I reply. "The question we have been discussing— 'Can it happen here?'—frames our answer in a certain direction, leading us to focus on the future and what is exceptional. It directs us away from structural violence, perhaps even atrocity crimes, which may be taking place right now.

"Some scholars have even spoken of structural genocide. Such concepts provide a way of thinking about the ongoing treatment of groups that have been victimized in the past and, despite the more spectacular forms of violence against them diminishing or ending—slavery, Jim Crow, Indigenous massacres and displacement, and so forth—are still being victimized in other ways that are nevertheless related to these dramatic events. Continuing discrimination is an obvious example. Mass incarceration is another possibility. *We Charge Genocide*, as we discussed, raises such possibilities."

* * *

"Unfortunately, we're out of time so we have to finish up our 'Tree of Life Teach-in,'" I tell the class. "Why don't we end with a vote?

"Everyone seems to agree that 'it can happen here,'" I note. "So how dangerous is the present moment? How many of you think the US should be under a high-risk red alert for genocide?"

A couple of hands go up.

"A moderate risk orange alert?"

The majority of students raise their hands.

"Mild risk yellow?"

The last few students raise their hands.

"What about atrocity crimes in general?" I continue. "How many of you think that the US is in a high-risk situation?"

Almost every student raises their hand.

"If there is serious risk, as most of you suggest," I say, "a next question is, How can we stop it from happening? I guess you will all give me the answers in your final policy briefs. As you know, I'm going to Cambodia next week for the verdict in Nuon Chea's trial. Several of our readings have argued that these sorts of tribunals are an important prevention mechanism in terms of deterrence.

"In the meantime," I finish, "we'll see how the midterm elections turn out tonight. Hopefully things will have calmed down by the time I get back next week."

5

Can It Be Prevented?

NOVEMBER 13, 2018, PHNOM PENH, CAMBODIA
"Pres. Trump's Nationalism Inspiring White Supremacists."

Things have not settled down by the time I reach my hotel in Phnom Penh near midnight after more than twenty-four hours of travel. Unable to sleep, I flip on the TV, tune in to Donald Trump's most hated "fake news" station, CNN, which flashes this headline. The story includes a tweet from GOP congressman Steve King, who warns, in keeping with his many past inflammatory statements, "We can't restore our civilization with somebody else's babies."

Now, just a week after my Tree of Life Teach-Ins and the midterm elections, worries about Trump's white power incitement continue. Trump, who embraced the term "nationalist" in October, is defending himself after French President Macron stated, "Nationalism is not patriotism." CNN headlines, "Trump says he's not a racist. That's not how white nationalists see it."[1]

Minor stories related to white power are also in the news. A controversy erupts about a group of Wisconsin high school students photographed giving the Nazi salute.[2] The FBI reports hate crimes rose 17 percent in 2017, with the rate of antisemitic ones even higher. In New Jersey, where I teach, there is a 76 percent rise, the fourth highest percentage in the nation. These upward trends continue in 2018.[3]

Meanwhile, in Washington, DC, police have just arrested Jeffrey R Clark Jr., an online acquaintance of Bowers who posted a photo of Bowers while warning, "Get used to it libtards. This was a dry run for things to come." Family members reported Clark to the FBI, telling them that Clark "fantasized about killing Jews and Blacks" and was heavily involved in white power extremism. According to the relatives, Clark attended Charlottesville, admired Timothy McVeigh, and wanted to help spark a "race revolution."[4]

On CNN, another story notes that white power actors say that despite Republican congressional losses, the midterm elections are actually a victory, in part because of Trump's racially tinged oratory. "This changed history," Anglin writes in the *Daily Stormer*. "It cleared away any of the remaining fog of confusion about what exactly we are dealing with in this country. . . . This is race war. Period."[5]

Race war. White power. Genocide. As I begin to doze off, CNN still on, I think of Khmer Rouge extremism and how, in just three days, the Trial Chamber will deliver its verdict in Nuon Chea's trial.

* * *

NOVEMBER 16, 2018, ECCC COURTROOM,
PHNOM PENH, CAMBODIA

Now I sit in the packed courtroom of the Extraordinary Chambers in the Courts of Cambodia (ECCC). I look at the witness stand where I testified two and a half years before, think of my exchange with Nuon Chea. There is electricity in the air as people await the court's decision about whether Nuon Chea and Khieu Samphan will be found guilty of atrocity crimes, including the charge about which I testified, genocide.

Transitional Justice

"Moving forward through Justice."

As I wait for the proceedings to commence, I glance down at the ECCC slogan, printed in orange on the back of the court's official booklet, which is given to visitors as they enter the court. It opens with statements from Cambodia's prime minister, Hun Sen, and the UN secretary-general, António Guterres.

Both speak to the meaning of the slogan.[6] Hun Sen emphasizes the suffering of Cambodians under the Khmer Rouge and how the court helps to "build a culture that will prevent the recurrence of such crimes." Guterres, in turn, states that such trials serve both to "end impunity and ensure accountability" and to help people "move forward" by strengthening the rule of law, building judicial capacity, empowering survivors, and helping them "search for the truth and find justice."

Such goals are often referred to as "transitional justice," an idea that emerged as the Cold War was ending.[7] While the transition was originally conceived of in terms of democratization, as postconflict societies moved away from authoritarianism, transitional justice now broadly encompasses efforts to deliver accountability and redress to victims of state crimes. In addition to tribunals like the ECCC, other mechanisms assisting in this process include truth-seeking efforts, memorialization, reparations, and institutional reforms.

After the Khmer Rouge were deposed, Cambodia undertook a number of redress efforts.[8] Some, like a 1993 UN-sponsored election and the ECCC, were undertaken in partnership with the UN and global actors. Other efforts, such as the construction of memorials, had been driven by the Cambodian government with some outside assistance.

Just the day before, I had visited Cambodia's most famous Khmer Rouge genocide memorial, the Tuol Sleng Museum of Genocidal Crimes, built on the site of the notorious S-21 security center where twelve thousand or more people were interrogated and killed. Established in 1979 in consultation with Vietnamese advisors, Tuol Sleng was meant both to inflame anger against the Khmer Rouge and to memorialize the crimes of the DK regime—a point that underscores the fact that transitional justice mechanisms are political creations, part aspiration, part compromise, and partly defined by the interests of the powerful.

While Tuol Sleng has changed over time, its structure remains roughly the same, chronicling the atrocities—interrogation, torture, and execution—that took place at S-21 and are framed as a microcosm of the larger DK atrocities. Among the most famous images from the site are mugshots of the prisoners, almost all of whom were killed. The commandant of S-21, Duch, was the first person tried at the ECCC and the focus of a book I wrote on the ECCC.[9] At one point, Nuon Chea supervised Duch's work at the security center and prison.

Atrocity Crimes Prevention

Transitional justice mechanisms like the ECCC are also meant to help prevent the recurrence of atrocity crimes, the issue the graduate students in my class on Atrocity Prevention and the International Human Rights Regime have been studying this semester. The risk-assessment tools they discussed last week during our Tree of Life Teach-In are another modality of prevention.

Earlier in the term, my students had read a book that, drawing on a public health metaphor, suggests thinking of atrocity crimes prevention as analogous to saving people from drowning in the currents of a dangerous river.[10] The most immediate intervention occurs "midstream" in the effort to pull drowning people out of the river (a situation in which mass violence has begun). It is also possible, of course, to intervene "upstream" (to prevent people from falling into the river in the first place) or "downstream" (to prevent people from drowning again in the future).

In class, we had discussed how, like all analogies, this one has limitations, such as potentially ignoring geopolitical enmeshments, overlooking the way interventions are mediated by power, and reinforcing stereotypes of victim passivity and external-actor heroics. But it nevertheless provides a useful way to think about prevention strategies.

From the perspective of this framework, transitional justice mechanisms like the ECCC and the Tuol Sleng memorial serve as downstream interventions, while monitoring and risk assessment are a key upstream prevention tool. Midstream interventions include things like peace talks, sanctions, or, most controversially, armed force. Some of the measures, like diplomacy and peacekeeping, may occur up-, mid-, or downstream.

My students have examined a host of actors and institutions working on atrocity prevention. While humanitarian law stretches far back in time, significant portions of the contemporary atrocity-prevention infrastructure emerged in what we discussed as "the two bursts of atrocity crimes prevention." The first burst took place after Nazi Germany, when the contemporary international human rights regime began to be constructed. The newly established UN played a key role in this process by creating internal human rights bodies and passing human rights declarations and conventions, including the 1948 UN Genocide Convention.

A second burst took place after the Rwandan genocide and other 1990s atrocities, when new institutions and initiatives were launched, including the UN Office of the Special Adviser of the Secretary-General on the Prevention of Genocide, which was created in 2004, and the Responsibility to Protect doctrine that was endorsed at the UN World Summit in 2005. The atrocity crimes prevention architecture now operates not just on a global level but also transnationally (for example, human rights and atrocity prevention NGOs), regionally (in Europe and Africa, among other places), and domestically (on both the governmental and grassroots levels).

The ECCC provides an illustration of how actors on all of these levels may intersect in a given initiative related to atrocity prevention.[11] Indeed, the audience gathered today at this global-national hybrid tribunal collaboration includes human rights and atrocity prevention actors from the UN, transnational NGOs, the Cambodian government, foreign aid agencies, and Cambodian civil society, including monks and civil parties.

The Nuon Chea Verdict

"All rise," the loudspeaker at the court instructs. Then the Trial Chamber judges walk in. After a few formalities, President Non shuffles his papers and begins reading. For two hours, he delivers the verdict in legal monotone.

President Non begins with a brief case history, noting the court's jurisdiction and procedural milestones, before turning to the charges.

Nuon Chea and his codefendant, Khieu Samphan, he states, are accused of being part of a "joint criminal enterprise" (JCE) that implemented five criminal policies: "(1) the repeated movement of the population from towns and cities to rural areas, as well as from one rural area to another; (2) the establishment and operation of cooperatives and worksites; (3) the establishment of security centres and execution sites. . . ."[12] Judge Non never looks up as he continues reading: "(4) the targeting of specific groups, including the Cham and Vietnamese, Buddhist and former Khmer Republic Officials . . . and (5) the regulation of marriage."

The direction of the verdict soon becomes clear. During DK, President Non announces, the Trial Chamber finds that "there was a widespread and systematic attack against the civilian population of Cambodia." The attack included "enslavement, forced transfer, murder, extermination, enforced disappearance, attacks against human dignity and political persecution." And, he continues, the court finds that "there is a nexus between this attack and the committed acts," one about which Nuon Chea and Khieu Samphan knew and with which they were involved.

"Historical Background," Judge Nil states, transitioning to the court's findings about the rise of the Khmer Rouge. "The Chamber finds that in 1959, TOU Samouth, POL Pot and NUON Chea began the process of creating a new Cambodian Communist Party." He notes the First Party Congress in 1960, when the revolutionaries formulated their Party Line and elected their leadership, which included Nuon Chea. "By 1969, the economy in Cambodia was flagging," President Non goes on, noting that the situation was further exacerbated by "devastating American bombing."

President Non is a third of the way through his reading, having turned to "Security Centres and Execution Sites" after finding that Khmer Rouge policy on cooperatives and worksites constituted crimes against humanity. At the main S-21 torture and execution center, President Non notes, prisoners "were brought to interrogation rooms handcuffed and blindfolded, their legs chained during questioning." Non Nil names the interrogation methods: "beatings with sticks, rods, electrical wire, whips and other tools; electroshocks; suffocation through covering the head with a plastic bag; covering the mouth and nose with a towel and pouring cold water from a kettle; and the extraction of toenails and fingernails."

"At the very least," President Non continues, "11,742 prisoners were executed . . . [many] by a blow to the neck with an iron bar, after which their throats were slit with a knife and their bodies disemboweled— and buried in mass graves." Nuon Chea, he notes, was directly involved in the chain of command that ordered these executions. At one point, Nuon Chea oversaw the running of the prison. Nuon Chea suddenly raises his hand. He requests to listen to the remainder of the proceedings from his holding cell.

"Disposition and Sentence," President Non announces an hour later, reaching the last section of the Trial Chamber Judgement. In the public gallery, everyone sits up.

"The Trial Chamber finds the Accused Nuon Chea to be GUILTY," President Non proclaims. President Non lists Nuon Chea's crimes against humanity ("murder, extermination, deportation, enslavement . . .") and war crimes ("willful killing, torture, inhuman treatment . . ."). Then President Non names it: "genocide by killing members of the Vietnamese and Cham groups." There is a murmur in the public gallery when the genocide conviction is announced and Nuon Cheea is sentenced to life imprisonment.

* * *

SATURDAY, NOVEMBER 17, 2018, NOIR & BLANC CAFÉ,
PHNOM PENH, CAMBODIA

The next day, I meet Bill Smith, the ECCC prosecutor who had questioned me during my 2016 testimony, at a local coffee shop. I want to interview him about the verdict and how my testimony had fit within the larger case.[13]

As we speak, Smith details some of the ECCC's major accomplishments, ranging from the groundbreaking civil party participation to justice achieved at last for mass human rights violations, an accounting important to victims, the rule of law, reconciliation, and deterrence.

Dieng's UN Office on Genocide Prevention has underscored this connection to prevention in a statement it issued about Nuon Chea's verdict.[14] "This conviction is a good day for justice," Dieng notes in the statement. "While criminal accountability is foremost a tool to provide justice and redress to victims, it also has an important preventative function as a deterrent as well as to help societies in reconciliation efforts and to deal with the past."

Eventually Smith and I turn to a discussion of how my expert testimony contributed to the case. A key purpose of expert testimony, Smith notes, is to help the judges gain perspective on the enormous amount of evidence. In this regard, my testimony had been important in explaining the dynamics and systematicity of mass violence.

Months after my testimony, Smith had given a keynote address at an international genocide conference where he had discussed how academics can contribute to tribunals through their research and by serving as expert witnesses. He had used my testimony as an example, noting my discussion of "the mechanics of genocide" and incitement, which was key to proving the genocide charge.

"All Dr. Hinton's prior hard work had paid off," Smith had concluded, "and he was able to make his contribution to the accountability and reconciliation process in Cambodia in one of the most salient possible ways." Smith's remarks pointed to a key goal of anthropology, using ethnographically informed research to develop comparative models that address larger questions about humanity and critical public issues like genocide.

Providing expert testimony is one way such knowledge can have real-world impact. Teaching is another. So, too, is writing books like this one, using comparative insights and the lessons of the past to unpack troubling issues like the global proliferation of white power extremism and, in the context of Trump's USA, the increased risk of domestic atrocity crimes.

Social Movements and Revitalization

Such comparison is also critical to prevention. And indeed, an understanding of the mechanisms, dynamics, and motivations involved in mass violence lays the basis for creating interventions that can help prevent it from taking place. For some, juxtaposing a genocidal regime like Khmer Rouge to white power extremists in the United States might seem like a stretch, even if they share violent ideologies. What such skeptics miss, however, are the temporal dynamics involved in mass violence and extremism, including the early stages of group formation and agitation.

Indeed, the Khmer Rouge, like Hitler and the Nazis, began as a smaller social movement that resembles that of white power extremists in some respects.[15] A key difference is that, amid a context of crisis and upheaval, the Khmer Rouge were able to expand their base of supporters and seize the levers of political control. If some social movements seek modest, specific changes, others are more radical, even revolutionary. Like the Khmer Rouge, many white-power-extremist groups seek revolutionary change, ranging from the creation of a white ethnostate to race war and the establishment of a new white-supremacist regime. This radical transformation, in turn, is premised on grievance (for example, loss of white power), key conceptual frames (like white genocide), modes of organizational action (ranging from group activities to Internet forums and acts of violence), and a transformative vision (white race renewal).

Anthropologists sometimes refer to social movements seeking such renewal as "revitalization movements."[16] These movements arise in moments of upheaval and stress, when people become disaffected with the current order and are drawn to groups and charismatic leaders promising renewal. Their revitalizing visions are sometimes couched in apocalyptic terms that divide the world into an "us" and a "them" who stand in the way of this better future and need to be eliminated. Once in power, revitalization movements consolidate control, reorganizing society and implementing new values and practices meant to enact the promised and sometimes utopian change. Most revitalization movements, however, never reach this stage, failing to gain widespread support and the power to implement radical change.

A number of genocidal regimes began as revitalization movements, including the Nazis, ISIS, and the Khmer Rouge. The Khmer Rouge, for example, swept to power in the midst of the Vietnam War, which led to massive US bombing, foreign incursions, economic stress, and seven years of civil war. Nuon Chea and his fellow revolutionaries played on class grievances, pinpointed capitalism and foreign interference as the root of oppression, promised the cure of a utopian future, and distinguished between the pure peasants and workers and the contaminating counterrevolutionaries blocking the path to this pure revolutionary order. Once in power, the Khmer Rouge reorganized society in terms of the Party Line, with its matrix of politics, organization, and consciousness.

While encompassing a broad range of groups and actors, white power extremism contains echoes of genocidal revitalization movements like the Khmer Rouge, a resonance underscored by the white genocide frame. For many white power extremists, the grievance is clear: the government is corrupt and pernicious, imposing a sociopolitical system that is leading to white race extinction. In this white genocide vision, there are pure revolutionaries who recognize the imminent dangers posed by evil culprits ranging from diabolical Jews to contaminating immigrant invaders.

To renew society, radical and even apocalyptic change is needed, not just race war but the eradication of the threat to a utopian white-supremacist order and homeland. This idea permeates the imaginings of white power extremists from Pierce and Lane to Bowers and the Charlottesville marchers who chanted "Blood and Soil!" and "You will not replace us!" As we will see, similar sorts of white genocide logics inform the actions of white power extremists across the globe, even if their white genocide concerns are inflected by local concerns.

Radicalization and the Flash, Line, and Hammer

These sorts of macrolevel, comparative frameworks also offer ways of understanding the pathways that do not just draw people to such movements but also motivate them to act. In terrorism and social-movements studies, this process is sometimes referred to as "radicalization."[17] The pathways to radicalization vary, having different causes and degrees of commitment that change over time and in response to circumstances. These pathways also may be more or less gradual or direct. Sometimes people join because of ideology; others may do so because of networks.

When teaching, I sometimes describe the process of radicalization through three related and interlocking metaphors: the flash, line, and hammer. *The Flash* represents extremist vision, the set of ideas that, like a bolt of lightning, illuminate the world in new ways and bathe it with meaning. The flip side, of course, is that this flash simultaneously blinds, erasing complexity and pushing contravening information out of sight.

This vision, which may be more formally organized as ideology (for example, the Khmer Rouge Party Line) or more loosely organized around conceptual frames (such as white genocide), diagnoses causes and provides solutions to grievances. It also helps adherents make sense of the world—offering order, certainty, identity, and meaning amid the tumult, hardships, and existential anxiety of their lives. These stressors may be linked to material, interpersonal, economic, or sociopolitical situations ranging from financial crisis to political strife. The solutions, in turn, may be apocalyptic and extreme.

For Nuon Chea and the Khmer Rouge, the Flash came from communist ideology applied to the conditions of Cambodian life and the "contradictions" that caused them. Their vision, which played upon class grievance and anger, offered a solution, the Party Line. Likewise, the Flash of white power extremism centers around issues like white genocide, the idea that white decline and impending extinction are taking place at the hands of malicious actors. This conceptual frame offers solutions such as ideological warfare, immigration restrictions, a white ethnostate, and apocalyptic race war. White power extremists have their own metaphor for those who suddenly experience the Flash that reveals such hidden "truths"—the Red Pill.

The Line, in turn, refers to the path that follows from the Flash, including its emphasis on identity and the other. Just as a line establishes a border between two sides, the Line entails action premised on a clear border between a pure, innocent, and victimized "us" and a contaminating "them" who are the source of the "problem"—a victimizer who has caused that about which the social movement is aggrieved. To solve "the problem," the extremist group organizes to take action in particular ways.

In this regard, the Line overlaps with what the Khmer Rouge referred to as "the Party Line"—an assemblage of politics, organization, and consciousness premised on us/them divisions and providing a path to cure. Along these lines, the Line centers on a set of intersecting beliefs and practices organized on a group level in a more or less loosely structured fashion (for example, formal membership in a group like Heimbach's and Hovater's Traditionalist Worker Party versus more anonymous participation in extremist chats on an Internet platform like 8chan).

If the Line refers to a pathway premised on group division, then, it also refers to organizational order. It is worth reiterating that, while a number of people may initially be drawn to extremist movements due to the vision of the Flash, others may join for more instrumental reasons (material gain, status, future opportunities) or due to their friend, peer, and community networks—or for a combination of reasons.[18] These motives may also emerge gradually and transform over time, such as when someone with milder racist attitudes joins a group primarily for community and only subsequently comes to hold hard-core white-power-extremist views after socialization and indoctrination.

There is, of course, a difference between white power banter on 8chan and killing people at Tree of Life—even if the two are interlinked. *The Hammer* refers to force, the action taken to implement the vision of the Flash and remedy the problems caused by "them." The degree of violence and force varies, in part due to circumstance, resources, and political opportunities. And individuals, operating with different degrees of commitment and within varying sets of personal, group-level, and institutional constraints, decide to take more or less radical forms of action.

If the Khmer Rouge agitated among the peasantry before coming to power, for example, they were able to systematically reorganize society to accord with their Line while "sweeping away" and "smashing" an enemy "them." White power extremists in the United States, in turn, engage in a wide spectrum of actions, ranging from putting up posters and trolling to demonstrating and carrying out violent attacks.

What white-power-extremist groups lack is direct access to the levers of power, the most forceful Hammer, even if they clearly state what they would do if they had it: engage in social engineering, ethnic cleansing, and race war. Many believe a race war has already begun, with the first skirmishes fought on metapolitical and institutional levels.

Deradicalization

These sorts of comparative frameworks provide a basis for developing prevention strategies, ideally ones that are adapted to the situation and based on the sort of context-rich understandings that scholars can help provide, especially those who have conducted ethnographic research on white power extremists. Anthropologists call this "thick description" in contrast to the "thin descriptions" that too often guide abstract and context-distant policy on issues like atrocity prevention.[19] Interventions can be undertaken at the macro-, meso-, and microlevels and at different phases, as suggested by the public health metaphor of upstream, midstream, and downstream prevention.

A number of interventions with extremist groups have focused on microlevel "deradicalization." Sometimes such efforts are led by individuals. Former white power extremists, for example, have spoken publicly about their experiences, explaining their paths to radicalization while sometimes seeking to deradicalize other white power extremists by offering dialogue, community, and job training.[20] Some have founded related groups and do public speaking, including media appearances.

Other people have sought long-term dialogue with white power actors, seeking to deradicalize them one by one. One of the more famous examples is the Black musician Daryl Davis, who has used dialogue to steer dozens of members away from the KKK. He even took a KKK Imperial Wizard who fired a gun at Charlottesville to the Museum of African American Culture and History in Washington, DC.[21]

As opposed to such efforts at dialogue and compassion, others seek to turn people from far-right extremism through methods ranging from youth education to increasing the cost of involvement. Doxing provides an example of the latter method, as extremists are publicly exposed and lose friends, family, and jobs. Lawsuits have increased the financial cost of extremism. The Southern Poverty Law Center has used this strategy to great effect, as have post-Charlottesville litigants. Counterprotesters now also mobilize in significant numbers in opposition to white-power-extremist rallies, as illustrated by the massive numbers who showed up at Unite the Right 2.

Given the centrality of social media and the Internet to contemporary white power extremists, deplatforming is yet another method that makes their work more difficult, denying them a public platform and the ability to conduct financial transactions using services like PayPal. Some of these efforts, such as Amazon's removal of Nazi-related books, have raised free speech concerns and clashed with the related commitment of technology actors to keep the Internet open to a wide range of views.[22] While no one is certain about their efficacy, such efforts appear to have made it harder for some white power extremists to operate and advocate for their cause—as Hovater noted during his Nordic Frontier podcast.

US law enforcement agencies like the FBI and Department of Homeland Security have also sought to counter extremism. They have often, however, been slow to act. This was true in the early 1980s when The Order went on its crime spree—though the FBI eventually mobilized a significant response.

However, after the 1990s, as militia movement activity subsided, these agencies turned their attention to other issues, especially the terrorist threat posed by groups like al-Qaeda and then ISIS. In 2009, a Department of Homeland Security report warned about the threat of white power extremism amid Obama's election, economic crisis, and ongoing war. It was also at this time that the social media explosion was getting underway.

The report was not just dismissed but sparked a conservative backlash and cutbacks.[23] When white power attacks did take place, they were dismissed by "lone wolf" and "hater" discourses that diverted attention from the broader structural issues and growing white-power-extremist movement. The Trump administration continued to largely ignore white power extremism and even canceled or defunded several deradicalization and counterterrorism training projects. There was minimal response after Charlottesville; the same was true after Tree of Life. This situation only began to change after a series of attacks in 2019.

* * *

NOVEMBER 20, 2018, PHNOM PENH INTERNATIONAL AIRPORT, CAMBODIA

"They're prepping for a race war. And they see Trump as their ray of hope."[24]

As I sit in the airport terminal waiting area, three days after the Nuon Chea verdict, I glance at a TV where this CNN headline catches my eye. The story centers on the far-right Suidlanders and other white power South African groups claiming that farmers are victims of white genocide, which they contend is manifest in the widespread murder of farmers and government appropriations of their lands.

The feature story begins with the violence in Charlottesville and Trump's two-sides remark before profiling Simon Roche, the South African Suidlander leader whom Kessler initially listed as a Unite the Right 2 speaker and who had attended Charlottesville the year before. Roche, the story reveals, had traveled through the United States for six months, meeting with US white power extremists to raise awareness of the impending genocide of South African farmers, an assertion not supported by crime rate statistics.[25]

These white genocide arguments found a receptive audience among the US far right—not just white power extremists but also mainstream politicians and news. Fox News' Tucker Carlson picked up the story, interviewing Ernst Roets, deputy head of a South African white farmer lobbying group, who complained of the targeting of white farmers and the threat to their survival. Before the May 2018 interview, Carlson warned on air that the South African government was expropriating land on the basis of skin color and that the State Department needed a more robust response.

After Carlson did an August 22 follow-up on the issue, Trump took to Twitter to instruct Secretary of State Pompeo to look into the matter. Trump's white genocide dog whistle was heard loud and clear by white power extremists. Former KKK leader David Duke, for example, tweeted "Thank you!" and posted a picture of a young white girl with a sign reading "STOP WHITE GENOCIDE."[26]

Meanwhile, Roche, Roets, and other South African white power actors traveled across the United States, getting together with Duke and other white power extremists.[27] Roets's tour included media interviews, meetings with far-right politicians, and, as the CNN story noted, even a photo opportunity with Trump's then national security advisor, John Bolton.[28]

The CNN feature concludes with a huge Suidlander bonfire, lit in the evening after a day of training exercises. The fire is set in the center of a circle of trees symbolizing an 1838 battle in which a small group of Afrikaaners defeated a much larger number of Zulu attackers. This Battle of Blood River is viewed as a sort of Afrikaaner's Alamo.[29]

The CNN reporter, David McKenzie, states that the Suidlanders are readying for a new battle, an apocalyptic race war. As lightning flashes in the background, Roche confirms, "We are preparing for a storm, like the canary in the coal mine, of the same anxieties and distresses that are being experienced in Western Europe and the USA." The camera zooms in on the flames of the Suidlander bonfire as Roche continues, "There is a pervasive sense amongst certain sectors of historically white societies, that those societies are being diluted."

"But when you use terms like 'diluted,'" McKenzie challenges Roche, "I think Nazism. I think eugenics. I think of all of these horrible things from the past."

Roche clips McKenzie's reply. "That's neurotic. The societies are, in demographic terms, being diluted."

With the camera focused on the blazing fire, Suidlanders seated on lawn chairs in the background, McKenzie cautions his listeners, "It's a dangerous mix and a warning about what can happen when extremes dominate a debate and reason gives way to fear." McKenzie is asking Fausset's "what makes a man start fires?" question. Roche is giving white genocide and great replacement answers.

~

If this CNN story is revealing in many respects, the South African white farmer awareness campaign underscores four key points about global white power extremism. First, as is the case in the United States, such extremism is not exceptional but a symptom of a worldwide system of white supremacy.[30] The colonial dynamics that fueled the establishment of the British colonies of North America took place around the world. While some colonies were focused on extracting resources and others on appropriating land, racial hierarchy, albeit manifesting in a variety of forms, was widely used to justify the capitalist expropriation of resources, territory, and labor. The Suidlander celebration of the Battle of Blood River speaks to the violence of this process in South Africa, which laid the basis for apartheid, one of the most extreme manifestations of systemic white supremacy in the world.

Second, the South African white farmer awareness campaign provides another illustration of the global connectedness of the white power extremist movement. Roche, Roets, and other South African white power actors traveled not just to the United States but to other parts of the globe promoting their cause—just as they promoted it globally using the Internet and social media. Australia considered issuing the white farmers fast-track visas.[31] In Europe, the South Africans also found receptive audiences in a context in which immigration was a key issue, one linked to the rise of populist leaders, far-right parties, and "great replacement" fears.

Third, while manifesting differently in places like South Africa, the white genocide frame circulates widely among global white-power-extremist groups, often intertwined with a sense of grievance (white victimization), apocalyptic threat (white race extinction), and what is viewed as a morally legitimate violent response (fighting the threatening nonwhite others).

Indeed, well before the South African white farmer delegations arrived in the United States, global white power extremists were mobilized around the idea of white genocide. This point was underscored by Norwegian shooter Anders Breivik's manifesto that harped on racial purity, demographic replacement, and cultural Marxism.

Breivik's attack partly inspired Brenton Tarrant's massacre of fifty people at a New Zealand mosque on March 15, 2019. Just before his attack, Tarrant published a manifesto that directly invoked "WHITE GENOCIDE," complaining of "the great replacement" of whites by immigrants, especially Muslims, the direct target of his ire.[32] Tarrant had "14" emblazoned on his semi-automatic. In addition to Breivik, Tarrant claimed to be inspired by Dylann Roof, who murdered nine African Americans at a Charleston church in 2015.

Tarrant's manifesto is another illustration of the global circulation of the white genocide frame, as well as the influence of a European version focused on replacement and manifest in *The Camps of the Saints*. As discussed earlier, such replacement discourses have had an increasing impact on US white power actors, including Stephen Miller and the alt-right.

This idea of great replacement was apparent in Nazi ideology, which valorized the German *volk*, asserted Aryan racial superiority and Germany's right to colonial-like conquest within Europe in the name of procuring "living space," and warned of the threat posed by "alien" Jews. This latter idea was dramatically portrayed in the Nazi propaganda film *The Eternal Jew*, which likened the Jewish threat to a rat infestation. In this line of replacement thinking, the host population under attack has the right to respond and destroy the threat, thereby purifying the polity.

While these ideas about replacement influenced Pierce, Lane, and the white genocide frame that emerged in the context of the United States, they had different inflections in Europe. In the 1960s, for example, the neofascist European New Right movement argued for the right to cultural difference, with culture standing in for older ideas linking race and place.[33] It was at this time that Alain de Benoist, drawing on Gramsci, began discussing the idea of metapolitics.

If the European New Right was antiliberal, anti-American, antiglobal, xenophobic, and anticapitalist, it ultimately sought to preserve white European purity—even if members of the New Right often disavowed overt racism and claimed they supported "the right to difference" around the globe, including in subjugated colonial populations.

New Right ideas often, and especially more recently, have focused on the threat of immigration—particularly Muslim immigration—and demographic replacement enabled by cultural Marxism, multiculturalism, political correctness, and liberalism. These ideas inspired Breivik's 2011 Norway attack and pervade his manifesto. The same is true of Tarrant's attack, which speaks extensively about white genocide and "the great replacement." This latter phrase was popularized by Renaud Camus's book, *Le Grand Remplacement*, published the same year as Breivik's attack. It was also around this time, and especially after the 2015 European immigration crisis, that there was renewed interest in *Camp of the Saints*.

This European "replacement" version of white genocide has circled back and influenced US white power actors, especially the alt-right. *A Fair Hearing*, for example, was published by the European far-right press, Arktos, which was founded by Friberg, the Swedish skinhead turned businessman whose essay on metapolitics appears in the volume.

Friberg is also a key point of connection between the European New Right in its more recent Identitarian iteration and the alt-right in the United States. Friberg has collaborated with Richard Spencer, who has referred to himself as an Identitarian, and even attended Charlottesville, where he was scheduled to speak.

This is just one of many examples of the global interconnections of white power extremism and its underlying white-supremacist logics. If earlier white power actors, like Pierce, made connections to their European counterparts, the interactions have been greatly enabled by social media and the Internet. The depth and breadth of these global connections is manifest in contexts ranging from Tarrant's manifesto to the immigration policy and replacement rhetoric of Stephen Miller and Trump.[34] Indeed, "The Snake" can be directly read as a parable regarding the danger of white genocide replacement by immigrants.

Interestingly, Tarrant named Trump as "a symbol of renewed white identity and common purpose," forcing administration officials to directly state that Trump was not a white supremacist.[35] Meanwhile, Trump, while offering condolences, invoked "the Hater" by claiming that the New Zealand attack was the work of a madman. "I think it's a small group of people that have very, very serious problems," he told reporters.[36] Critics were quick to argue that, as had been the case in Charlottesville, his statements fell short of condemning white power extremism and that Trump had repeatedly stirred up the sort of anti-Muslim and anti-immigrant animus that helped drive Tarrant's attack.[37]

Just a month earlier, Christopher Paul Hasson, a Coast Guard officer, was arrested for plotting mass attacks. He wanted to further the white power cause and yearned for a "white homeland."[38] Muslim "scum" immigration was a particular target of his ire. Like Tarrant, Hasson was inspired by Breivik, the global white power movement, and the idea of white genocide. "I am dreaming of a way to kill almost every last person on earth," he wrote.

While Hasson was arrested before he could attack, John T. Earnest was not. Inspired by Tarrant and Bowers, Earnest killed one person and injured three on April 27, 2019, at Chabad of Poway synagogue. If his gun had not jammed, he likely would have killed many more.[39]

Like Tarrant, Earnest wrote a manifesto in which he harped on white genocide fears and even included a passing reference to the "Day of the Rope" killings in *The Turner Diaries*. Earnest praised Hitler while inveighing against the evil of Jews who, he said, "planned genocide of the European race" with the help of their "puppets," Latinos and Blacks ("spics and niggers") who were not "intelligent enough" to recognize they were being used. "I hate them," Earnest emphasized, something he signified with frequent slurs.

If Hasson's electronic messages suggested support of Trump, Earnest held Trump in contempt, referring to Trump as a "Zionist, Jew-loving, anti-White, traitorous cocksucker." Earnest said his political ideology was "not wanting to go extinct." He also drew motivation from the on-line communities where many white power extremists dwell. He announced his attack on 8chan, providing links to his manifesto and a livestream.[40] Another user encouraged him to get a "high score," a euphemism Earnest used in his manifesto, which, in imitation of Tarrant's, was filled with Internet in-joke "shitposting."

In his last 8chan post, Earnest thanked other users. "Keep up the infographic redpill threads," he encouraged. "I've only been lurking for a year and a half, yet what I've learned here is priceless."[41] Besides suggesting his more recent conversion to the white power cause, Earnest's post invoked "the red pill," the key far-right extremist metaphor for revelation.

Earnest's invocation of red-pilling likely referred to simplified infographics about racial difference and Jewish power that routinely were posted on 8chan. However, the term also has a strong gender inflection.[42] White power actors likely repurposed the term from the men's rights movement, which argues that mechanisms like women's rights, feminism, and cultural Marxism have created a system of female domination—one in which sexual decisions are based on wealth, appearance, and status and denied to large numbers of men, some of whom, as noted earlier, identify as involuntary celibates, or "incels."

Like the white power movement, the men's rights movement is hypermasculine and built on a sense of victimhood and grievance. Those who have taken the "red pill" believe they see the truth of an oppressive misandrist system. Many dialogue in Internet forums like Reddit and 4chan. Some join far-right male-empowerment groups like the Proud Boys. A few have launched shooting attacks. Members of the movement also organized to vote for Trump.

For white power extremists like Earnest, "red pilling" refers to white genocide insight, such as seeing that a Jewish-controlled system is driving white race extinction. As is the case with the men right's movement, this supposed revelation is related to grievance and a corresponding sense of righteousness legitimating violent and even revolutionary actions that right the wrongs. This idea directly informs *The Turner Diaries* and Lane's "White Genocide Manifesto." And it appears in the manifestos of white power extremists, including Earnest, who described his violence as an act of sacrifice and racial "self-defense" amid a race war that had already begun.

These more recent attacks provide further illustrations of the fourth aspect of white power extremism that the Suidlanders underscore: while long present, white power extremism has become more overt and widespread over the past decade. This trend has been driven by a number of factors: the affordances of new media and the Internet, population dislocations due to violence and war, immigration, economic stresses and global financial crisis, and the rise of populist and far-right leaders, some of whom lean in authoritarian directions.[43]

Like Trump, Putin, and Hungarian prime minister Viktor Orbán, some already held office. Other far-right leaders and parties have risen in popularity in France, Italy, Sweden, Austria, the Netherlands, and Greece, among other places. Even in Germany, a country that has undertaken extensive Holocaust education and transitional justice efforts, the rise of the far-right Alternative for Germany has been accompanied by white-power-extremist attacks and widespread threats against national, regional, and local politicians.[44]

Atrocity crimes prevention actors have taken notice. Shortly before the Tree of Life attack, Dieng, the UN special advisor on genocide prevention, issued a statement warning about the rise in xenophobia, hate crimes, dehumanization of immigrants, ultranationalism, and far-right populism in European countries like Italy, Hungary, and Germany.[45]

Dieng reiterated the point in his press release on the Nuon Chea verdict. "At a time when we are witnessing a dangerous disregard for fundamental rights and international legal norms and standards in many parts of the world," Dieng stated, "this decision sends a strong message, in the region and globally, to those who commit, incite or condone atrocity crimes that sooner or later they will be held accountable."[46]

In May 2019, Dieng would liken the situation to Nazi Germany in the 1930s. The same month Secretary-General António Guterres underscored this point in announcing a major UN initiative to combat hate. "Around the world," Guterres stated, "we are seeing a disturbing groundswell of xenophobia, racism, and intolerance. . . . Neo-Nazi and white supremacy movements are on the march." Alluding to Trump and other far-right populists, Guterres warned, "Public discourse is being weaponized for political gain with incendiary rhetoric that stigmatizes and dehumanizes minorities, migrants, refugees, women and any so-called other."[47]

Noting that the UN was established in the backdrop of World War II, Guterres stated that the UN's identity is "rooted in the nightmare that ensues when virulent hatred is left unopposed for too long. Today, I fear, we have reached another acute moment in battling this demon." With Dieng by his side, Guterres mandated his offices to take action before it is too late. Back at Rutgers, my students have been wondering why no one in the United States is similarly sounding the atrocity crimes alarm.

* * *

NOVEMBER 27, 2018, RUTGERS UNIVERSITY, NEWARK, NJ
"Maybe we also need transitional justice here in the USA."

A week and half after the verdict, a graduate student in my course on Atrocity Prevention and the International Human Rights Regime offers this suggestion. Today's class focuses on transitional justice and the ECCC. After recounting my experience of attending the verdict, I had noted Dieng's statement linking transitional justice initiatives like the Khmer Rouge tribunal to atrocity crimes prevention.

Our discussion then turned to "downstream" prevention. The student had discussed transitional justice mechanisms in other parts of the world: Germany's Holocaust reparations, Argentinian memorialization efforts, and the South African Truth and Reconciliation Commission. Then the student suggested that these sorts of transitional justice efforts are needed in the United States.

"Some would say we already have them," another student says. "My high school teachers taught about slavery and the civil rights movement. And we studied the Holocaust a lot. In terms of memorialization, we have Martin Luther King Jr. Day. And he's got a monument in DC."

"So does Christopher Columbus," the first student counters. "There's also one at Columbus Circle in New York City. And remember Robert E. Lee and all the Confederate monuments. They're like monuments celebrating white supremacy."

"And no one has paid reparations. There's nothing resembling the Cambodia court or the South African TRC," a third student adds.

"Politicians don't want to talk about reparations," a fourth student notes. "And you can't have transitional justice if you don't want to look at the past."

"That's a critical point," I say. "In many ways, vision is at the heart of atrocity crimes prevention. You can only prevent what you see. And what you see is informed by your assumptions, institutions, practices, and 'toolkit' of responses. In many ways, atrocity crimes prevention is also about envisioning possibilities, what philosophers sometimes call 'moral imagination.'"

"And politics," a student notes.

"Sadly, yes," I agree. "The politics is always there, often from start to finish."

"What do you mean by 'moral imagination'?" another student asks. "And how exactly does it relate to transitional justice and prevention?"

~

While philosophers have long discussed the concept, moral imagination might be loosely defined as "thinking about" and "thinking beyond" a morally charged situation.[48] Genocide and atrocity crimes are just such events that call for moral imagination. So, too, are white power extremism and the systemic white supremacy with which it is enmeshed. To "think about" such a situation is to consider, as we had discussed in class, the background assumptions, institutions, practices, frames, and politics that inform it. "Thinking beyond" involves reimagining things in ways that resolve ethical dilemmas and create new paths forward.

My student had engaged in just such an act of moral imagination by suggesting that the United States needs a transitional justice process, a thought that transposes an idea from one domain ("downstream" atrocity crimes prevention) to another (the United States, which is usually assumed not to be in need of transitional justice) to reimagine a situation (the ethical challenges posed by the US history of white supremacy). Doing so, by extension, would potentially both provide redress and mitigate the possibility of future atrocity crimes—which is precisely the sort of "new path" the moral imagination seeks. This exercise of "thinking beyond," of course, is bound up with "thinking about" systemic white supremacy past and present.

Similarly, the *We Charge Genocide* petition, while deeply political, was also an exercise in moral imagination. It "thought about" the long history of white supremacy in the United States even as it sought to mobilize the UN Genocide Convention to consider redress. Du Bois's

1947 "Appeal to the World: Statement of Denial of Human Rights to Minorities in the Case of Citizens of Negro Descent in the United States of America and an Appeal to the United Nations for Redress" did much the same. Both petitions, however, were largely ignored due to power and politics. These efforts were part of a history of denial, obfuscation, and minimization of past US atrocity crimes perpetrated not just against Blacks but against Native Americans and other nonwhite groups.

Perhaps the most significant moment of attempted redress, post–Civil War Reconstruction, was reversed as segregation and Jim Crow laws were imposed. For many Blacks, the unfulfilled promise of "forty acres and a mule" reparations speaks to the continuing lack of accountability for US atrocity crimes. This sort of historical amnesia and denial leads to a lack of understanding about the possibility that similar sorts of violence could take place in the present—as well as the ways in which historical injustices continue to reverberate.

Some recent, if halting, steps to provide redress for past US atrocity crimes have been made. The morning before Kessler's Unite the Right 2 rally in Washington, DC, for example, I visited the National Museum of the American Indian and the Museum of African American History and Culture. These museums discuss the issue of genocide and atrocity crimes, especially the latter museum, which leads the visitor through a detailed consideration of enslavement, Jim Crow, and segregation. But this national museum on the African American experience was only opened in late 2016.

And even more recently, in April 2018, the National Memorial for Peace and Justice launched in Montgomery, Alabama. Focused on the victims of white supremacy, the memorial is highlighted by hundreds of hanging steel columns—representing the counties in which over forty-four hundred lynchings took place—that tower above visitors.

In interviews at the time, Bryan Stevenson, the founder, said the museum was established to help address the historical silence about enslavement and its aftermaths.[49] A similar silence, Stevenson notes, surrounds the genocide of Native Americans, which laid the basis for the treatment of African Americans. Few people, Stevenson observes, acknowledge that the wealth and success of the United States was built on slave labor and Jim Crow, institutions premised on a white-supremacist ideology and system that endure.

⌁

Others have emphasized a different transitional justice mechanism: reparations. One of the key problems with reparations, however, is cost. If Germany paid huge sums after the Holocaust, other countries are hesitant not just to do so but to undertake acts that might make them criminally liable, such as acknowledging and apologizing for historical injustices and atrocity crimes. Turkey, which refuses to acknowledge the Armenian genocide, is one notorious example.

The same is true of the United States. Although there are different sorts of reparations and ways of calculating cost, some have noted that the amounts could run into the billions and even trillions of dollars. While reparations for Native Americans and African Americans have long been discussed, the idea gained more attention under Obama, who also showed an openness to acknowledgment and apology.

It was in this context that Ta-Nehisi Coates wrote a 2014 *Atlantic* essay, "The Case for Reparations," which sparked broad debate.[50] Coates offers a detailed study of racist housing policy as part of his larger argument that African Americans are owed reparations for hundreds of years of economic expropriation and servitude dating back to early enslavement. As a precedent, Coates points to Germany's Holocaust reparations even as he considers possible amounts (in the billions) and emphasizes the importance of acknowledgment and education. These sorts of ideas would later be discussed in House hearings and by Democratic candidates in the lead-up to the primaries for the 2020 presidential election.

While massive monetary reparations currently seem unlikely—and indeed, a House resolution to set up a commission on reparations languished for decades before hearings were held in 2019—there are other possible models. The ECCC provides one example of how reparations can be made in a context where there is a dearth of funds. Instead of money, the court has provided "collective and moral reparations" to civil parties by supporting initiatives focused on education, prevention, documentation, mental and physical health care, and commemoration. These sorts of projects, as well as ones centered on job training and other forms of economic support, could be incorporated into an initial US reparations award.

Canada offers another model that could be effective in the context of the United States: a truth commission. Established in 2008 as part of a court case that included a government apology, the Truth and Reconciliation Commission of Canada (2008–15) sought to address the injustices perpetrated by the Indian Residential Schools, which operated for over 150 years.[51] These sorts of boarding schools, it is worth noting, were also widespread in the United States, even if this history has been largely ignored. In fact, Richard Henry Pratt, founder of the Carlisle Indian Industrial School in Pennsylvania, famously said it was necessary to "kill the Indian . . . and save the man."

After conducting extensive research and offering a platform for survivors to speak, the Canadian commission found that a range of abuses took place, including widespread physical and sexual abuse, and that the separation of children from their families was cultural genocide. The commission made a number of nonbinding recommendations, and its documents and materials were housed in a newly created National Centre for Truth and Reconciliation.

If not all of the commission's recommendations have been implemented and not everyone is satisfied, the Canadian efforts at redress have gone much further than those in the United States. Like other transitional justice efforts across the globe, the Canadian commission provides an example of what is possible. While there are many reasons to undertake these sorts of redress efforts in the United States, such initiatives also would create a key "downstream" prevention buffer by raising awareness and combating bias, ignorance, and denial. To date, however, the United States has shown too little moral imagination in this regard, though there have been some local-level attempts like the Greensboro TRC, which grappled with the legacy of a notorious 1979 KKK attack in the city.[52]

~

To its credit, the United States has taken important steps to promote international atrocity crimes prevention, particularly under Obama, who formalized the government's prevention apparatus and established an Atrocities Prevention Board.[53] More recently, Congress passed the Elie Wiesel Genocide and Atrocities Prevention Act to further strengthen these infrastructures.

These governmental efforts, however, are predominantly directed outward and usually focused on "less developed" countries, a pattern also characteristic of the international atrocity crimes prevention regime as well as related academic research. Indeed, while some scholars have considered links between the Trump administration and Nazi Germany, few have examined the potential for atrocity crimes in the United States.[54] Dieng's and Guterres's warnings about the rise of hate speech stand out in this regard since they were turning the atrocity crimes prevention lens back on the United States and Europe.

There are a number of reasons for this outward orientation of the US atrocity crimes prevention approach. "American exceptionalism" likely plays a role since people often assume that it is unlikely that atrocity crimes could take place in the United States given its "unique" moral status and human rights safeguards. This assumption has eroded somewhat following Trump's assault on the US system of check and balances, but few people have considered the possibility that genocide and atrocity crimes could take place on US soil, its long history notwithstanding.

Systemic white supremacy also informs the US approach as well as the larger international human rights and atrocity crimes prevention regime. The long-standing trope of "the savage" is implicit in the outward orientation—the assumption that "those sorts of things" are done by more "primitive" people in places like Cambodia, Syria, and Rwanda, not in the United States or Europe.

In this framing, the "international community" is positioned as a savior who bestows the gift of democracy, justice, and human rights on the "savages."[55] These sorts of criticisms have been directed at transitional justice mechanisms, including the ECCC and the International Criminal Court, which has been criticized for focusing its prosecution on places like Africa while ignoring possible atrocity crimes committed by actors such as the United States in Afghanistan and Iraq.[56]

Some scholars have made this sort of argument directly about the atrocity crimes prevention regime, noting that related initiatives may be informed by political interests, systemic white supremacy, and neo-imperialism.[57] The notion of the Responsibility to Protect has also been critiqued in this regard, particularly in relationship to its use to legitimate intervention in Libya in 2011.

As illustrated by the *We Charge Genocide* and "Appeal to the World" petitions, political interests have also informed the outward US approach to human rights and atrocity crimes prevention. Just as "Dixiecrats" fought to make sure that the United States would not be held accountable for enslavement and Jim Crow, so, too, do contemporary political actors work to keep the atrocity crimes prevention lens trained away from the issue of white supremacy.

Following the 2019 House hearings on reparations, for example, Senate majority leader Mitch McConnell dismissed the idea, stating, "I don't think we need reparations for something that happened 150 years ago."[58] In response, Ta-Nehisi Coates, the author of "The Case for Reparations" and a witness at the House hearings, noted that systemic white supremacy continued through Jim Crow and into the present.

Similarly, political interests and systemic white supremacy have also informed the US domestic response to white power extremism. As opposed to examining the systemic aspects of white power extremism, the domestic approach has largely been filtered through the individualizing lens of "the Hater," with Homeland Security and the FBI more focused on "lone wolves" and foreign terrorist threats. When analysts have raised the alarm about white power extremism, conservatives have pushed back.[59] Trump's "two sides" remark also reflected this long-standing attempt to steer attention away from the issue of white power. Only after a series of high-profile shootings in 2019 would the policy finally shift somewhat, with domestic terrorism being elevated as a priority. The connections to systemic white supremacy, however, remain unexplored.

This situation calls for moral imagination—a "thinking about" and a "thinking beyond" white power extremism and the threat of atrocity crimes in the United States. There are steps that could be taken to address this situation. The purview of existing US atrocity crimes prevention infrastructures could be expanded to include domestic threats. So, too, could the scope of the domestic agencies like the FBI and Homeland Security be broadened. Another option would be to create a US national mechanism dedicated to domestic atrocity crimes prevention, as a handful of countries in other parts of the world have done.[60]

On the state level, Holocaust and genocide education has been mainstreamed into classrooms in many parts of the country. While sometimes encompassing atrocity crimes in US history, such curricula could be expanded to include modules on atrocity crimes prevention and the risk assessment of current domestic threats, including those posed by white power extremism. Likewise, more research and scholarship could be inflected in this direction. The university center I direct, for example, has recently launched a Global Consortium on Bigotry and Hate in collaboration with partners around the world.

Undertaking such initiatives demands both the "thinking about" and the "thinking beyond" of moral imagination. A key first step is recognizing the challenge at hand. As noted earlier, Dieng's and Guterres's statements stand out in this regard. They note that hate speech, incitement, and dehumanization are key risk factors. And they underscore the need to monitor extremist movements that have the potential to gain access to the levers of power, thereby paving the path to genocide and atrocity crimes.

This possibility in the United States may seem remote. And indeed, most extremist social movements never gain power. To return to the revitalization framework, most of these movements are unable to mainstream their message, gain a mass following, and implement their often-apocalyptic visions of renewal. But some have. The Nazis provide one example. So too do ISIS and the Khmer Rouge. Before they took power, all three of these groups started out as small-scale revitalization movements with apocalyptic visions.

Some might contend that they were only able to gain power in a context of tumult and upheaval. And this is certainly true—even as their path to power had begun long before they seized control. The Nazi example further underscores the point that the process can even be fostered through democratic mechanisms.

Literature can help us "think beyond" our assumptions and consider such possibilities. In the early 1930s, with European fascism on the rise, Sinclair Lewis observed a number of danger signs in the United States: white power extremism, socioeconomic stressors, demagoguery, social movement mobilization, the language of revitalization and renewal, hate speech, and a lack of moral imagination echoed by the common remark, "It can't happen here." His novel, like books by authors ranging from Jack London to Philip Roth, envisions what can happen when moral compass is lost, hate speech turns into action, the seemingly unimaginable happens, and atrocity crimes ensue.[61]

Many of the issues Lewis noted in the 1930s and depicted in his novel resonate with the situation in the United States during the Trump presidency, including the erosion of the safeguards meant to protect human rights and ensure democratic processes. Donald Trump was not Buzz Windrip, the fictional demagogue in *It Can't Happen Here* who is unexpectedly voted into office, strips Congress and the Supreme Court of power, and empowers his extremist Brownshirt-like Minute Men militia to commit abuses and even atrocity crimes. But it is incumbent upon us all to consider such possibilities in the present. Early recognition of the warning signs is a key first step to prevention.

Along these lines, this book has been an exercise in moral imagination, one that "thinks about" white power extremism and the lessons of the past to consider a precarious moment in US history under Trump. If Buzz Windrip had his Minute Men, Trump had white-power-extremist followers, many of whom were armed, were highly motivated by the white genocide frame, and believed that a race war had already begun. While new in some ways, as we have discussed, the alt-right and other white-power-extremist groups who became more visible during Trump's presidency were not exceptional: they were a symptom of a system of white supremacy that dates back to the beginning of US history. Their numbers, visibility, and networking, however, grew during the Trump presidency.

Many white power extremists felt a connection to Trump. Trump, in turn, made racially coded dog whistles to them, which were received loud and clear. He complained about "fake news" and referred to media outlets as "enemies of the people." It was the same thing that white power extremists, including Pierce, had argued for years, often invoking the myth of Jewish-controlled media and world conspiracy. It was also the language the Khmer Rouge used to restrict freedom of speech and target enemies during DK.[62]

And this is just one of many instances in which President Trump used the language of demonization, apocalyptic threat, and revitalizing transformational change. Even as he sought to erode the legitimacy of the media, Trump undercut US democratic institutions and checks and balances—key buffers against atrocity crimes—ranging from his relentless attacks on the Mueller investigation to his attempts to ignore congressional oversight and his critiques of judges whose decisions he disliked. He pardoned a Navy Seal who committed atrocity crimes and lauded authoritarian leaders. And he emerged from his congressional impeachment hearings with greater control over Senate Republicans and the Department of Justice, even if his momentum was stopped by the 2020 coronavirus pandemic and economic collapse.

This, at least, is how things looked during the Trump presidency, when the risk of atrocity crimes escalated. People inside the Trump administration acknowledged the danger and volatility of the situation, even as some worked to curb Trump's "worst inclinations."[63]

If not a rigid ideologue, Trump was a demagogue who trafficked in the ideology of white supremacy while using fear and hate to stir up his audiences. His rhetoric, which echoed a long history of US white power populism, directly tapped into contemporary white genocide fears. Indeed, during his presidency, Trump directly and indirectly invoked white victimization and more broadly positioned himself as a victim.

As he demonized nonwhite others, Trump tied his oratory to a message of renewal—"Make American Great Again"—that many read as an implicit statement on race ("Make America White Again"). And Trump brought white power actors, some openly aligned with the alt-right, into the White House. One, Stephen Miller, was directly involved in orchestrating an immigration policy that was responding to white genocide "great replacement" fears. Trump's use of "The Snake" in political speeches underscored this point.

If white power extremists lacked direct access to the levers of power, then, they had an administration aligned with their white genocide concerns. Meanwhile, hate crimes and the number of hate groups spiked,[64] as did animus against "illegal aliens" threatening an "infestation" on the border. Such "undocumented immigrants" were poised to be victims of Trump administration atrocity crimes; some suggest they were, as illustrated by the "concentration camp" and family-separation debate.[65] This situation further heightened the possibility that extremist violence— even atrocity crimes and genocide—against Jews, the queer community, and people of color could take place in the United States.

So, yes, the warning signs for atrocity crimes were present in the United States during the Trump administration. The United States had armed and organized white-power-extremist groups motivated by the idea of white genocide and race war. And it had a president who offered them racist dog whistles, was strongly anti-immigrant, incited hate, praised authoritarian leaders, demonized the media, and repeatedly sought to undermine the country's democratic system. He even invoked civil war.

Almost a century later, we would do well to heed Sinclair Lewis's warnings and face the fact that atrocity crimes can happen here. The United States is a post-genocide society, one in which systemic white supremacy continues to impact our politics and way of life. In this regard, Trump's presidency, if a dangerous moment, was not an anomaly or exceptional. It aligned with a long history of horrific atrocity crimes.

Conclusion

The Bird

AUGUST 4, 2019, CHAUTAUQUA INSTITUTION, NEW YORK
Nuon Chea's toes turn black with rot. Then he dies.

"Nuon Chea, Khmer Rouge's Infamous 'Brother Number Two,' Dies at 93," the *Washington Post* headlines. "World's Most Evil Man Dies: He Hated Education and Pushed Ethnic Supremacy," proclaims a *Daily Kos* post.[1]

The day before Nuon Chea's August 4, 2019, death, a shooter strikes in the name of white genocide, killing twenty-four people and injuring two dozen more at an El Paso Walmart frequented by Hispanics. Moments before the attack, the shooter, twenty-one-year-old Patrick Crusius, posts a four-page manifesto, "The Inconvenient Truth about Me," explaining his motives.

The manifesto begins by expressing Crusius's "support" for Tarrant, the Christchurch shooter, claiming that Tarrant's manifesto, "The Great Replacement," inspired him. "This attack is a response to the Hispanic invasion of Texas," the second line of Crusius's manifesto states. "They are the instigators, not me. I am simply defending my country from cultural and ethnic replacement brought on by an invasion." This "invasion," Crusius imagines, threatens whites by increasing economic stress, race mixing, the number of Democratic voters, and environmental destruction, which is further fueled by corporate greed. "If we can get rid of enough people," Crusius contends, "then our way of life can become more sustainable."

After explaining his motives, Crusius describes his choice of "gear," including bullets that fragment. He claims that his ideology has been in place for years and "predates Trump." Crusius concludes by saying that he is "honored to lead the fight to reclaim my country from destruction." At the end of the text, Crusius lists the URL of a white power website, which states that its goal is to "accelerate the 'cultural wave' theorized by European New Right thinkers and implemented by the American Alt Right."

Images of Crusius circulate in the media as people search for answers, asking once again, *Why?* Just a week earlier, a gunman had opened fire at the Gilroy Garlic Festival, killing three and injuring thirteen others. He left no manifesto, but his social media directed readers to a book, written over a hundred years ago, which is popular in white power circles. 14 Words Press, founded by David Lane, the author of the "White Genocide Manifesto," even reprinted a version of the text that includes a preface by Lane's wife.

And, in the early morning of August 4, hours before Nuon Chea's death in Cambodia, a gunman wearing body armor opens fire in a Dayton, Ohio, entertainment district. In thirty-two seconds, he shoots twenty-six people, killing nine. While his motives are unclear, his attack, coming on the heels of Gilroy and El Paso, helps catalyze a renewed US debate about Trump, guns, and white power extremism.

* * *

"Why does this happen in America?"

Reverend Gene Robinson, Chautauqua's senior pastor, asks this question during the Sunday morning service on August 4, hours after the second shooting. I sit in what many consider the heart of the Chautauqua Institution, a forty-four-hundred-seat open-air amphitheater, packed full today.

"Why are guns meant for the military in the hands of civilians?" Reverend Robinson continues. "And at the southern border nine hundred more children have been separated from their parents," he adds to applause. "We may have lost our moral compass as a nation and a people."

～

Founded in 1874 on the banks of Chautauqua Lake in western New York, the Chautauqua Institution began as a camp for Sunday school teachers.[2] While it retains its religious roots, Chautauqua now presents itself as an educational "summer retreat for the mind, body, and soul" where visitors, many of whom are religious and most of whom are older and white, may select from the weekly themes that guide the programming.

It would be easy, however, to spend a week at Chautauqua focused on religion or recreation, not the current events that fill our televisions and social media streams. Because the institution is located on the banks of Lake Chautauqua, people walk and bike on paved paths crossed by tree groves. With residential housing on the edges of the gated grounds, Chautauqua is centered around the amphitheater where Reverend Robinson is speaking, which dates back to the event platform used during the first Sunday School Assembly.[3] Recently refurbished, the amphitheater now has a cutting-edge stage and sound system, necessary for feature orchestra, dance, lecture, and other entertainment events held each evening—and the massive organ that accompanies religious services.

The amphitheater is bordered by a grass quad with a library and shops, including a popular ice cream stand. In the other direction, a red brick pedestrian path leads past houses of worship to the Hall of Philosophy, where, among other things, an afternoon Interfaith Lecture Series is held.

This week, Chautauqua's theme is "Grace: A Celebration of Extraordinary Gifts." Being agnostic, I was not particularly excited when I first heard this would be the thematic focus during the week of my visit. For me, the idea of grace conjures images of evangelical preachers giving fiery sermons about God-given goodness, beneficence amid a world of suffering and sin. And indeed, the promotional description for the week explains, "Grace, as defined by religious terms, is the means by which we receive an unearned gift, one we're not worthy of."[4] My presumption, however, is wrong. "Beyond religion," the description goes on, "what does grace look like in the secular world? When is grace difficult? In talking across differences? In compromise? In the face of adversity? We look at the moments in which grace is most needed."

Over the course of this week, Chautauqua will consider such questions from a variety of perspectives, many, but not all, religious. The concept of grace will be most deeply explored in the daily afternoon Interfaith Lecture Series, but is discussed elsewhere, including the weekly Sunday morning service, which marks the beginning of the thematic week and features a guest chaplain. This week's chaplain is Reverend Barbara Lundblad, a lesbian Lutheran pastor and professor. Like Reverend Robinson, she will grapple with the issue of moral compass and the question everyone is asking about the shootings: "Why?"

~

As usual, public commentators are providing easy first answers spotlighting the Hater. Critics point the finger at Trump for his inflammatory speech.[5] Some note the connection between Trump's "invasion" language and Crusius's manifesto. Several Democratic presidential candidates call him a racist.

Others contend that the attacks are, as one op-ed puts it, proof that "Trump Is a White Nationalist Who Inspires Terrorism."[6] The essay quotes an FBI agent who says Trump "is basically the fuel that's been poured onto a fire" of white power extremism. Meanwhile, and coincidentally, Cesar Sayoc, the Trump fanatic turned mail bomber, is sentenced to twenty years. In his sentencing memo, Sayoc's lawyers state, "In this darkness [of his personal struggles], Mr. Sayoc found light in Donald J. Trump."[7]

Responding to such criticism, Trump's acting chief of staff, Mick Mulvaney, points to a different Hater, claiming that the shootings are the acts of "sick people" who "spew hate." Mulvaney adds, "You cannot be a white supremacist and be normal in the head."[8] Calls increase for Trump to directly condemn white power extremism. He does so while reading stiffly from a teleprompter and echoing Mulvaney in characterizing the "evil attacks" as the work of "twisted monsters." Trump suggests that mental illness, video games, and social media are to blame.

Some people push back on these individualizing "Hater" arguments, pointing toward structure and power. The *New York Times* editorial board calls for recognition that "We Have a White Nationalist Terrorist Problem." After 9/11, the editorial states, the United States and its allies mobilized to address the threat posed by Islamic extremists, but they have failed to do so in the United States.[9] The sense of urgency around the growing threat of white power extremism is only heightened when, in the days that follow the shootings, there is an attack in Norway and dozens of arrests related to domestic terrorism are made in the United States.[10]

Despite repeated warnings, the government is said to remain hesitant to respond robustly to the white-power-extremist threat because of the connections between white nationalism and Trump's base.[11] Some critics extend this line of thinking, arguing that there is direct link among the Trump administration, white power extremists, and systemic white supremacy.

A *New York Times* columnist contends that white nationalists in the government and white power extremists are two sides of the same coin, as both seek to maintain a system of white dominance.[12] Both, the author states, are firmly anti-immigrant and seek to diminish the rights (and numbers) of people of color through policies ranging from voting restrictions and border walls to, in the case of white power extremists, violence and intimidation.

More white power ties to the government are revealed after the shooting. A State Department official is placed on leave for his white nationalist views. Meanwhile, reports suggest that there are white nationalist sympathizers in the police, military, and border police forces, a point recently highlighted by the discovery of a border patrol Facebook group that includes racist posts.[13]

Other commentators note that this situation is neither exceptional nor new but linked to a long history of systemic white supremacy in the United States. Presidential candidate Joe Biden is among those who make this point.[14] At an August 7 Iowa rally, Biden reiterated his 2020 presidential campaign theme that the United States is "in a battle for the soul of this nation"—one reflected by a litany of Trump actions ranging from his assault on democratic safeguards to his fanning "the flames of white supremacy" through incitement, including his recent language inveighing against immigrant "invaders" that was echoed in Crusius's manifesto.

If dangerous, Biden contended, Trump's actions are not unique. "America's history is not a fairy tale," Biden told the crowd. "The battle for the soul of the nation has been a constant push and pull for 243 years between the American ideal that says we're all created equal and the harsh reality that racism has long torn us apart" and that enslavement and the KKK are part of the country's history. Biden concluded by invoking American exceptionalism, noting that "when we're at our best, we believe in honesty, decency, treating everyone with respect, leaving nobody behind, giving hate no safe harbor, [and] demonizing no one," a "uniquely American code" that stands "as a beacon to the world."

Biden's comments about "American values" and "the battle for the soul of the nation" invoked the idea that Reverend Robinson had mentioned and is being widely discussed in public following the shootings: moral compass. In its most basic sense, a moral compass is a guide for moral behavior. If it can help a person distinguish between right and wrong, moral compass also provides direction in complex, morally charged situations.

Sometimes the term is used in reference to individuals, such as Biden's depiction of Trump or some conservative commentators' suggestion that a lack of moral compass, not guns, was the reason for Crusius's attack.[15] Biden's invocations of "American values" illustrate the broader sense of moral compass, which is also used to refer to societies and nations. Reverend Robinson had used the term in this manner with his collective "we."

Although ethical values stand at the center of the moral compass, one problem arises because these standards may vary. If different groups and individuals have different values, then how is it possible to judge the morality of their actions since a person may act in ways we view as unethical even as they claim to do so on moral grounds? Nuon Chea, for example, argued that he acted for a moral good: liberating the poor from oppression. Similarly, as we saw, white power extremists claim moral grounds through their use of the white genocide frame. Crusius's manifesto also made such moral claims. In my discipline, anthropology, there has been enormous debate about this issue, often inflected through the concept of cultural relativism.[16] As we shall see, Grace, dignity, and moral compass offer one path out of this seeming paradox.

In the week that follows while I am at Chautauqua, the topic of moral compass will come up repeatedly as speakers and audiences consider the shootings, the state of the nation, and ethical action. As they proceed, Chautauquans will ask what can be done to prevent such violence and how they can help. Reverend Lundblad offers an answer.

* * *

"A word out of place."

Reverend Lundblad frames her sermon around these words on the Monday morning after the attacks. Lundblad leaves the podium often as she talks to the amphitheater audience about Isaiah 35, saying it is a verse of hope that seems misplaced in a narrative of scripture focused on destruction.

I listen but mainly think of the shootings and Nuon Chea's death the day before. I wonder whether she will address the attacks, which dominate the news. Chautauqua has a long history of grappling with these sorts of political issues, hosting dignitaries, presidents, world leaders, and media personalities, often in the morning lecture series that follows the ecumenical service. This week's lectures are being moderated by Krista Tippett, who hosts the public radio program *On Being*.[17]

"Sometimes a word out of place exposes evil and injustice," Reverend Lundblad continues. "Sometimes a word out of place envisions something new." She makes the transition to El Paso and Dayton by describing her visit to a Nazi prison in Berlin that included a timeline charting the implosion of democracy and a display about the systematic targeting of Jews, Roma, homosexuals, and others. Lundblad says she was particularly struck by a propaganda poster featuring a Nazi eagle protecting an Aryan family with blond hair. Many contemporary white power extremists draw on such imagery. I think of the New Jersey European Heritage Association website, which features pictures of white families with the caption, "Our European race is in a struggle for survival, don't sit idly by as we fight for existence."

"The Nazi party did everything in its power to make sure those who did not fit this poster would be eliminated," Lundblad states. Then she asks, "Would I have spoken out against what happened in Germany if I lived then? That's a historical question I cannot answer." She flips to the present. "The more pressing question is, 'Barbara, will you say something now in this country in the face of hatred and racism?'"

To help make the shift to the present, she cites Toni Morrison, who will die later in the day. "Toni Morrison writes about the power and problem of language," Lundblad notes. "She says we hunger for a way to articulate who we are and what we mean, but that the language we have inherited is not neutral. It's embedded within history. Language is not neutral. The words paint a picture."

She turns to Trump. "Our president has called Baltimore a disgusting rat- and rodent-infested place," Lundblad continues. "He called sanctuary cities infested and claimed that immigrants pour into and infest parts of our country. The key word here is 'infest.'"

Lundbald is referring to a controversy that emerged in July when Trump attacked four congresswomen of color, tweeting that they should "go back and help fix the totally broken and crime infested places from which they came." Days later, at a North Carolina rally, Trump failed to intervene when the crowd began to chant about one of them, "Send her back! Send her back! Send her back!"

As was the case with his Charlottesville remarks, Trump, after coming under criticism, first sought to gaslight the incident (saying he had intervened to stop the chant) before backtracking and calling the chanting crowd "incredible patriots." Meanwhile, critics condemned Trump for making racist remarks that echoed past US xenophobia and current white power extremism. The House of Representatives officially rebuked him.

Rep. Ilhan Omar, the primary target of Trump's ire at the rally, penned a *New York Times* op-ed in which she claimed the rally would be "a defining moment in American history" and that, echoing Biden's campaign launch video, there was a "fight for the soul of our nation" taking place as Trump acted like a demagogue and mounted racist attacks.[18]

Trump was undeterred. Within a week, he sparked a new controversy by referring to the Baltimore district of Rep. Elijah Cummings, who had condemned conditions at the southern border, as a "disgusting, rat- and rodent-infested mess."

While Trump had political reasons for inflaming hate—rallying his base, deflecting attention from recent immigration-policy setbacks, and seeking to align the Democratic Party with its far left elements—he also was likely reacting to strong criticism from "the squad" of congresswomen, including a June remark by Rep. Alexandria Ocasio-Cortez claiming that the United States was running "concentration camps" on its southern border and was endangered by "an authoritarian and fascist presidency."[19] After facing criticism, she tweeted an expert essay supporting the use of the term and noted that the United States had run concentration camps before, such as the Japanese internment camps during World War II. She finished, "We should not fund the caging of kids & families."

"Human beings do not infest any place," Lundblad continues, drawing applause. She returns to Morrison to underscore her point. "Language is not neutral. . . . When we hear a word like 'infest,' when it refers to immigrants or people in the inner cities, we turn those people into vermin. And what do you do with vermin? You want to get rid of it." This, she states, is what motivated Crusius in El Paso: "He wanted to get rid of Mexican immigrants and Mexicans who live there." She cites Martin Luther King Jr., who famously said, "In the final analysis, racism is evil because its ultimate logic is genocide."

The day of the Gilroy shooting, *New York Times* columnist Charles Blow had invoked the same quotation while arguing, following Trump's remarks about Baltimore and many other comments about infestation, that "Trump is a racist. Say that out loud."[20] Blow and other critics contend that Trump's racist language is systematic, as illustrated by the hundreds of times he has used words like "invasion," "alien," and "killer" at his rallies, including a recent incident at a Florida rally where Trump semi-joked that the only way to stop the "invasion" was to "shoot them." Trump, his critics note, frequently uses such language on Twitter and in his political campaigning, as illustrated by his midterm election rhetoric and his campaign's use of the word "invasion" in over two thousand Facebook ads.[21]

Lundblad's "word out of place" sermon is meant to prevent the normalization of such language. "We need to speak up," she says. "All of us have a sphere of influence. A family. Other relatives. People we work with. A cards club. A yoga class." Each person, she urges, must be "a witness" and work "to expose" the language of hate.

* * *

Expose and Envision. A Word out of Place. The power of language. These ideas recur in Chautauqua lectures in the days that follow as speakers continue to grapple with the attacks. The discussions are inflected by the theme of Grace and Chautauqua's emphasis on dialogue, which dates back to its origins and long-standing work on interfaith engagement.

This week, the idea of dialogue emerges most directly during Tippett's interviews, in which she and her guests sit facing each other in plush chairs on the amphitheater stage. On Monday, she interviews two women who promote dialogue through "The People's Supper" program, which brings groups together to have meaningful conversations about difficult topics, including race. They speak of the need to "interrogate whiteness" and the importance of learning "how to be together" in the aftermath of the shootings.

The Wednesday morning interview features Richard Blanco, a gay Latino immigrant poet who reads a poem he wrote for Obama's second inauguration. Blanco emphasizes consideration of the stories into which each person is born, which structure the paths upon which they walk in life. Through language, he says, people can come to share and understand one another's "stories," an idea that infuses his poetry.

He reads a poem about the death of immigrants attempting to cross the Rio Grande River, an issue that arose in public debate in late June 2019 when a photo of a dead father and his daughter, lying face down on the muddy banks of the river, circulated in the media. To emphasize the importance of dialogue and understanding, Blanco recalls a Zulu greeting in which two people lock eyes and say, "I see you."

If these morning interviews center on dialogue, the 2:00 p.m. Interfaith Lectures most directly consider the issue of Grace. The first is given on Monday by Rabbi Rami Shapiro in the Hall of Philosophy, a smaller open-air speaking venue with Doric columns set in a grove of trees. The audience overflows into a nearby grass field, where people sit in lawn chairs gazing at the podium where Shapiro stands. A line of tapestries, their colors forming a Rainbow Flag, hangs behind him.

Shapiro tells the audience that the Jewish notion of Grace is simply conveyed by a repeated phrase in a nineteenth-century Hasidic song, which he teaches to them. "I am alive, I am alive, I'm alive," the Hall of Philosophy crowd sings several times. "And who is this aliveness, I am."

The biblical word "Lord," Shapiro explains to the audience, is a mistranslation.[22] It originally was a verb, not a noun, referring to an effervescent aliveness in which, as transitory beings, we momentarily partake. Humans become distanced from this aliveness through their fictions and ideologies, ranging from our sense of self to religious doctrine. This aliveness, the reality we call "God," is Grace, he says. It encompasses both good and bad. The shootings, he tells the audience, were therefore part of Grace but done by people blinded from this "aliveness" by their fictions.

Shapiro's argument dovetails in interesting ways with the interfaith talks that follow. Wednesday's speaker, Abdullah S. Daar, states that, even as he approaches Grace from a Muslim perspective, he and Rabbi Shapiro are perennialists who believe that all religions point to an ultimate truth about a reality that is obscured and difficult to comprehend.[23]

The Muslim idea of Grace, Daar says, involves appreciation of this oneness of humanity, a point he underscores with his talk title, "Garment of Destiny," taken from a Martin Luther King Jr. quotation: "In a real sense, all life is interrelated, all men are caught in an inescapable network of mutuality, tied in a single garment of destiny." Like Shapiro, Daar notes the danger of ideological certainty, which leads to the intolerance and fear that fuel violence, including this week's mass shootings.

* * *

"How can evil be explained?" Reverend Robinson asks on Friday. Robinson tells the audience gathered in the Hall of Philosophy that he has asked the Zen Buddhist Abbott Roshi Bodhin Kjolhede to respond to this question in today's interfaith conversation, held on the last day of the Chautauqua thematic week.

"I don't know," Kjolhede later answers, telling the audience that these are the most famous words in Zen philosophy. Kjolhede also gives a perennialist answer, saying that the question speaks to an ultimately unknowable reality that all religions explore. The Zen Buddhist perspective emphasizes Being and use of meditation to strip away the thoughts, feelings, and memories that cloud consciousness and thereby distance each person from awareness of it. It is a bit like the inverse of original sin, he explains. If, like Shapiro and Daar, Kjolhede sees the roots of violence and evil in illusory thinking that misdirects us from the transience of

Being, Kjolhede inflects it through the Buddhist notions of cause and effect. Karma.

As I sit listening to Kjolhede talk about grace, evil, and karma, I think of Nuon Chea's Buddhist funeral, which concluded today in Cambodia.[24] Hundreds of people attended the funeral: family, friends, supporters, and former Khmer Rouge colleagues. Nuon Chea's daughter told reporters that her father was "a good man" and had done "nothing wrong. He struggled for the people." A former Khmer Rouge soldier, in turn, called Nuon Chea a "nationalist" and a "hero."

Survivors had a different view. Some bitterly noted the irony of Nuon Chea's long life and elaborate funeral given that the Khmer Rouge banned Buddhism and dumped the bodies of hundreds of thousands of their victims in mass graves without ceremony. Others were more forgiving, such as a survivor who stated, "I no longer hate him because it's been a long time."

A belief in karma informs this latter attitude. Human beings like Nuon Chea commit bad deeds because they are blinded by delusion (ignorance, misperception, bewilderment), aversion (repulsion, anger, hate), and attachment (craving, desire, greed)—the three "poisons" and sources of suffering with which all human beings constantly struggle. In the end, they receive their due, the karmic return on their sins—being reborn in the Buddhist hells.

For Buddhists, then, Grace follows from the Awareness that comes with equanimity and being present in a world conditioned by karma and impermanence. Such understanding provides the basis for letting go of vindictiveness while seeing the reasons that lead someone like Nuon Chea to commit horrible crimes.

From this perspective, Nuon Chea's moral compass was broken. As he and his followers noted, Nuon Chea had fought for a good: improving the plight of the oppressed and the poor. But he did so in a "bewildered" (ignorant) manner, one bound up with the hatred (aversion) of others and the desire (attachment) for power that would lead the Khmer Rouge to seek a utopian end regardless of the human cost.

Shapiro, Daar, and Kjolhede similarly spoke of this sort of bewilderment during their lectures on Grace. If Kjolhede foregrounded the ignorance that misdirects us from Being, Shapiro, speaking the day after the shootings, said that such violence occurs because people are misguided by fictions that blind them to the Aliveness in which all human beings partake and that is Grace. Daar likewise linked the violence to ideological certainty while emphasizing the interconnectedness of human beings partaking in a shared "garment of destiny"—a mutuality that demands compassion and respect for the dignity of others, including their basic rights.

Their reflections provide a way to think about moral compass, one in which Grace serves as the centering compass rose. In contrast to "the Flash" of ideological conviction that often drives violent extremists like Nuon Chea and white power shooters, Grace involves Awareness and the deep understanding of context and respect for the human dignity that comes with it.

This emphasis on dignity dovetails with the idea of human rights. It is mentioned in the first line of the Universal Declaration of Human Rights, which calls for "recognition of the inherent dignity . . . of all members of the human family." Dignity, then, provides an ethical standard to guide moral behavior. If scholars have debated the meaning and relativity of the term, it has a legal and consensual universality insofar as it has become ensconced as a key international human rights norm and codified in related conventions, declarations, and laws.[25]

This human rights emphasis on dignity was inflected by Nazi atrocity crimes and exemplified by the extreme degradations of human life during the Holocaust. Here again we see how the lessons of the past can inform the present, since they provide an example of what can happen when extremists hold power and abuse outgroups—and serve as a barometer for assessing such possibilities in the current moment.

Besides this respect for the dignity of others, the Awareness of Grace also involves deep understanding of context, the concrete ground in which abstract moral standards are applied and moral assessments made. If Grace (Awareness) is the center rose of moral compass, we might think of its four primary points as Discernment ("looking beneath" surface understandings), Orientation ("looking back" to see how the past aligns with the present), Perspective ("looking at" the situation at hand, structural forces in play, and views of those involved), and Foresight ("looking ahead" to consider future possibilities and imagine new paths forward, the work of the moral imagination).

In a sense, this book is centered around these four cardinal points. The "Charlottesville Lessons" and "The Hater" chapters, for example, illustrate Discernment as they seek to "look beneath" the surface understandings of political discourse and everyday terms of speech—ranging from Trump's "two sides" remark on Charlottesville to the ways in which hate individualizes racism and violence and thereby diverts from structure, history, and power.

"White Genocide," in turn, centers on Orientation and Perspective as it examines the history of systemic white supremacy, the historical pathways that gave rise to the white genocide frame, and the views of contemporary white-power-extremist groups. The last two chapters and this conclusion, in turn, are more focused on Foresight, a "looking ahead" to consider the threat of atrocity crimes in the United States and possible pathways to prevent such assaults on human dignity from happening.

* * *

"There's a tribute to Toni Morrison at the library," Reverend Robinson announces at the end of Kjolhede's talk. "People are invited to bring something brief they can read. It will be a celebration of her writing and the ways she has contributed to all of us."

I follow the central pedestrian walkway from the Hall of Philosophy to the Chautauqua library, a two-story, red-brick colonial fronting a rectangular green space where children are playing in the hot summer afternoon. Some people read passages from Morrison's novels, others read selections from her prose. Many of the excerpts take up issues of language, race, power, and how literature helps spark moral imagination.

These themes all appear in Morrison's 1993 Nobel Prize address, which many commentators are discussing in the wake of Morrison's death. It begins with a story. "Once upon a time," Morrison's lecture starts, "there was an old woman. Blind but wise."[26] The woman, who "is the daughter of slaves, black, [and] American," is approached by a group of youths who, challenging her, say, "Old woman, I hold in my hand a bird. Tell me whether it is living or dead."

After a long silence, the woman replies that she does not know whether the bird is dead or alive but that "it is in your hands" and thus the youths have responsibility for its fate. In so doing, "The blind woman shifts attention away from assertions of power to the instrument through which that power is exercised."

Reading "the bird as language and the woman as a practiced writer," Morrison turns to an interpretation of the story, at times given from the perspective of the blind woman, in terms of language and power. While there are many nuances to Morrison's address, one key idea centers on the danger of language used for "nefarious purposes," especially when supporting a totalizing view. For Morrison, language, like the "bird in the hand" of the youths, can be more or less alive. It deadens under domination that "thwarts the intellect, stalls conscience, suppresses human potential."

Such domination encompasses a wide range of "policing languages of mastery," not just "obscuring state language" but also the obscuring language of the media, academia, science, and law. Language that diminishes others, ranging from sexism to racism, likewise reflects "the bottomed-out mind" and must be rejected since it stifles knowledge and the "mutual exchange of ideas." Language that is alive, in turn, is generative and illuminates "the actual, imagined and possible," "surges toward knowledge," "arcs toward the place where meaning may lie," and indeed "may be the measure of our lives."

Morrison underscores these points through a narrative shift in the last part of her address as she imagines a dialogue that takes place between the old woman and visitors to whom she has recounted the story of the bird-in-the-hand youths. The visitors challenge her to consider a different reading of the youth's intent, one in which their question was in fact a query about the meaning of life and an invitation to teach them "how to see without pictures" and to "show us belief's wide skirt and the stich that unravels fear's caul." Instead of remaining stuck in her position of elevated social status and superior knowledge, she was being asked by the youths to jointly "make up a story" that creates "us at the very moment it is being created." For Morrison, this sort of openness and dialogue is the counterpoint to "dead language" and provides a path to knowledge and understanding.

While coming from a different disciplinary terrain, Morrison's ideas intersect in many ways with those of the Frankfurt School. If Adorno wrote "Education after Auschwitz," Morrison might have written "Education after Jamestown" as she emphasized how language, in its open and dialogic forms, can be emancipatory and stand against structures of domination, especially racism. This emphasis on power and domination, categorization, critical reflection, empathy, respect for others, resistance, and combating prejudice and bigotry dovetails directly with key concerns of Adorno and his Frankfurt School colleagues.

These themes also emerged during the Chautauqua discussions of Grace—not just in the Interfaith Lectures emphasizing Awareness but also in Tippett's amphitheater dialogues and Lundblad's "a word out of place" sermon and exhortation to "expose and envision." To use Morrison's phrase, all these speakers sought ways to counter "deadened," "calcified," and violent languages of domination, including the language of white supremacy that Trump often deployed as he demeaned nonwhite others and played on white genocide great replacement fears.

As I sit on the Chautauqua lawn, watching as the readers take their turns reading excerpts from Morrison's work, I think about the El Paso Walmart shooting, Crusius's echo of Trump's warnings about the danger of immigrant "invasion," children separated from their parents on the southern border, and what might transpire next, including the possibility of genocide and atrocity crimes.

Several readers frame their Morrison reading in relation to Trump's USA, a topic Morrison herself wrote about in a 2016 postelection *New Yorker* essay titled, "Making America White Again." I think of "The Snake," an Aesop fable set to music by a Black artist and then turned by Trump into a campaign speech harangue. Trump's rendering of the story, like so much of his political rhetoric, epitomized the "dead," oppressive language about which Morrison warned. Instead of being open and affording multiple points of view, "The Snake" stifled conversation and reduced literature to a singular message and perspective. "Think of it in terms of immigration," he instructed his crowds. There was no space for dialogue, critical reflection, or alternative views. Instead, Trump's language reflected the sort of "coldness" and "blindness" that Adorno had warned led to Auschwitz.

If this book began with Trump's "The Snake," it ends by counterposing it to Morrison's "bird" of language. For Morrison, language can liberate but also kill. And thus each of us bears an ethical responsibility for this "bird in the hand." When used with awareness and moral imagination, language provides a path to navigate dangerous and fraught situations, like the sway of white power during Trump's presidency.

As the end of Morrison's address shows, when the old woman's visitors challenge her to reimagine the intent of the youths she assumed were malicious, this path may involve difficult and uncomfortable conversations. It requires a moral compass, respecting the dignity of others, and sometimes, as Lundblat, drawing on Morrison, underscores, speaking "a word out of place." Although dialogue is often not easy, it provides a space for critical reflection, self-awareness, empathy, respect for others, and creative meaning making. And so Morrison finishes her address by reimagining the old woman's reply to the youths. She tells them that she trusts them with the bird of language, for which she realizes they seek to take responsibility. "You have truly caught it," she says to them. "How lovely it is, this thing we have done—together."

EPILOGUE

"Angry mobs are trying to tear down statues of our Founders, deface our most sacred memorials, and unleash a wave of violent crime in our cities," Donald Trump states at his Mount Rushmore rally, held to mark the Fourth of July and punctuated by fireworks.[1] Behind him the stone faces of Washington, Jefferson, Lincoln, and Roosevelt stare.

Prior to Trump's arrival, Native American protesters had held aloft signs reading, "You are on Stolen Land," "Trump—Mt. Rushmore— White Supremacy," and "#Land Back." A Sioux tribal leader explained that, to his community, "Mount Rushmore is a symbol of white supremacy and racial injustice in this country and . . . the four faces carved on that mountain are the four faces of colonizers who have committed genocide on Indigenous people."[2] Ironically, Trump supporters had yelled "Go Home!" at the protesters while Trump's speech would complain of white victimization and suggest the threat of white genocide.

"The American people," Trump goes on, "will not allow our country, and all of its values, history, and culture, to be taken from them." The crowd, predominantly white and sprinkled with red Trump shirts and "Make America Great Again" caps, replies, "USA! USA! USA!"

Trump names the enemy, "far-left fascism," which, he will suggest the following day, includes "the radical left, the Marxists, the anarchists, the agitators, [and] the looters."[3] These radicals, he tells the crowd, use "Cancel Culture" to advance their aims, "shaming dissenters and demanding total submission from anyone who disagrees. This is the very definition of totalitarianism, and it is completely alien to our culture and our values."

Far-left fascism, Trump continues, is found in schools and the media and "demands absolute allegiance. If you do not speak its language, perform its rituals, recite its mantras, and follow its commandments, then you will be censored, banished, blacklisted, persecuted, and punished." To applause, Trump tells the crowd he will not let this happen.

"Make no mistake," Trump warns, "this left-wing cultural revolution is designed to overthrow the American Revolution. In doing so, they would destroy the very civilization that . . . has lifted humanity to new heights of achievement, discovery, and progress. To make this possible, they are determined to tear down every statue, symbol, and memory of our national heritage." The goal of this new enemy that wants to "erase our heritage," Trump states, "is the end of America." The crowd boos at Trump's suggestion of white genocide.

～

Trump remains unwilling to hold "a bird in the hand." Instead, he continues to invoke "The Snake" of hate and division, often with white genocide inflections. It remains a key part of his "Make America Great Again" messaging and a pillar of his political oratory.

He began his 2016 presidential bid with warnings of Islamic terror, Mexican rapists, and immigrant menace from the South. During the 2018 midterm elections, he ramped up this xenophobic message again as he inveighed against southern border immigrant "caravans" and "infestations." By the time of his 2020 presidential campaign launch, Trump was able to boast about a booming economy—and spoke of changing his slogan to "Keep America Great!"—but nevertheless continued to inveigh against immigration dangers. At a February 10, 2020, rally in New Hampshire, Trump even reprised "The Snake," noting that crowds at his last few rallies had been asking him to read it and stressing that it was about illegal immigration.[4]

At the time, Trump's reelection prospects looked promising. He had weathered impeachment proceedings, having been acquitted just the week before his New Hampshire rally, where he referred to his impeachment as a "hoax" while positioning himself as a victim. Meanwhile, the economy remained strong, with the stock market reaching an all-time high two days after the rally. His poll numbers were moving in a similar direction. Some worried, however, that in the aftermath of his acquittal, Trump was showing less regard than ever for democratic safeguards and was expanding his power in authoritarian directions.[5]

Then a 9/11-like moment struck—the kind that can destabilize a country and constitutes a key risk factor for genocide and atrocity crimes. Even as Trump was on the campaign trail in New Hampshire and other rally sites, the coronavirus disease 2019 (COVID-19) pandemic was spreading across the United States. By the time of Trump's Mount Rushmore address, the pandemic had already afflicted 2.8 million people in the United States (and more than eleven million worldwide), hospitalizing hundreds of thousands while killing nearly 130,000 people (and over 500,000 across the globe).[6] When the COVID-19 trendlines in the United States first began to rise sharply in late February, the economy and stock market sputtered before collapsing in March 2020 as businesses shut down and tens of millions of jobs were being lost. Many condemned Trump for holding the rally at Mount Rushmore amid a new surge in cases.

If the risk of atrocity crimes in the United States had been moderately high before, it further intensified as the crisis unfolded. White power extremists sought to weaponize the virus and spread Jewish-conspiracy theories about COVID-19's origin that circulated worldwide. Gun sales in the United States spiked, as did "yellow peril" animus toward people of Asian descent. Meanwhile, Trump began referring to COVID-19 as the "foreign" or "Chinese" virus. His son retweeted a "Kung-Flu" meme, a racially tinged term Trump would later deploy.[7]

Many far-right extremists responded to his messaging.[8] The New Jersey European Heritage Association (NJEHA), for example, posted social media messages with hashtags like "#StopTheInvasionOfAmerica," "#SealTheBorders," and "#BuildA40FootWall." The group also affixed posters on everything from stop signs to New Jersey Transit ticket machines that included slogans like "Open Borders is the Virus," "Diversity Means no White People," "Stop Coronavirus / Deport All Illegal Aliens

/ Close the Borders / Stop Immigration," "Stand Your Ground," "Feminism is Cancer," "Black Crimes Matter," "There is a War on Whites," "[Jewish] (((Media))) is the Virus!" and "Mass Immigration is White Genocide."

Trump would also encourage anti-coronavirus lock-down protesters, many linked to far-right gun groups, to "LIBERATE" several states led by Democratic governors.[9] When critiqued for using the language of incitement, Trump responded by calling the protesters "great people," a remark that reminded some of his Charlottesville "two sides" comments.

Trump's "LIBERATE" tweet also led to a surge of Internet traffic centered on "boogaloo," a meme increasingly used by white power extremists and gun groups to refer to insurrection and civil war. The term had also circulated at a January 2020 gun-rights rally in Richmond, Virginia, which many had feared would lead to Charlottesville-like violence—especially after the FBI arrested members of a white-power-extremist group that was planning attacks at the rally in the hope of sparking a race war that would lead to the creation of a white ethnostate.[10]

More broadly, concerns rose that global unrest could increase and populist leaders would use the coronavirus crisis to invoke emergency powers and consolidate power—a possibility that, to return to the UN "Framework of Analysis" risk factors, increases *Instability* and can even serve as a *Trigger* for atrocity crimes.[11] The concerns about Trump were amplified by the erosion of long-standing checks and balances during his administration, his civil war threats, and his apparent turn to once again center his 2020 campaign against Biden around white grievance and victimization, racism, and xenophobia. Meanwhile, Stephen Miller, in keeping with his great replacement white genocide aims, sought to use the crisis to further tighten immigration restrictions. On July 15, the Southern Poverty Law Center would place Miller on its extremist watch list.[12]

∾

The situation in the United States underwent another dramatic turn on May 25, when an African American man, George Floyd, suffocated to death while a Minneapolis police officer knelt on his neck, ignoring Floyd's repeated pleas of "I can't breathe."[13] Videos of Floyd's killing went viral and sparked mass Black Lives Matter protests that spread across the United States and even abroad. If, at first, the protests centered on police violence against Blacks, they soon expanded to include calls for addressing structural racism more broadly.

Some of the protests turned violent or enabled looting.[14] In response, Trump threatened to use military force against those he described via Twitter as "THUGS." Invoking an infamous 1967 phrase used by a Miami police chief to justify a crackdown on Blacks, Trump posted, "When the looting starts, the shooting starts." Twitter added a label to his tweet warning that it "glorified violence." If Trump sought to blame "antifa and the radical left" for the rioting, looting, and violence, evidence emerged that white power extremists hoping to spark a boogaloo civil war were the ones more heavily involved and who posed a significant threat to domestic security.[15]

A few days after Floyd's killing, the protests reached the White House. At one point, the Secret Service rushed Trump to a secure bunker, an event that became public and further amplified the argument—already circulating due to his poor response to the pandemic—that Trump was weak and unable to meet the moment. He responded with a "law and order" message and the threat of force.

On June 1, as protests continued across the country, Trump stated that he was "mobilizing all available Federal resources—civilian and military—to stop the rioting and looting." If local officials were unable to "dominate the streets," Trump warned, "I will deploy the United States military and quickly solve the problem for them."[16]

Moments before he began speaking, a host of law enforcement agencies, including military police, had used massive force, including tear gas and helicopters, to clear peaceful protesters from Lafayette Square. After finishing his address, Trump and a number of officials—including

Secretary of Defense Mark Esper and the chairman of the joint chiefs of staff, Mark Milley, who was dressed in a battle camouflage uniform—walked across the square to St. John's Episcopal Church for a photo-op where Trump help up a Bible.

Immediately, there was an enormous outcry as Trump appeared ready to use military force on US civilians and reportedly wanted ten thousand active-duty troops sent to Washington, DC.[17] Former top military officials denounced Trump's actions. Milley apologized. And Esper, contradicting Trump, backtracked on the need for military force. Nevertheless, Trump would later send paramilitary-like federal agents into cities like Portland, Oregon, even as he continued to suggest that he might not respect the results of the 2020 election.

Commentators warned that Trump's militarization had strong fascist echoes and that "it could happen here" as Trump further eroded democratic safeguards. A global atrocity crimes monitor issued an alert for the United States, along with Iraq and Sudan, while others warned that the risk of domestic atrocity crimes in the United States was sharply rising.[18] Given the ongoing pandemic, economic collapse, and protests, the atrocity crimes "heat map" alert for the United States was now glowing light to medium red.

If the protests would taper off in June, the debate about structural racism continued, with large numbers of people in the United States viewing the issue as significant and supporting the Black Lives Matter movement.[19] To an extent that seemed almost unimaginable when I was at Chautauqua in 2019, the issue of systemic white supremacy was now being broadly discussed—not just at scholarly conferences or in the media, but in local communities and everyday social media domains like Instagram, Facebook, and Twitter.

While people discussed the longer-term and institutional changes needed to address structural racism, especially but not only in terms of policing, racist symbols became a focus of attention since they were highly visible and action often could be taken more quickly. Corporations began to change racially inflected brands like Aunt Jemima syrup and Uncle Ben's rice.[20] Sports teams with Native American names like the "Redskins" and "Indians" did the same. NASCAR banned the Confederate flag, while Mississippi dropped a Confederate battle symbol from its flag. Even Disneyland indicated it would remove "Song of the South" references from a ride.

Monuments became the most visible locus of change. If the battle to remove the Robert E. Lee statue in Charlottesville had been going on for years and continued to be litigated in court, monuments associated with systemic white supremacy were defaced, graffitied, and toppled by protesters or taken down by municipalities.[21] Confederate monuments to Lee, Jefferson Davis, Stonewall Jackson, and others fell across the South and other parts of the country. So too did markers of slavery and colonial conquest, including those commemorating Christopher Columbus. Figures like King Leopold II of Belgium were also targeted by protesters abroad. Protesters even tried to take down the Andrew Jackson memorial in Lafayette Square. Eventually, the antistatue movement turned to somewhat less obvious figures who expressed racist views, owned slaves, or otherwise were associated with white supremacy, including Thomas Jefferson, Theodore Roosevelt, and even George Washington.

～

All of these events formed the backdrop of Trump's Mount Rushmore Fourth of July address. He spoke as a president greatly weakened by a devastated economy and his lackluster response to the COVID-19 pandemic and the Black Lives Matter protests that followed George Floyd's murder. His approval ratings were falling to new lows.[22] And his reelection prospects, which had been promising at the start of the year when the economy was booming, now looked grim.

In response, Trump once again turned to white power themes that he sought to make more palatable by mixing in occasional references to Black leaders and the antislavery movement. His address, which centered on heritage and history and the demonization of others, had distinct echoes of Charlottesville. Trump was also returning to the long-standing "Southern Strategy" of using coded racist language while playing on white racial concerns and culture war issues. He spoke at length about American exceptionalism and Manifest Destiny. "No nation has done more to advance the human condition," Trump stated at the start of his address. "And no people have done more to promote human progress."[23]

Nevertheless, he warned, "As we meet here tonight, there is a growing danger that threatens every blessing our ancestors fought so hard for, struggled, [and] bled to secure." Far-left fascists—"bad, evil people"— were on a "merciless campaign to wipe out our history, defame our heroes, erase our values, and indoctrinate our children." Such remarks about the "left-wing cultural revolution" and destruction of the nation directly echoed white-power-extremist discourses about cultural Marxism and white genocide.

If, during the 2016 and 2018 elections, Trump had previously demonized foreigners and immigrant border threats, he was now turning this rhetoric inward with a racialized gaze that spotlighted people of color and their "radical left" white allies who had joined with them to protest systemic racism.[24] Some commentators noted that the domestic situation in the United States was volatile given Trump's increasingly divisive rhetoric, targeting of domestic minorities, white victimization narrative, and multiple ongoing crises (the pandemic, economic collapse, and domestic protests) that were increasing the risk threat across the globe.

Just prior to the Mount Rushmore address, a group of global leaders and activists issued "A Call to Defend Democracy," warning that authoritarian regimes and leaders worldwide were using the COVID-19 crisis to enhance their powers and erode democracy. Others warned that extremist groups, ranging from ISIS to white power extremists in the United States, were taking advantage of the pandemic to promote their causes. A number of human rights and prevention experts, in turn, cautioned that the United States was at heightened risk for atrocity crimes even as health experts warned that the pandemic could lead to "one of the most unstable times in the history of our country." Meanwhile, critics continued to worry about Trump's "fascist" tendencies and that he would refuse to leave office even if defeated—though others, echoing some of the authors in the *Can It Happen Here?* volume, argued that, if damaged, the democratic safeguards in the United States were still working.[25]

* * *

JULY 7, 2020, RUTGERS UNIVERSITY, NEWARK, NJ

It is in this context of widespread discussion of structural racism and heightened atrocity crimes risk that I receive two e-mails that will alter my teaching once more, catalyzing my decision to start my Fall 2020 undergraduate human rights class with a George Floyd Teach-In on structural racism. A last lesson from teaching in Trump's USA.

This Teach-In will echo the earlier ones. It will begin with the premise that Trump is a symptom, not an aberration. And it will be guided by a rule: try not to talk about Trump. Instead, the students will examine the underlying structural realities that Trump's dramatic presidency and personality masked. More broadly, this lesson continues to bring together anthropology, genocide studies, and critical race studies to explore the relationship of white power and genocide—while putting Adorno's "Education after Auschwitz" into conversation with *We Charge Genocide*.

The first e-mail, on July 7, is from historian Jonathan Holloway, the new president of Rutgers University, who announces that, due to the COVID-19 crisis, university teaching for the Fall 2020 semester will be largely online.[26] The second is Holloway's introductory e-mail message to the university community sent just the week before as he started his position. Holloway, the first African American president of Rutgers and an expert on race, had discussed the challenges posed by the pandemic before noting that "we are also living in a moment of global racial awakening," one that required "repair and rebuilding." Throughout the country, he went on, people were "calling for concrete commitments to address this nation's systemic inequities."

As Holloway's e-mails suggest, these calls impacted higher education more generally. On the one hand, there has been increasing demand for teaching about structural racism. If there has been enormous interest in books on race and racism, scholars and educators are also addressing such issues in courses, lectures, and even some teach-ins.[27] On the other hand, critics have also called for structural transformations within the halls of academia. These calls have been widespread and featured in the flagship *Chronicle of Higher Education*.

One visible manifestation of these changes has focused on symbols of structural racism, including buildings named after those implicated in systemic white supremacy. At Princeton University, Woodrow Wilson's name has been removed from the prestigious School of Public and International Affairs. Rutgers is likewise considering changing the names of several buildings as part of an ongoing project examining how the university's past is bound up with structural racism.[28]

But the calls for change extend far beyond name changes and include things like bias training, diversification, campus safety, promotion, financial aid, and power structures. As is the case with institutions and groups across the country, academic disciplines are also examining their own enmeshments with structural racism. This is true in my discipline of anthropology as sometimes heated debates have broken out over how, its long-standing antiracism scholarship and advocacy notwithstanding, the field is also implicated in the projects of colonialism and imperialism, historically predicated on conceptions of savagery and biological race, and continuing to struggle with bias within the discipline.[29]

Education, of course, has long been a key aspect of systemic white supremacy. Enforced illiteracy was a tool of enslavement. Indigenous children were forced to attend boarding schools. During Jim Crow, Black children were required to attend racially segregated schools. Even after the *Brown v. Board of Education* decision and civil rights movement, Blacks and other people of color continued to face educational hurdles such as discrimination, de facto educational segregation, and poorly funded and often inferior schools.[30]

Many of the Rutgers–Newark students who take my classes have faced these kinds of challenges, which the COVID-19 crisis and move to online learning only amplified. Indeed, part of the perniciousness of structural racism is the way it intertwines across multiple domains. Thus, beyond the already existing racial inequities in education, many students of color from Newark and the surrounding areas are now dealing with additional hurdles like finding Internet access for online education and living in homes that have been severely disrupted by the pandemic. A host of studies have demonstrated that communities of color have been disproportionately impacted by COVID-19, and Newark is no exception. Indeed, the health care sector is another key area of structural racism in the United States. For many Rutgers–Newark students of color, then, the already existing challenge of online classes is amplified by structural racism in education, wealth distribution, housing, and health care.[31] My George Floyd Teach-In must take such issues into account.

* * *

NOTES TOWARD A GEORGE FLOYD TEACH-IN ON STRUCTURAL RACISM AND "EDUCATION AFTER 1492"

All of these domains of structural racism, along with others, ranging from voter suppression to mass incarceration, were flagged in *We Charge Genocide*. Accordingly, I decide that it will serve as one of the key texts for my four-part Fall 2020 George Floyd Teach-In on structural racism. The three-hour undergraduate human rights class will start with basic background on Floyd's murder and subsequent calls for police reform and then address structural racism more generally. After discussing the social construction of race, we will turn to a discussion of the concept of structural racism.[32] The students will be tasked with coming up with their own definitions of structural racism as together we work toward something along the lines of "an interwoven set of ideas, practices, and institutions underpinning racial inequality and, in its more extreme forms like systemic white supremacy, racial domination."

With this definition in hand, the students will be first tasked with explaining how structural racism operates in terms of law enforcement, with each student selecting a related example of an idea (for example, assumptions about Black criminality like the long-standing "Black brute" caricature),[33] practice (such as racial profiling, stop-and-frisk, and a disproportionate readiness to use lethal force against people of color, ranging from shootings to the chokehold that killed George Floyd), and institution (like mass incarceration) that undergirds this domain.

After a discussion of the legibility of structural racism (the ways it is more or less seen and taken for granted), the students will be asked to create a list of other ideas, practices, and institutions undergirding structural racism that became more visible during the Floyd protests—as well as those that remain invisible, like the use of racially inflected language in everyday conversation.[34] This open-ended discussion will likely range far and wide and touch upon issues like redlining, disparities in wealth and economic opportunity, and racial stereotypes.

During our discussion, we will refer back to the categories of structural racism identified in *We Charge Genocide* as the students consider the extent to which things in the United States have changed over the last seventy years since the petition was published. I plan for the class to also discuss the recent debates over symbols, ranging from the names of sports teams to the monuments that were dismantled or removed.

The monuments will serve as a transition to the third part of the George Floyd Teach-In, focusing on an examination of structural racism in its systemic white-supremacy-domination form. It is only then that we will start to speak about Trump as the students put Trump's Mount Rushmore address into conversation with Frederick Douglass's 1852 "The Meaning of July Fourth for the Negro" speech, which was being widely discussed as Trump gave his remarks and also echoes the remarks made by Native American protesters.[35]

In the pre-Civil War backdrop of enslavement, Douglass asked, "What, to the American slave, is your 4th of July? I answer; a day that reveals to him, more than all other days in the year, the gross injustice and cruelty to which he is the constant victim. To him, your celebration is a sham . . . your national greatness, swelling vanity." In a statement reminiscent of *We Charge Genocide*, Douglass's speech argues that the Fourth of July is "a thin veil to cover up crimes which would disgrace a nation of savages. There is not a nation on the earth guilty of practices more shocking and bloody than are the people of the United States, at this very hour." The juxtaposition of this speech with the "heritage and history" and American exceptionalism themes of Trump's address will open up a larger discussion of the legibility of systemic white supremacy past and present.

To conclude the George Floyd Teach-In, the students will situate structural racism in relationship to the structure-agency debate and critical pedagogy. After discussing Trump as symptom as opposed to being exceptional, the students will reconsider Adorno's "Education after Auschwitz" in light of systemic white supremacy. As noted in the introduction, the Frankfurt School was directly focused on the emancipatory potential of critical self-awareness, which was necessary for understanding structure and power. If Adorno framed his essay in terms of the horrors of Auschwitz, his arguments are easily recast in terms of, as Douglass put it, the "shocking and bloody" history of systemic white supremacy in the United States. In this sense, we might talk about the need for "Education after Jamestown" in the United States or, in the context of global history and colonialism, "Education after 1492," the year Christopher Columbus reached the Americas.

Just as there is a huge Holocaust education effort in the United States, so too might there be one to address and make more legible the genocide and atrocity crimes committed against Black and Brown people in the United States—beginning with Jamestown's settler colonialism, destruction of Indigenous communities, and enslavement. The George Floyd protests appear to have opened the door further to this sort of more robust reckoning with the devastating violence that resulted from systemic white supremacy.

In this sense, Trump's presidency was a dramatic but brief episode in a long history of white power and structural racism. Nevertheless, there are key lessons that may be gleaned from his presidency, ones condensed in this book's "it can happen here" theme. As we have seen, genocide and atrocity crimes have taken place throughout US history, and they can happen again. Meanwhile, the violence of the past reverberates into the present in the form of structural racism and systemic white-supremacy domination.

And, as *We Charge Genocide* contends, the current situation of Blacks—as well as Native Americans—could arguably be considered an ongoing genocide, particularly if one takes a long-duration perspective. Many scholars of genocide and atrocity crimes would disagree with this claim. But I would counter that it is at least an in-depth conversation the field must have and that the field needs to be critically rethought in light of systemic white supremacy and the Holocaust prototype assumptions that inform much of its research.[36]

Only through these sorts of reckonings with the past and acknowledgment of systemic white supremacy in the present is repair possible. This point returns us to Morrison's "bird-in-the-hand" parable, with its emphasis on open-ended dialogue and moral imagination. Her Nobel Prize address is directly concerned with how dialogue and critical awareness may counter the totalizing and obfuscating "policing languages of mastery."

As discussed earlier, repair can take many forms. Sometimes it centers on breaking the silences imposed by such languages and the systems of domination in which they are enmeshed, including systemic white supremacy. The truth-seeking aspirations of transitional justice provide one example of how such initiatives are undertaken in an attempt to explain what happened and why during violent and repressive moments of history—like the atrocities committed in the United States against Indigenous peoples, the enslaved, and other communities of color. While truth commissions and trials do this in different ways, truth seeking may also take place through reparative and educational efforts.

And indeed, in the aftermath of the George Floyd killing and structural racism protests, there have been renewed calls for reparations.[37] Ideally, the United States might undertake a suite of such initiatives, such as a truth commission that includes symbolic reparations and recommendations for financial ones like monetary payments or scholarship programs. As noted earlier, the Canadian Truth and Reconciliation Commission provides an example of how this can be done.

If such a transitional justice initiative in the United States will take time, more immediate action can take place on the level of education, another key dimension of transitional justice. Adorno and the Frankfurt School focused on education for precisely this reason since larger structural change is usually difficult and slow. My experience of teaching during Trump's presidency models some possibilities, ranging from holding teach-ins in response to related current events to more broadly extending pedagogy from an "Education after Auschwitz" orientation to one that also focuses on systemic white supremacy.

The recognition that "it can happen here" is premised on comprehending that "it has happened here." Only then can we begin to find paths to diminish the recurrence of genocide and atrocity crimes. An important first step is to understand and acknowledge the persistence of structural racism in the United States and the history of white supremacy from which it arises. Trump was a dramatic symptom of this largely masked and pernicious system.

For me, this is a key last lesson learned from Trump's presidency, one that lays the ground for the moral imagination to grapple with systemic white supremacy in new ways. A crucial place to begin is with critical pedagogies. One of the signs held by a Native American protester at Trump's Mount Rushmore rally suggests a starting point. It read, "The Most Dangerous Immigrants Arrived in 1492."

After the Nazis, Adorno called for "Education after Auschwitz." We now need "Education after Jamestown" and "Education after 1492." Such a reorientation would facilitate fresh forms of thinking and acts of moral imagination, ones that envision new paths forward that fully recognize it has happened here before and can happen again.

ACKNOWLEDGMENTS

It would be impossible to thank all of the people who have supported this project. During the writing process, my family has provided help in many different ways, including talking about the ideas as they formed and reading over drafts. My thanks and love go to my family and my wife, who read over the entire manuscript just before it went to press. Thanks also go to my father and late mother, for their support. I'd like to acknowledge my brothers and their families, as well as my in-laws.

I'd also like to recognize my colleagues at the Rutgers Center for the Study of Genocide and Human Rights (CGHR), Nela Navarro and Stephen Eric Bronner. Nela and Steve, as well as Tom LaPointe, have been great colleagues for many years and helped create a vibrant intellectual atmosphere in which to consider issues related to the concerns of this book. Most recently, the Center has launched a Global Consortium on Bigotry and Hate with partners around the world. I'm grateful for the conversations and opportunity to discuss and present on issues discussed in this book, particularly at the Consortium workshop at the Norwegian Center for Holocaust and Minority Studies.

I have also had the opportunity to give talks on white genocide and related issues at various conferences and would like to acknowledge the feedback I received. Of particular note was the "Second Annual Natalie Mayer Holocaust and Genocide Studies Lecture" I gave at Pacific Lutheran University where I first pulled together the argument of this book. In particular, I'd like to thank Prof. Kirsten Christensen and the sponsor, Natalie Mayer, for their hospitality, feedback, and support. Two other talks were also quite valuable in this regard, presentations I gave at Boston University and the New School for Analytical Psychology (NSAP) in Seattle. My thanks go to Timothy Longman, Lane Gerber, and the members of NSAP for providing me with the opportunity to speak about this project.

I would also like to thank my many other colleagues and students at Rutgers, including the Department of Sociology and Anthropology and Division of Global Affairs. Various offices at Rutgers, including the Office of the Chancellor, Faculty of Arts and Sciences, RU Global, and Research Council, also provided sabbatical time, grants, or other forms of support to facilitate this research—as did a grant from the New Jersey Center for Gun Violence Research that helped me complete the manuscript. The ideas expressed in this book are, of course, my own and do not necessarily reflect the views of these institutions. My thanks also go to my department chair, Chris Duncan, and administrator, Dawn Wilson. I greatly appreciate their assistance during this project.

Once written, a book needs to find a publishing home. In this regard, I very much appreciate all that my editor, Jennifer Hammer, has done to support the publication of this book. Indeed, she is one of the most efficient and supportive editors with whom I have had the pleasure of working. A number of anonymous reviewers provided important feedback and suggestions, which are much appreciated and greatly strengthened the manuscript. Different staff members at NYU Press have also provided critical assistance, including Ellen Chodosh, Laura Ewen, Mary Beth Jarrad, Veronica Knutson, Alexia Traganas, adam b. bohannon, Emily Wright, and other members of the editorial, production, and marketing teams.

I would also like to thank Dirk Moses, Victoria Sanford, and Cathy Schlund-Vials for their comments on the manuscript. There are many other people who have contributed to this project in one way or another, including Fredrik Barth, Paul Boxer, Youk Chhang, Daniel Feierstein, Louis Harrison, Jim Lance, Charles Nuckolls, Robert Paul,

Robert Ruffini, Bradd Shore, Mark Urken, Andrew Woolford, Richard Wilson, and Carol Worthman. I also want to thank the staff at the coffee shops where I wrote parts of this book, including Cafe Grumpy, Paper Plane, and, especially, Raymonds and Local Coffee. There are no doubt many other deserving people I have left off this brief list of acknowledgments, and my thanks go to them as well.

NOTES

PREFACE

1 Alex Hinton, "Trump's Helter Skelter," Project Syndicate, October 9, 2020, https://www.project-syndicate.org, accessed October 10, 2020. Examples of others warning of violence included Rosa Brooks, "What's the Worst That Could Happen?," *Washington Post*, September 3, 2020, www.washingtonpost.com, accessed October 8, 2020; James Waller, "'I Didn't Know If I Was Going to Be Seen Again': The Escalating Risk of Mass Violence in the United States," Stanley Center for Peace and Security, October 8, 2020; "The U.S. Presidential Election; Managing the Risks of Violence," International Crisis Group, October 28, 2020, www.crisisgroup.org, accessed November 8, 2020; Simon Adams, "It Could Happen Here: The US Election and the Threat of Violence," Global Centre for the Responsibility to Protect, October 30, 2020, https://www.globalr2p.org, accessed November 1, 2020.

INTRODUCTION. THE SNAKE

1 Brooke Bobb, "Hillary Clinton's Plane vs. Donald Trump's Plane: The Other Debate," *Vogue*, September 26, 2016, www.vogue.com.

2 The details and quotations from this rally are based on "Presidential Candidate Donald Trump Rally in Vienna, Ohio," C-Span, March 14, 2016, www.cspan.org.

3 Alexander Laban Hinton, *Why Did They Kill? Cambodia in the Shadow of Genocide* (Berkeley: University of California Press, 2005).

4 "Will Fascism Come to America? (A Symposium)," *Modern Monthly* 8, no. 8 (1934): 453–78.

5 Michael Meyer, "Introduction," *It Can't Happen Here* by Sinclair Lewis (New York: Signet, 2014), v–xv; Jason Daley, "The Screenwriting Mystic Who Wanted to Be the American Führer," *Smithsonian Magazine*, October 3, 2018, www.smithsonian-mag.com. See also A. James Rudin, "The Dark Legacy of Henry Ford's Anti-Semitism," *Washington Post*, October 10, 2014, www.washingtonpost.com.

6 See, for example, Annika Neklason, "When Demagogic Populism Swings Left," *Atlantic*, March 3, 2019, www.theatlantic.com.

7 Sinclair Lewis, *It Can't Happen Here* (New York: Signet, 2014).

8 Lewis, *It Can't Happen Here*, 17.

9 Aimé Césaire, *Discourse on Colonization* (New York: Monthly Review, 1972); Zygmunt Bauman, *Modernity and the Holocaust* (Cambridge: Polity, 1989). The

phrase "citadel of Western civilization" is from Theodor Adorno, Else Frenkel-Brunswik, Daniel J. Levinson, and R. Nevitt Sanford, *The Authoritarian Personality* (New York: Norton, 1950), v.

10 Samuel H. Flowerman, "Portrait of the Authoritarian Man," *New York Times*, April 23, 1950, 28–31, www.nytimes.com.

11 Adorno et al., *The Authoritarian Personality*, vii.

12 Adorno et al., *The Authoritarian Personality*, 973.

13 Samuel H. Flowerman, "Mass Propaganda in the War against Bigotry," *Journal of Abnormal and Social Psychology* 42, no. 2 (1947): 429–39.

14 Andrew Joyce, "'Modify the Standards of the In-Group': On Jews and Mass Communications," *Occidental Observer*, January 14, 2020, www.theoccidentalob-server.net.

15 Andrew Marantz, *Antisocial: Online Extremists, Techno-Utopians, and the Hijacking of the American Conversation* (New York: Viking, 2019); "The Overton Window," MacKinac Center for Public Policy, www.mackinac.org, accessed October 31, 2020; Maggie Astor, "How the Politically Unthinkable Can Become Mainstream," *New York Times*, February 26, 2019, www.nytimes.com.

16 Max Horkheimer and Theodor W. Adorno, *Dialectic of Enlightenment* (Stanford, CA: Stanford University Press, 2007). See also Stephen Eric Bronner, *Reclaiming the Enlightenment: Toward a Politics of Radical Engagement* (New York: Columbia University Press, 2004).

17 Adorno et al., *The Authoritarian Personality*, 747, 749, 976. Peter E. Gordon, "The Authoritarian Personality Revisited: Reading Adorno in the Age of Trump," *Boundary 2* 44, no. 2 (2017): 31–56. For a discussion of how such ideas relate to genocide more broadly, see A. Dirk Moses, "Genocide and Modernity," in *The Historiography of Genocide*, ed. Dan Stone (New York: Routledge 2008), 156–93.

18 Theodor W. Adorno, *Critical Models: Interventions and Catchwords* (New York: Columbia University Press, 1998), 191.

19 Adorno, *Critical Models*, 195.

20 John Levi Martin, "*The Authoritarian Personality*, 50 Years Later: What Lessons Are There for Political Psychology?" *Political Psychology* 22, no 1. (2001): 1–26; Gordon, "The Authoritarian Personality Revisited."

21 See Christopher Vials, *Haunted by Hitler: Liberals, the Left, and the Fight against Fascism in the United States* (Amherst: University of Massachusetts Press, 2014); Bill V. Mullen and Christopher Vials, eds., *The U.S. Anti-Fascism Reader* (New York: Verso, 2020).

22 Gordon, "The Authoritarian Personality Revisited"; Vials, *Haunted by Hitler*.

23 Jane Velencia, "This Donald Trump Rally Looks like a Scene from Nazi Germany," *HuffPost*, March 5, 2016, www.huffpost.com; Sam Sanders, "#MemeOfTheWeek: Comparing Trump to Hitler," NPR, March 11, 2016, www.npr.org. See also Peter W. Stevenson, "The Hitler-ification of Donald Trump," *Washington Post*, March 7, 2016, www.washingtonpost.com. On the *Time Magazine* cover featuring Trump,

see Donald Von Drehle, "Donald Trump's Wild Ride," *Time Magazine*, March 3, 2016, www.time.com.

24 David A. Fahrenthold, "Trump Recorded Having Extremely Lewd Conversation about Women in 2015," *Washington Post*, October 8, 2016, www.washingtonpost.com; Clark Mindock, "Trump's Sexual Assault Allegations: The Full List of Women Who Have Accused the President," *Independent*, December 2, 2019, www.independent.co.uk.

25 Michael Barbaro and Megan Twohey, "Shamed and Angry: Alicia Machado, a Miss Universe Mocked by Donald Trump," *New York Times*, September 27, 2016, www.nytimes.com; Asawin Suebsaeng, "Miss Universe Alicia Machado: Donald Trump a 'Nazi Rat,'" *Daily Beast*, April 13, 2017, www.dailybeast.com; Cristina Maza, "Trump Tried to Have Sex with Teenage Beauty Queen Alicia Machado While He Fat-Shamed Her, Former Miss Universe Claims," *Newsweek*, April 9, 2018, www.newsweek.com.

26 Jacey Fortin, "Dress like a Woman? What Does That Mean?" *New York Times*, February 3, 2017, www.nytimes.com.

27 Alexandra Minna Stern, *Proud Boys and the White Ethnostate: How the Alt-Right Is Warping the American Imagination* (Boston: Beacon, 2019).

28 Kathleen Belew, *Bring the War Home: The White Power Movement and Paramilitary America* (Cambridge, MA: Harvard University Press, 2018); Kathleen M. Blee, *Inside Organized Racism: Women in the Hate Movement* (Berkeley: University of California Press, 2003).

29 See, for example, Sarah Posner and David Neiwert, "How Trump Took Hate Groups Mainstream," *Mother Jones*, October 14, 2016, www.motherjones.com; David Leonhardt and Ian Prasad Philbrick, "Donald Trump's Racism: The Definitive List," *New York Times*, January 15, 2018, www.nytimes.com.

30 Alex Hinton, "Trump's Helter Skelter," Project Syndicate, October 9, 2020.

31 Beverly Gage, "Reading the Classic Novel That Predicted Trump," *New York Times*, January 17, 2017, www.nytimes.com; Samuel Clowes Huneke, "An End to Totalitarianism," *Boston Review*, April 16, 2020, bostonreview.net.

CHAPTER 1. CHARLOTTESVILLE TEACH-IN

1 Staff, "Neo-Nazis and White Supremacists Cheer Trump's Most Recent Remarks," Agence France-Press, August 16, 2017, www.afp.com; Glenn Thrush and Maggie Haberman, "Trump Gives White Supremacists an Unequivocal Boost," *New York Times*, August 15, 2017, www.nytimes.com. For a version of the AAA letter and additional information, see the American Anthropological Association's "Understanding Race after Charlottesville" web page, www.americananthro.org.

2 See Mullen and Vials, *The U.S. Anti-Fascism Reader*.

3 The term "gaslighting" was popularized by a 1944 Ingrid Bergman film, *Gaslight*, which centers on a husband's psychological manipulation of his wife in order to make her doubt reality. The term now also refers to political attempts to

manipulate voters by altering their perception of and creating doubt about the reality of events and has been used with specific reference to Trump's mistruths, lies, distortions, and invocations of "fake news." See, for example, Amanda Carpenter, *Gaslighting America: Why We Love It When Trump Lies to Us* (New York: Broadside Books, 2018); Stephanie Sarkis, "Donald Trump Is a Classic Gaslighter in an Abusive Relationship with America," *USA Today*, October 3, 2018, www.usatoday.com.

4 Gregory Krieg, "14 of Trump's Most Outrageous 'Birther' Claims—Half from after 2011," CNN, September 16, 2016, www.cnn.com.

5 Ta-Nehisi Coates, "The First White President," *Atlantic*, October 2017, www.theatlantic.com.

6 Rebecca Sinderbrand, "How Kellyanne Conway Ushered in the Year of 'Alternative Facts,'" *Washington Post*, January 22, 2017, www.washingtonpost.com.

7 Travis M. Andrews, "Sales of Orwell's '1984' Spike after Kellyanne Conway's 'Alternative Facts,'" *Washington Post*, January 25, 2017, www.washingtonpost.com.

8 Hannah Arendt, "Truth and Politics," *New Yorker*, February 25, 1967, 78, www.newyorker.com; Zoe Williams, "Totalitarianism in the Age of Trump: Lessons from Hannah Arendt," *Guardian*, February 1, 2017, www.theguardian.com.

9 Brian Stelter, "Trump Averages a 'Fake' Insult Every Day. Really. We Counted," CNN, January 17, 2018, www.cnn.com.

10 Mike Wendling, "The (Almost) Complete History of 'Fake News,'" BBC, January 22, 2018, www.bbc.com.

11 Michael M. Grynbaum, "Trump Calls the News Media the 'Enemy of the American People,'" *New York Times*, February 17, 2017, www.nytimes.com.

12 Amber Phillips, "'Our Democracy Will Not Last': Jeff Flake's Speech Comparing Trump to Stalin, Annotated," *New York Times*, January 17, 2018, www.nytimes.com.

13 Philip Bump, "Half of Republicans Say the News Media Should Be Described as the Enemy of the American People," *Washington Post*, April 26, 2018, www.washingtonpost.com.

14 Glenn Kessler, Michelle Ye Hee Lee, and Meg Kelly, "President Trump's List of False and Misleading Claims Tops 1,000," *Washington Post*, August 22, 2017, www.washingtonpost.com; Glenn Kessler, Salvador Rizzo, and Meg Kelly, "President Trump Has Made More Than 20,000 False or Misleading Claims," *Washington Post*, July 13, 2020, www.washingtonpost.com.

15 Alison Flood, "'Post-Truth' Named Word of the Year by Oxford Dictionaries," *Guardian*, November 15, 2016, www.theguardian.com.

16 "About Chancellor Cantor," Rutgers University, www.newark.rutgers.edu, accessed October 31, 2020.

17 See, for example, Amy Harmon, "How Much Racism Do You Face Every Day?" *New York Times*, January 20, 2020, www.nytimes.com.

18 See, for example, Wendy Brown, ed., "Feminist Theory and the Frankfurt School," *Differences* 17, no. 1 (2006), www.dukejournals.edu; Judith Butler,

Gender Trouble: Feminism and the Subversion of Identity (New York: Routledge, 2006); Césaire, *Discourse on Colonization*; Achille Mbembe, *Critique of Black Reason* (Durham, NC: Duke University Press, 2017); Edward Said, *Orientalism* (New York: Vintage, 1989). For a consideration of critical theory in relationship to Trump, see Gordon, "The Authoritarian Personality Revisited" and Bernard E. Harcourt, "Counter-Critical Theory: An Intervention in Contemporary Critical Thought and Practice," *Critical Times* 1, no. 1 (2018): 5–22.

19 Paolo Friere, *Pedagogy of the Oppressed* (New York: Bloomsbury, 2018); Henry A. Giroux, *On Critical Pedagogy* (New York: Bloomsbury, 2020); bell hooks, *Teaching to Transgress: Education as the Practice of Freedom* (New York: Routledge, 1994); Gayatri Chakravorty Spivak, *Outside in the Teaching Machine* (New York: Routledge, 2008).

20 Josh Harkinson, "Meet the White Nationalist Trying to Ride the Trump Train to Lasting Power," *Mother Jones*, October 27, 2016, www.motherjones.com.

21 See also "analysis," *Oxford English Dictionary*, www.oed.com, accessed October 31, 2020.

22 "Marshall Sahlins Part I," *Resistance and Revolution: The Anti-Vietnam War Movement at the University of Michigan, 1965–1972*, accessed September 9, 2020, www.umich.edu.

23 "Understanding Race after Charlottesville," American Anthropological Association, accessed August 31, 2017, www.americananthro.org.

24 What follows is based on "Charlottesville: Race and Terror," *VICE News Tonight*, August 14, 2017, www.vice.com.

25 Monica Davey and Julie Bosman, "Protests Flare after Ferguson Police Officer Is Not Indicted," *New York Times*, November 24, 2014, www.nytimes.com.

26 "Christopher Cantwell," Southern Poverty Law Center, www.splcenter.org, accessed October 31, 2020.

27 Joe Heim, "Recounting a Day of Rage, Hate, Violence, and Death," *Washington Post*, August 14, 2017, www.washingtonpost.com.

28 Kevin Drum, "Donald Trump's Race-Baiting Presidency: A Listicle," *Mother Jones*, June 3, 2019, www.motherjones.com.

29 Jamelle Bouie, "Why Richard Spencer Matters," *Slate*, May 22, 2017, slate.com; Eileen Johnson, "Moments of Rupture: Confederate Monuments and a Southern Town's Search for Its Identity," *Politic*, April 12, 2017, thepolitic.org; American Historical Association, "Statement on Confederate Monuments," August 28, 2018, www.historians.org. See also Ian Shapira, "Inside Jason Kessler's Hate-Fueled Rise," *Washington Post*, August 11, 2018, www.washingtonpost.com.

30 Farah Stockman, "Who Were the Counterprotestors in Charlottesville?" *New York Times*, August 14, 2017, www.nytimes.com.

31 George T. Shaw, ed., *A Fair Hearing: The Alt-Right in the Words of Its Members and Leaders* (Budapest: Arktos, 2018); George Hawley, *Making Sense of the*

Alt-Right (New York: Columbia University Press, 2019); Graeme Wood, "His Kampf," *Atlantic*, June 2017, www.theatlantic.com.

32 "Flags and Other Symbols Used by Far-Right Groups in Charlottesville," Southern Poverty Law Center, August 12, 2017, www.splcenter.org.

33 "Flags and Other Symbols"; "Origins of Neo-Nazi and White Supremacist Terms and Symbols," United States Holocaust Memorial Museum, www.ushmm.org, accessed October 31, 2020.

34 Azzmador (with Andrew Anglin), "Charlottesville: Why You Must Attend and What to Bring and Not to Bring!" *Daily Stormer*, August 8, 2018, daillystormer.su.

35 "RACE: Are We So Different?," American Anthropological Association; "Statement on Race," American Anthropological Association, May 17, 1998, www.americananthro.org.

36 "Statement on Race."

37 On anthropology, race, and white supremacy, see Lee D. Baker, *From Savage to Negro: Anthropology and the Construction of Race, 1896–1954* (Berkeley: University of California Press, 1998); Aisha M. Beliso-DeJesús and Jemima Pierre, "Introduction: Toward an Anthropology of White Supremacy," *American Anthropologist*, December 31, 2019, www.americananthropologist.org; see also the various essays in the related special issue of *American Anthropologist* on "The Anthropology of White Supremacy." Recent ethnographies of European white power and neofascism include Nitzan Shoshan, *The Management of Hate: Nation, Affect, and the Governance of Right-Wing Extremism in Germany* (Princeton, NJ: Princeton University Press, 2016); Benjamin R. Teitelbaum, *Lions of the North: Sounds of the New Nordic Radical Nationalism* (New York: Oxford University Press, 2017); Douglas R. Holmes, *Integral Europe: Fast-Capitalism, Multiculturalism, Neofascism* (Princeton, NJ: Princeton University Press, 2010).

38 For examples of these caricatures, see the Jim Crow Museum of Racist Memorabilia (www.ferris.edu).

39 Sarah Mervosh and Niraj Chokshi, "Reagan Called Africans 'Monkeys' in Call with Nixon, Tape Reveals," *New York Times*, July 31, 2019, www.nytimes.com.

40 Ian Haney López, *Dog Whistle Politics: How Coded Racial Appeals Have Reinvented Racism and Wrecked the Middle Class* (New York: Oxford University Press, 2015).

41 Julia Jacobs, "DeSantis Warns Florida Not to 'Monkey This Up,' and Many Hear a Racist Dog Whistle," *New York Times*, August 29, 2018, www.nytimes.com; Eugene Scott, "2018: The Year of Dog Whistle Politics," *Washington Post*, November 14, 2018, www.washingtonpost.com.

42 Johnson, "Moments of Rupture"; see also American Historical Association, "Statement on Confederate Monuments."

43 Alexander Burns, "Joe Biden's Campaign Announcement Video, Annotated." *New York Times*, April 25, 2019, www.nytimes.com.

44 Colby Itkowitz, "Trump Defends Charlottesville Comments by Praising a Confederate General," *Washington Post*, April 26, 2019, www.washingtonpost.com.

45 Steve Cortes, "Trump Didn't Call Neo-Nazis 'Fine People': Here's Proof," *RealClear Politics*, March 21, 2019, www.realclearpolitics.com; Joel B. Pollak, "Blue State Blues: 'Facts First' CNN Must Retract Charlottesville Hoax," *Breitbart*, March 15, 2019, www.breitbart.com.

46 Greg Wilford, "Heather Heyer: Charlottesville Neo-Nazi Rally Organizer Describes Protester's Death as 'Payback,'" *Independent*, August 20, 2017, www.independent.co.uk.

CHAPTER 2. THE HATER

1 Josh Dawsey, "Trump Derides Protections for Immigrants from 'Shithole' Countries," *Washington Post*, January 12, 2019, www.washingtonpost.com.

2 Ibram X. Kendi, "The Day 'Shithole' Entered the Presidential Lexicon," *Atlantic*, January 13, 2019, www.theatlantic.com.

3 "White Supremacists Praise Trump's Inflammatory Immigration Remarks," Anti-Defamation League, January 12, 2018, www.adl.org.

4 What follows is based on Richard Fausset, "A Voice of Hate in America's Heartland," *New York Times*, November 25, 2017, www.nytimes.com; Richard Fausset, "I Interviewed a White Nationalist and Fascist: What Was I Left With?" *New York Times*, November 25, 2017, www.nytimes.com.

5 Marc Lacey, "Readers Accuse Us of Normalizing a Nazi Sympathizer: We Respond," *New York Times*, November 26, 2017, www.nytimes.com.

6 On "Rosebud" as a metaphor for a question in need of a missing answer or explanation, see Peter Bradshaw, "Citizen Kane and the Meaning of Rosebud," *Guardian*, April 25, 2015, www.theguardian.com. *Citizen Kane* is also a favorite of Trump, who has offered his own interpretations of what "Rosebud" signifies; see David Canfield, "Donald Trump Once Did a Surprisingly Introspective Interview with Errol Morris about Citizen Kane," *Slate*, October 25, 2016, slate.com.

7 Howard Fineman, *The Thirteen American Arguments: Enduring Debates That Define and Inspire Our Country* (New York: Random House, 2009).

8 Kay Whitlock and Michael Bronski, *Considering Hate: Violence, Goodness, and Justice in American Culture and Politics* (Boston: Beacon Press, 2015); see also Jack Levin, *The Violence of Hate: Understanding Harmful Forms of Bias and Bigotry* (New York: Rowman & Littlefield, 2016).

9 See, for example, Belew, *Bring the War Home*.

10 On the difficulties of using the term "extremism," see J. M. Berger, *Extremism* (Cambridge: MIT Press, 2018); Shoshan, *The Management of Hate*; Robert Futrell, Pete Simi, and Anna A. Tan, "Political Extremism and Social Movements," in *Wiley-Blackwell Companion to Social Movements*, ed. David A. Snow, Sarah A. Soule, Hanspeter Kriesi, and Holly McCammon (London: Wiley-Blackwell, 2019),

618–34. On the use of "white supremacist," see Vann R. Newkirk II, "The Language of White Supremacy," *Atlantic*, October 6, 2017, www.theatlantic.com.

11 "Christopher Cantwell," Southern Poverty Law Center.

12 Yoni Appelbaum, "The Banality of White Nationalism," *Atlantic*, November 26, 2017, www.theatlantic.com.

13 Mallory Simon and Sara Sidner, "Inside the GM Plant Where Nooses and 'Whites-Only' Signs Hung," CNN, January 17, 2019, www.cnn.com; Mallory Simon and Sara Sidner, "Black Workers Describe Details of 'Living Hell' at UPS Center in Ohio," CNN, March 15, 2019, www.cnn.com; "Hate Map—Ohio," Southern Poverty Law Center, www.splcenter.org, accessed October 31, 2020. On socioeconomic distress in Ohio, see also J. D. Vance, *Hillbilly Elegy: A Memoir of a Family and Culture in Crisis* (New York: Harper, 2016); Vegas Tenold, *Everything You Love Will Burn: Inside the Rebirth of White Nationalism in America* (New York: Nation Books, 2018).

14 "In 2019, 31 Hate Groups Were Tracked in Ohio," Southern Poverty Law Center, www.splcenter.org, accessed October 31, 2020.

15 See, for example, "Extremists React to Trayvon Martin Controversy," Southern Poverty Law Center, August 25, 2012, www.splcenter.org.

16 Adorno et al., *The Authoritarian Personality*; G. M. Gilbert, "Hermann Goering, Amiable Psychopath," *Journal of Abnormal and Social Psychology* 43 (1948): 211–29.

17 Hannah Arendt, *Eichmann in Jerusalem: A Report on the Banality of Evil* (New York: Penguin, 2006); Stanley Milgram, *Obedience to Authority: An Experimental View* (New York: Harper & Row, 1974); Philip Zimbardo, *The Lucifer Effect: Understanding How Good People Turn Evil* (New York: Random House, 2008).

18 Christopher R. Browning, *Ordinary Men: Reserve Police Battalion 101 and the Final Solution in Poland* (New York: HarperCollins, 1992); Wendy Lower, *Hitler's Furies: German Women in the Nazi Killing Fields* (New York: Houghton Mifflin Harcourt, 2013).

19 Ian Kershaw, *The Nazi Dictatorship: Problems and Perspectives of Interpretation* (London: Arnold, 2000).

20 Doris L. Bergen, *War and Genocide: A Concise History of the Holocaust* (Lanham, MD: Rowman & Littlefield, 2016), 45.

21 Bergen, *War and Genocide*, 45.

22 Brandy X. Lee, *The Dangerous Case of Donald Trump: 27 Psychiatrists and Mental Health Experts Assess a President* (New York: Thomas Dunne, 2017); Peter Baker and Maggie Haberman, "Trump, Defending His Mental Fitness, Says He's a 'Very Stable Genius,'" *New York Times*, January 6, 2018, www.nytimes.com.

23 The biographical details that follow are from Gina Chon and Sambath Teth, *Behind the Killing Fields: A Khmer Rouge Leader and One of His Victims* (Philadelphia: University of Pennsylvania Press, 2010), 18 ff. See also Nuon Chea's ECCC testimony and Thet Sambath and Rob Lemkin, *Enemies of the People*, Old Street

Films, 2009 (www.enemiesofthepeoplemovie.com). Parts of this text on Nuon Chea are adapted from Alexander Laban Hinton, "What Makes a Man Start Fires?" in *Pre-Genocide: Warnings and Readiness to Protect*, ed. Anders Jerichow and Cecilie Felicia Stockholm Banke (Copenhagen: Humanity in Action, 2018), 83–93.

24 Chon and Teth, *Behind the Killing Fields*, 20.

25 This paragraph on Pol Pot is based on David P. Chandler, *Brother Number One: A Political Biography of Pol Pot* (Boulder, CO: Westview Press, 1999); see also Thet and Chon, *Behind the Killing Fields*.

26 Thet and Chon, *Behind the Killing Fields*, 30.

27 This paragraph is based on Thet and Chon, *Behind the Killing Fields*, 61; Pol Pot, *Long Live the Nineteenth Anniversary of the Communist Party of Kampuchea: Speech by Pol Pot, Secretary of the Central Committee of the Kampuchean Communist Party Delivered on September 29, 1977* (Phnom Penh: Democratic Kampuchea Ministry of Foreign Affairs, 1977).

28 Chandler, *Brother Number One*; Pol Pot, *Long Live*; Thet and Chon, *Behind the Killing Fields*.

29 Pol Pot, *Long Live*, 28.

30 Pol Pot, *Long Live*, 33.

31 Pol Pot, *Long Live*, 38.

32 Chandler, *Brother Number One*.

33 Pol Pot, *Long Live*, 57–58.

34 Kara Critchell, Susanne C. Knittel, Emiliano Perra, and Ugur Ümit Üngör, "Editor's Introduction," *Journal of Perpetrator Research* 1, no. 1 (2017): 1–27; Kai Ambos, "Criminologically Explained Reality of Genocide, Structure of the Offense and the 'Intent to Destroy' Requirement," in *Collective Violence and International Criminal Justice: An Interdisciplinary Approach*, ed. Alette Smeulers (Antwerp: Intersentia, 2010), 153–73; Timothy Williams and Dominik Pfeiffer, "Unpacking the Mind of Evil: A Sociological Perspective on the Role of Intent and Motivations in Genocide," *Genocide Studies and Prevention* 2, no. 1 (2017): 72–87.

35 Kathleen M. Blee, "Ethnographies of the Far Right," *Journal of Contemporary Ethnography* 36, no. 2 (2007): 119–28. On some of the ethical issues involved in such research, see Benjamin R. Teitelbaum, "Collaborating with the Radical Right: Scholar Informant Solidarity and the Case for an Immoral Anthropology," *Current Anthropology* 60, no. 3 (2019): 414–35.

36 Jo Becker, "How Nationalism Found a Home in Sweden," *New York Times*, August 11, 2019, www.nytimes.com; Teitelbaum, *Lions of the North*.

37 "Interview: Andreas Johansson (Nordic Resistance Movement)," *Herrenblut*, October 24, 2018, www.herrenblut.com; "Nordic Frontier #51: Tony Hovater—A Voice of Hatred," Nordic Frontier, January 30, 2018, www.spreaker.com.

38 Nick Sorasaniti, "Donald Trump Releases Plan to Combat Illegal Immigration," *New York Times*, August 16, 2015, www.nytimes.com.

CHAPTER 3. WHITE GENOCIDE

1　See "Defend DC from White Supremacy: #AllOutDCWeekend of Events," It's Going Down, itsgoingdown.org, August 11, 2020.

2　Adi Robertson, "Two Months Ago, the Internet Tried to Banish Nazis: No One Knows If It Worked," *Verge*, October 9, 2017, www.theverge.com.

3　"Charlottesville: An Overview of the Legal Case," Integrity First For America, April 19, 2018, www.integrityfirstforamerica.org.

4　Andrew Anglin, "Official *Daily Stormer* Position: Don't Go to 'Unite the Right 2'; We Disavow," *Daily Stormer*, August 5, 2018, dailystormer.su.

5　Shapira, "Inside Jason Kessler's Hate-Fueled Rise"; "Jason Kessler on His 'Unite the Right' Rally Move to D.C.'," National Public Radio, August 10, 2018, www.npr. org.

6　See, for example, "Jason Kessler," Southern Poverty Law Center, www.splcenter. org, accessed October 31, 2020.

7　Jamie Ross, "The Battle against Kremlin Propaganda Network RT," *Daily Beast*, May 22, 2018, www.dailybeast.com.

8　Masha Gessen, "Why the Tree of Life Shooter Was Fixated on the Hebrew Immigrant Aid Society," *New Yorker*, October 27, 2018, www.newyorker.com.

9　"Remarks by President Trump at the 91st Annual Future Farmers of America Convention," The White House, October 27, 2018, www.whitehouse.gov.

10　James S. Robbins, "Synagogue Shooter Hated Donald Trump and Shows What Real Hatred, Anti-Semitism Looks Like," *USA Today*, October 29, 2018, www. usatoday.com.

11　Alan Zimmerman, "Synagogue President: A Straight Line from our Charlottesville Ordeal to Pittsburgh Shooting," *USA Today*, October 28, 2018, www.usatoday.com; see also Dana Milbank, "Trump's America Is Not a Safe Place for Jews," *Washington Post*, October 28, 2018, www.washingtonpost.com.

12　Meghan Keneally, "A Look Back at Trump's Comments Perceived by Some as Encouraging Violence," *ABC News*, October 19, 2018, www.abcnews.go.com; "Divider in Chief? Trump in His Own Abrasive Words," *France 24*, October 30, 2018, www.france24.com; Jan Ransom, "Trump Will Not Apologize for Calling for Death Penalty over Central Park Five," *New York Times*, June 18, 2019, www. nytimes.com.

13　Christina Caron, "Trump Mocks LeBron James's Intelligence and Calls Don Lemon 'Dumbest Man' on TV," *New York Times*, August 4, 2018, www.nytimes. com; Michael D. Shear and Eileen Sullivan, "Trump Calls Omarosa Manigault Newman 'That Dog' in His Latest Insult," *New York Times*, August 14, 2018, www. nytimes.com. On Trump's history of racist remarks, see Leonhardt and Philbrick, "Donald Trump's Racism."

14　Noah Weiland, "Before 'Unite the Right' Rally, Trump Does Not Condemn Supremacists," *New York Times*, August 11, 2018, www.nytimes.com.

15 Matt Zapotosky, Annie Gowen, Sari Horwitz, and Cleve R. Wootson Jr., "Who Is Cesar Sayok? What We Know about the Suspected Mail Bomber Arrested in Florida," *Washington Post*, October 26, 2018, www.washingtonpost.com; Kristin Lam, "Pipe Bomb Suspect Cesar Sayoc Describes Trump Rally as 'New Found Drug,'" *USA Today*, April 23, 2019, www.usatoday.com.

16 "ADL Calls on Leaders to Redouble Efforts to Counter Hate after FBI Reports Hate Crimes Jumped 17 Percent," Anti-Defamation League, November 13, 2018, www.adl.org.

17 Lenny Bernstein, Sari Horwitz, and Peter Holley, "Dylann Roof's Racist Manifesto: 'I Have No Choice,'" *Washington Post*, June 20, 2015, www.washington-post.com; "Dylann Roof May Have Been a Regular Commenter at Neo-Nazi Website the *Daily Stormer*," Southern Poverty Law Center, June 22, 2015, www.splcenter.org.

18 The discussion of systemic white supremacy that follows draws on Eduardo Bonilla-Silva, "Rethinking Racism: Toward a Structural Interpretation," *American Sociological Review* 62, no. 3 (1997): 479–80; Michael Omi and Howard Winant, *Racial Formation in the United States* (New York: Routledge, 2015); Joe R. Feagin, *The White Racial Frame: Centuries of Racial Framing and Counter-Framing* (New York: Routledge, 2013). For an early iteration of this perspective, see W. E. B. Du Bois, *The Philadelphia Negro* (New York: Oxford University Press, 2014); Franz Fanon, *Black Skins, White Masks* (New York: Grove, 1967).

19 Patrick Wolfe, "Settler Colonialism and the Elimination of the Native," *Journal of Genocide Research* 8, no. 4 (2006): 387–409; Raphael Lemkin, *Axis Rule in Occupied Europe: Laws of Occupation, Analysis of Government, Proposals for Redress* (Washington, DC: Carnegie Endowment for International Peace, 1944), 79. See also A. Dirk Moses, ed., *Empire, Colony, Genocide: Conquest, Occupation, and Subaltern Resistance in World History* (New York: Berghahn, 2008).

20 Feagin, *The White Racial Frame*; Ibram X. Kendi, *Stamped from the Beginning: The Definitive History of Racist Ideas in America* (New York: Nation Books, 2016).

21 Roxanne Dunbar-Ortiz, *An Indigenous Peoples' History of the United States* (Boston: Beacon, 2015); Ned Blackhawk, *Indians and Empire in the Early American West* (Cambridge, MA: Harvard University Press, 2006); Wolfe, "Settler Colonialism"; Andrew Woolford, Jeff Benvenuto, and Alexander Laban Hinton, eds., *Colonial Genocide in Indigenous North America* (Durham, NC: Duke University Press, 2014); Andrew Woolford, *This Benevolent Experiment: Indigenous Boarding Schools, Genocide, and Redress in Canada and the United States* (Lincoln: University of Nebraska Press, 2015).

22 Patrick Brantlinger, *Dark Vanishings: Discourse on the Extinction of Primitive Races, 1800–1930* (Ithaca, NY: Cornell University Press, 2003); Feagin, *The White Racial Frame*.

23 Feagin, *The White Racial Frame*; Kendi, *Stamped from the Beginning*; Omi and Winant, *Racial Formation*.

24 Feagin, *The White Racial Frame*; Omi and Winant, *Racial Formation*; Kendi, *Stamped from the Beginning*.

25 Evelyn Nakano Glenn, "Settler Colonialism as Structure: A Framework for Comparatives Studies of U.S. Race and Gender Formations," *Sociology of Race and Ethnicity* 1, no. 1 (2015): 54–74.

26 John Kuo Wei Tchen and Dylan Yeats, eds., *Yellow Peril! An Archive of Anti-Asian Fear* (New York: Verso, 2014).

27 Omi and Winant, *Racial Formation*; Feagin, *The White Racial Frame*; Bonilla-Silva, "Rethinking Racism"; Glenn, "Settler Colonialism."

28 The discussion of the three waves of the KKK that follows draws on Linda Gordon, *The Second Coming of the KKK: The Ku Klux Klan of the 1920s and the American Political Tradition* (New York: Liveright, 2017); "Ku Klux Klan: A History of Racism," Southern Poverty Law Center, March 1, 2011, www.splcenter.org.

29 Kathleen M. Blee, *Women of the Klan: Racism and Gender in the 1920s* (Berkeley: University of California Press, 2008); Gordon, *The Second Coming*; Blee, *Inside Organized Racism*.

30 See, for example, Joshua Rothman, "When Bigotry Paraded through the Streets," *Atlantic*, December 4, 2016; Richard Yeselson, "The Return of the 1920s," *Atlantic*, December 30, 2015, 2, www.theatlantic.com.

31 Mae M. Ngai, "The Strange Career of the Illegal Alien: Immigration Restriction and Deportation Policy in the United States, 1921–1965," *Law and History Review* 21, no. 1 (2003): 69–107; Matthew Frye Jacobson, *Whiteness of a Different Color: European Immigrants and the Alchemy of Race* (Cambridge, MA: Harvard University Press, 1999); Brent Staples, "How Italians Became White," *New York Times*, October 12, 2019, www.nytimes.com.

32 Lawrence Dinnerstein, *Antisemitism in America* (New York: Oxford University Press, 1994).

33 Philip Roth, *The Plot against America* (New York: Vintage, 2005).

34 Gordon, *The Second Coming*; Southern Poverty Law Center, "Ku Klux Klan: A History of Racism"; Belew, *Bring the War Home*.

35 Belew, *Bring the War Home*.

36 Libby Nelson, "'Why We Voted for Donald Trump': David Duke Explains the White Supremacist Charlottesville Protests," *Vox*, August 12, 2017, www.voxcom.

37 For a discussion of historical conspiracy theory uses of "new world order," see John Feffer, "Conspiracy Theories Are Obsessed with the Wrong 'New World Order,'" *Nation*, December 17, 2018.

38 Belew, *Bring the War Home*.

39 Marc Edelman, "Hollowed Out Heartland, USA: How Capital Sacrificed Communities and Paved the Way for Authoritarian Populism," *Journal of Rural Studies*, November 10, 2019, www.sciencedirect.com.

40 On the Overton window and white power extremism in the social media age, see Marantz, *Antisocial*.

41 Brantlinger, *Dark Vanishings*. On the origin of the idea of white genocide, see Paul Jackson, "'White Genocide': Post-War Fascism and the Ideological Value of Evoking Existential Conflict," in *The Routledge History of Genocide*, edited by Cathie Carmichael and Richard C. Maguire (New York: Routledge, 2015), 207–26; Devan A. Feshami, "Fear of White Genocide: Tracing the History of a Myth from Germany to Charlottesville," *Lapham's Quarterly*, September 6, 2017, www.laphamsquarterly.org; Cynthia Levine-Rasky, "The 100-Year-Old Rallying Cry of 'White Genocide,'" *Conversation*, July 8, 2018, theconversation.com; A. Dirk Moses, "'White Genocide' and the Ethics of Public Analysis," *Journal of Genocide Research* 21, no. 2 (2019): 201–13.

42 James Q. Whitman, *Hitler's American Model: The United States and the Making of Nazi Race Law* (Princeton, NJ: Princeton University Press, 2018).

43 The biographical details and quotations that follow are, unless noted otherwise, drawn from William Pierce, "The Radicalizing of an American," *National Vanguard*, 1978, www.nationalvanguard.org.

44 This paragraph draws on "William Pierce," Southern Poverty Law Center, www.splcenter.org, accessed March 8, 2019.

45 Robert S. Griffin, *The Fame of a Dead Man's Deeds: An Up-Close Portrait of White Nationalist William Pierce* (Bloomington, IN: 1st Books, 2001), 114, 115, 116.

46 "What Is the National Alliance?" National Alliance website, natall.com, accessed October 31, 2020.

47 Andrew Macdonald [William Pierce], *The Turner Diaries* (Hillsboro, WV: National Vanguard Books, 1978), iii–iv.

48 "Explosion of Hate: The Growing Danger of the National Alliance," Anti-Defamation League, 2000, www.adl.org, accessed October 31, 2020.

49 "National Alliance," Southern Poverty Law Center, www.splcenter.org, accessed October 31, 2020.

50 Belew, *Bring the War Home*.

51 James Coates, *Armed and Dangerous: The Rise of the Survivalist Right* (New York: Hill and Wang, 1995); Belew, *Bring the War Home*; Kevin Flynn and Gary Gerhard, *The Silent Brotherhood: The Chilling Inside Story of America's Violent Anti-Government Militia Movement* (New York: Signet, 1990).

52 Griffin, *Fame of a Dead Man's Deeds*, 209.

53 Griffin, *Fame of a Dead Man's Deeds*, 221.

54 "Christian Identity," Anti-Defamation League, www.adl.org, accessed October 31, 2020; Coates, *Armed and Dangerous*.

55 Belew, *Bring the War Home*, 105.

56 Belew, *Bring the War Home*, 116; see also Griffin, *Fame of a Dead Man's Deeds*, 212.

57 Griffin, *Fame of a Dead Man's Deeds*, 216.

58 Louis R. Beam, "Leaderless Resistance," *Seditionist* 12 (February 1992), www. louisbeam.com. See also Belew, *Bring the War Home*.

59 David Eden Lane, *Deceived, Damned, and Defiant: The Revolutionary Writings of David Lane* (St. Maries, ID: 14 Words Press, 1999).

60 Lane, *Deceived*.

61 George Michael, "David Lane and the Fourteen Words," *Totalitarian Movements and Political Religions* 10, no. 1 (2009): 43–61.

62 Lane, "White Genocide Manifesto," in *Deceived, Damned, and Defiant*.

63 Glenn, "Settler Colonialism"; Feagin, *The White Racial Frame*; Blee, *Inside Organized Racism*; Belew, *Bring the War Home*; Stern, *Proud Boys*.

64 See Moses, "'White Genocide.'" I would also like to thank one of my reviewers for noting this point. On ontological resonance, see Hinton, *Why Did They Kill?*

65 Belew, *Bring the War Home*, 187 ff.

66 Belew, *Bring the War Home*.

67 See Belew, *Bring the War Home*, 214; On Pierce's denials of a connection to McVeigh, see Griffin, *Fame of a Dead Man's Deeds*, 167 ff.

68 "Explosion of Hate," Anti-Defamation League, January 6, 2013, www.adl.org; Griffin, *Fame of a Dead Man's Deeds*, 11–12; J. M. Berger, "The Turner Legacy: The Storied Origins and Enduring Impact of White Nationalism's Deadly Bible," International Centre for Counter-Terrorism, September 16, 2016, 27, icct.nl.

69 Griffin, *Fame of a Dead Man's Deeds*, 130, 399.

70 Weiyi Cai Simone Landon, "Attacks by White Extremists Are Growing: So Are Their Connections," *New York Times*, April 3, 2019, www.nytimes.com.

71 "Explosion of Hate," Anti-Defamation League, www.adl.org.

72 "Stormfront," Southern Poverty Law Center, www.splcenter.org, accessed October 31, 2020.

73 Lane, "White Genocide Manifesto," in *Deceived, Damned, and Defiant*.

74 Daryl Johnson, *Hateland: A Long Hard Look at America's Extremist Heart* (New York: Prometheus, 2019); Marantz, *Antisocial*.

75 Sam Biddle, "Facebook Allowed Advertisers to Target Users Interested in 'White Genocide'—Even in Wake of Pittsburgh Massacre," *Intercept*, November 2, 2018, theintercept.com.

76 Peggy Levitt and Sally Merry, "Vernacularization on the Ground: Local Uses of Global Women's Rights in Peru, China, India, and the United States," *Global Networks* 9, no. 4 (2009): 44–161.

77 See, for example, Erving Goffman, *Frame Analysis: An Essay on the Organization of Experience* (New York: Harper and Row, 1974). For a review of framing and social movements, see Robert D. Benford and David A. Snow, "Framing Processes and Social Movements: An Overview and Assessment," *Annual Review of Sociology* 26 (2000): 611–39. On framing, see also Alexander Laban Hinton, *Man or Monster? The Trial of a Khmer Rouge Torturer* (Durham, NC: Duke University Press, 2016).

78 Feagin, *The White Racial Frame*.

79 Gordon, *The Second Coming*; Blee, *Inside Organized Racism*; Betty A. Dobratz and Stephanie L. Shanks-Meile, *The White Separatist Movement in the United States* (New York: Twayne, 1997).

80 George T. Shaw, "An Alternative to Failure," in *A Fair Hearing: The Alt-Right in the Words of Its Members and Leaders*, ed. George T. Shaw (Budapest: Arktos, 2018), ix–xv. The following discussion is based on Shaw, *A Fair Hearing*. For discussion of the alt-right and white power extremism in the social media age, see Hawley, *Making Sense of the Alt-Right*; Stern, *Proud Boys*; Marantz, *Antisocial*; Johnson, *Hateland*.

81 Daniel Friberg, "Metapolitics," in *A Fair Hearing*, 179–82. On Friberg, see Teitelbaum, *Lions of the North*. On the genealogy of metapolitics, see Stern, *Proud Boys*.

82 George T. Shaw, "Dismantling Anti-White Newspeak," in *A Fair Hearing*, 191.

83 Shaw, "An Alternative to Failure," xii.

84 Evan McLaren, "Ground Zero at Charlottesville," in *A Fair Hearing*, 51.

85 Shaw, "An Alternative to Failure," xiii–xiv.

86 Tenold, *Everything You Love Will Burn*.

87 "Traditionalist Worker Party," Southern Poverty Law Center, www.splcenter.org, accessed October 31, 2020.

88 Tenold, *Everything You Love Will Burn*.

89 "Traditionalist Worker Party."

90 "Traditionalist Worker Party."

91 Marwa Eltagouri and Avi Selk, "How a White Nationalist's Family Came to Blows over a Trailer Tryst," *Washington Post*, March 14, 2018, www.washingtonpost.com.

92 "Traditionalist Worker Party," Internet Archive Wayback Machine, web.archive.org, accessed September 9, 2020; see also "How to Fix America: The Traditionalist Worker Party Platform TWP," Bitchute, www.bitchute.com, accessed September 9, 2020.

93 "Criminal Complaint," *USA v. Robert Bowers*, U.S. District Court, October 27, 2018.

94 "Anti-Semitic Incidents Surged Nearly 60% in 2017, according to New ADL Report," Anti-Defamation League, February 27, 2018, www.adl.org; "In 2019, 21 Hate Groups Were Tracked in New Jersey," Southern Poverty Law Center, www.splcenter.org, accessed October 31, 2020.

95 "Unite the Right 2 Highlights Challenges Facing Alt Right, Other White Supremacists," Anti-Defamation League, August 15, 2018, www.adl.org.

96 "New Jersey European Heritage Association (NJEHA)," Anti-Defamation League, www.adl.org, accessed September 20, 2018; New Jersey European Heritage Association website, www.njeha.com, accessed October 19, 2018; "New Jersey European Heritage Association" Gab website, https://gab.com/NJEHA, accessed October 19, 2018.

97 Daryl Lamont Jenkins, "Neo-Nazis Run out of Princeton, NJ!" *Mississippi Link*, January 14, 2019. See also posts from the Twitter handle, "AntiFash Gordon," https://twitter.com/AntiFashGordon, accessed November 14, 2018.

CHAPTER 4. COULD IT HAPPEN HERE?

1 Madeline Albright, *Fascism: A Warning* (New York: HarperCollins, 2018); Cass R. Sunstein, ed., *Can It Happen Here? Authoritarianism in America* (New York: HarperCollins, 2018). See also Steven Levitsky and Daniel Ziblatt, *How Democracies Die* (New York: Crown, 2018); Timothy Snyder, *On Tyranny: Twenty Lessons from the Twentieth Century* (New York: Tim Duggan Books, 2017).

2 Jason Staley, *How Fascism Works: The Politics of Us and Them* (New York: Random House, 2018).

3 Magnus Linden, "'Trump's America and the Rise of the Authoritarian Personality," *Conversation*, February 16, 2017, thecoversation.com; John Gartner, "Donald Trump's Malignant Narcissism Is Toxic: Psychologist," *USA Today*, May 4, 2017, www.usatoday.com; Lee, *The Dangerous Case of Donald Trump*.

4 Jason Kessler, "Yes, Virginia (Dare), There Is Such a Thing as White Genocide," VDare, June 19, 2017, vdare.com. Just days after Unite the Right 1, in an interview with White Rabbit Radio, Kessler also noted how his speakers, including Cantwell, would have discussed white genocide if the rally hadn't been canceled. He also included a white genocide activist from South Africa on his initial list of speakers for Unite the Right 2. Given Kessler's past statements, then, it was not surprising that white power extremists espousing white genocide views were present at Charlottesville and participated in his Unite the Right 2 march in Washington, DC.

5 On white-power-extremist misuses of the concept of genocide, see Moses, "White Genocide," and A. Dirk Moses, "White Genocide: The Far Right and the Center-Right," keynote address at the "Bigotry and Hate in the U.S." conference, Rutgers University, Newark, April 27, 2019.

6 "Framework of Analysis for Atrocity Crimes: A Tool for Prevention," United Nations Office on Genocide Prevention and the Responsibility to Protect, October 3, 2014, www.un.org.

7 "Statement by Adama Dieng, United Nations Special Adviser on the Prevention of Genocide, on the Situation in Idlib, Syrian Arab Republic," United Nations Press Release, September 6, 2018, www.un.org.

8 See, for example, Kevin Davis, Angelina Fisher, Benedict Kingsbury, and Sally Engle Merry, eds., *Governance by Indicators: Global Power through Classification and Rankings* (New York: Oxford University Press, 2012); Sally Engle Merry, *The Seductions of Quantification: Measuring Human Rights, Gender Violence, and Sex Trafficking* (New York: Cambridge University Press, 2016).

9 William L. Patterson, *We Charge Genocide: The Crime of Government against the Negro People* (New York: International Publishers, 1951); Carol Anderson, *Eyes off*

the Prize: The United Nations and the African American Struggle for Human Rights, 1944–1955 (New York: Cambridge University Press, 2003).

10 Patterson, *We Charge Genocide*, xvi, 3, 7.

11 Raphael Lemkin, "Nature of Genocide," *New York Times*, June 14, 1953.

12 Lemkin, *Axis Rule in Occupied Europe*.

13 A. Dirk Moses, "Raphael Lemkin, Culture, and the Concept of Genocide," in *The Oxford Handbook of Genocide Studies*, ed. Donald Bloxham and A. Dirk Moses (New York: Oxford University Press, 2010), 19–41; Douglas Irvin-Erickson, *Raphael Lemkin and the Concept of Genocide* (Philadelphia: University of Pennsylvania Press, 2016).

14 On the boarding schools, see Woolford, *This Benevolent Experiment*.

15 See Anderson, *Eyes off the Prize*; Benjamin Meiches, "The Charge of Genocide: Racial History, Political Discourse, and the Evolution of International Institutions," *International Political Sociology* 13 (2019): 20–36.

16 Bonilla-Silva, "Rethinking Racism"; Feagin, *The White Racial Frame*; Omi and Winant, *Racial Formation*.

17 On "new racism," see, for example, Eduardo Bonilla-Silva, *Racism without Racists; Color-Blind Racism and the Persistence of Racial Inequality in America* (New York: Rowman & Littlefield, 2017).

18 Omi and Winant, *Racial Formation*.

19 Rick Perlstein, "Exclusive: Lee Atwater's Infamous 1981 Interview on the Southern Strategy," *Nation*, November 13, 2012, thenation.com; see also Marantz, *Antisocial*, 30.

20 Bonilla-Silva, *Racism without Racists*; Feagin, *The White Racial Frame*; Omi and Winant, *Racial Formation*. See also Michelle Alexander, *The New Jim Crow: Mass Incarceration in the Age of Colorblindness* (New York: New Press, 2020); "The 1619 Project," *New York Times Magazine*, August 14, 2019, www.nytimes.com.

21 On dehiscence, see Hinton, *Man or Monster?*

22 Feagin, *The White Racial Frame*.

23 Wil Haygood, "Why Won't Blackface Go Away? It's Part of America's Troubled Cultural Legacy," *New York Times*, February 7, 2019, www.nytimes.com; Cleve R. Wootson Jr., "The Lengthy History of White Politicians Wearing Blackface—and Getting a Pass," *Washington Post*, February 16, 2019, www.washingtonpost.com.

24 Dylan Rodriguez, "Inhabiting the Impasse: Racial/Racial-Colonial Power, Genocide Poetics, and the Logic of Evisceration," *Social Text* 33, no. 3 (2015): 19–44; Joao Costa Vargas, *Never Meant to Survive: Genocide and Utopias in Black Diaspora Communities* (New York: Rowman & Littlefield, 2008).

25 "Plan of Action for Religious Leaders and Actors to Prevent Incitement to Violence That Could Lead to Atrocity Crimes," United Nations Office on Genocide Prevention and the Responsibility to Protect, www.un.org, accessed October 31, 2020.

26 Tal Kopan, "Donald Trump Retweets 'White Genocide' Twitter User," CNN, January 22, 2016, www.cnn.com.

27 Aaron Sankin and Will Carless, "President Trump Is Pushing White Nationalist Ideas into the Mainstream," *Washington Post*, August 24, 2018, www.washington-post.com. On Trump's more indirect white genocide messaging, see, for example, Michael Harriot, "Donald Trump's Top 10 Most Racist Conspiracy Tweets," *Root*, August 24, 2018, www.theroot.com.

28 Simon Lancaster, "Why Donald Trump Resembles a Hitler Tribute Act," *Total Politics*, February 26, 2018, www.totalpolitics.com.

29 Rich Higgens, "POTUS & Political Warfare," May 2017, reproduced in Jana Winter and Elias Groll, "Here's the Memo That Blew up the NSC," *Foreign Policy*, August 10, 2017, foreignpolicy.com.

30 William S. Lind, "The Roots of Political Correctness," *American Conservative*, November 19, 2009, www.theamericanconservative.com. On cultural Marxism, see Samuel Moyn, "The Alt-Right's Favorite Meme Is 100 Years Old," *New York Times*, November 13, 2018, www.nytimes.com; Jason Wilson, "'Cultural Marxism': A United Theory for Rightwingers Who Love to Play the Victim," *Guardian*, January 18, 2015, www.theguardian.com.

31 Higgens, "POTUS and Political Warfare"; on Trump's remark, see "Transcript: Donald Trump's Speech Responding to Assault Accusations," National Public Radio, October 13, 2016, www.npr.org.

32 Winter and Groll, "Here's the Memo."

33 Winter and Groll, "Here's the Memo."

34 Michelle Goldberg, "Stephen Miller Is a White Nationalist: Does It Matter?" *New York Times*, November 18, 2019, www.nytimes.com; Andrew Kaczynski, "Speechwriter Who Attended Conference with White Nationalists in 2016 Leaves White House," CNN, August 22, 2018; Rosie Gray, "Emails Link Former Homeland Security Official to White Nationalists," *Atlantic*, August 28, 2018, www.theatlantic.com.

35 "Stephen Miller's Affinity for White Nationalism Revealed in Leaked Emails," Southern Poverty Law Center, November 12, 2019, www.splcenter.org.

36 "Miller Pushed Racist 'Camp of the Saints' Beloved by Far Right," Southern Poverty Law Center, November 12, 2019, www.splcenter.org; Julia Hahn, "'Camp of the Saints' Seen Mirrored in Pope's Message," *Breitbart*, September 24, 2015, www.breitbart.com.

37 Jean Raspail, *The Camp of the Saints* (New York: Charles Scribner, 1975); Elian Peltier and Nicholas Kulish, "A Racist Book's Malign and Lingering Influence," *New York Times*, November 22, 2019, www.nytimes.com.

38 Jason DeParle, "How Stephen Miller Seized the Moment to Battle Immigration," *New York Times*, August 17, 2019, www.nytimes.com; Katie Rogers and Jason DeParle, "The White Nationalist Websites Cited by Stephen Miller," *New York Times*, November 18, 2019, www.nytimes.com.

39 Marantz, *Antisocial*, 55.

40 Katie Rogers, "Before Joining White House, Stephen Miller Pushed White Nationalist Theories," *New York Times*, November 13, 2019, www.nytimes.com; see also Jayashri Srikantiah, and Shirin Sinnar, "White Nationalism as Immigration Policy," *Stanford Law Review Online* 71 (2019): 197–209.

41 Sara Sidner and Rachel Clarke, "Former *Breitbart* Editor: Stephen Miller Is a White Supremacist; I Know, I Was One Too," CNN, December 16, 2019, www.cnn.com.

42 Marcy Oster, "Stephen Miller Claims Anti-Semitism from Democrats Who Want Him Fired for His White Nationalist Views," *Forward*, December 23, 2019, forward.com; "Stephen Miller," Southern Poverty Law Center, www.splcenter.org, accessed October 31, 2020.

43 Jeremy W. Peters, Michael M. Gyrnbaum, Deith Collins, Rich Harris, and Rumsey Taylor, "How the El Paso Killer Echoed the Incendiary Words of Conservative Media Stars," *New York Times*, August 11, 2019, www.nytimes.com; Chauncy Devega, "Media Expert: How Tucker Carlson and Fox News Have Mainstreamed 'Unfettered White Nationalism,'" *Salon*, July 18, 2019, www.salon.com; Adam Serwer, "The White Nationalists Are Winning," *Atlantic*, August 10, 2018, www. theatlantic.com.

44 Luke O'Neil, "Laura Ingraham Isn't an Outlier, She's the Mainstream," *Observer*, August 10, 2018, observer.com.

45 Joseph Bernstein, "Data Shows Tucker Carlson Is the *Daily Stormer*'s Favorite Pundit," *Buzzfeed*, November 28, 2018, www.buzzfeednews.com; Oliver Darcy, "Tucker Carlson's Top Writer Resigns after Secretly Posting Racist and Sexist Remarks in Online Forum," July 11, 2020, www.washingtonpost.com; Pete Hegseth, *American Crusade: Our Fight to Stay Free* (New York: Center Street, 2020).

46 Mark Joyella, "Fox News Ends 2019 with Biggest Prime Time Ratings Ever," *Forbes*, December 11, 2019; Amanda Marcotte, "The Alt-Right Isn't Dead: It Was Just Taken Over by Fox News," *Salon*, December 6, 2018, www.salon.com.

47 Matt Gertz, "Fox News Is Pushing White Nationalism because the Murdochs Want It To," *Media Matters*, August 8, 2019, www.mediamatters.org; Jonathan Mahler and Jim Rutenberg, "How Rupert Murdoch's Empire of Influence Remade the World," *New York Times*, April 3, 2019, www.nytimes.com; Lachlan Cartwright, Loyd Grove, Andrew Kirell, Noah Schatman, and Justic Baragona, "Fox News Staffers Erupt over Network's Racism: Bosses 'Created a White Supremacist Cell,'" *Daily Beast*, July 17, 2020, www.thedailybeast.com.

48 Marantz, *Antisocial*; Katie Rogers, "White House Hosts Conservative Internet Activists at a 'Social Media Summit,'" *New York Times*, July 11, 2019, www.nytimes. com; Alex Kaplan, "Here Are the Extremist Figures Going to the White House Social Media Summit," *Media Matters*, July 9, 2019; Siva Vaidhyanathan, "From Trump to Fox News to 8chan: The Web of White Supremacist Rhetoric Is Wide," *Guardian*, August 6, 2019, www.theguardian.com.

49 Belew, *Bring the War Home*, 4.

50 George Hawley, "The Demography of the Alt-Right," Institute for Family Studies, August 9, 2018, ifstudies.org.

51 Gary Langer, "1 in 10 Say It's Acceptable to Hold Neo-Nazi Views," *ABC News*, August 21, 2017, www.abcnews.go.com. See also "New Poll: Some Americans Express Troubling Racial Attitudes Even as Majority Oppose White Supremacists," UVA Center for Politics, September 14, 2017, www.centerforpolitics.org.

52 "Subcommittee on Military Personnel Hearing: Alarming Incidents of White Supremacy in the Military; How to Stop It?" House Armed Services Committee, February 11, 2020, www.armedservices.house.gov; Will Carless and Michael Corey, "To Protect and Slur," *Reveal News*, June 14, 2019, www.revealnews.org.

53 Anonymous, "I Am Part of the Resistance inside the Trump Administration," *New York Times*, September 5, 2018, www.nytimes.com.

54 Robin Wright, "Is America Headed for a New Kind of Civil War?" *New Yorker*, August 14, 2017, www.newyorker.com.

55 Nicholas Kristof, "We Will Survive: Probably," *New York Times*, March 6, 2019, www.nytimes.com; see also Lawrence Douglas, *Will He Go? Trump and the Looming Election Meltdown in 2020* (New York: Twelve, 2020).

56 Mary B. McCord, "Armed Militias Are Taking Trump's Civil War Tweets Seriously," *Lawfare*, October 2, 2019, www.lawfareblog.com; Astead W. Herndon, "'Nothing Less Than a Civil War': These White Voters on the Far Right See Doom without Trump," *New York Times*, December 28, 2019, www.nytimes.com.

CHAPTER 5. CAN IT BE PREVENTED?

1 Mallory Simon and Sara Sidner, "Trump Says He's Not a Racist: That's Not How White Nationalists See It," CNN, November 13, 2018, www.cnn.com.

2 Adeel Hassan, "Photo of More Than 60 Students Giving Apparent Nazi Salute Is Being Investigated," *New York Times*, November 12, 2018, www.nytimes.com.

3 Hannan Adely, "Hate Crimes Up 76 Percent in New Jersey, FBI Says," *Northjersey. com*, November 13, 2018, www.northjersey.com.

4 Spencer S. Hsu and Peter Hermann, "D.C. Man Arrested on Gun Charge after Relatives Alert Police to His Alleged White Nationalist Outbursts," *Washington Post*, November 13, 2018, www.washingtonpost.com.

5 Simon and Sidner, "Trump Says He's Not a Racist."

6 "An Introduction to the Khmer Rouge Trials (7th Edition)," ECCC, Phnom Penh, Cambodia, August 11, 2017, www.eccc.gov.kh.

7 On transitional justice and the ECCC, see Alexander Laban Hinton, *The Justice Facade: Trials of Transition in Cambodia* (New York: Oxford University Press, 2018).

8 See Hinton, *The Justice Facade*.

9 Hinton, *Man or Monster?*

10 James Waller, *Confronting Evil: Engaging Our Responsibility to Prevent Genocide* (New York: Oxford University Press, 2016).

11 See Hinton, *The Justice Facade*. On the international human rights regime, see Jack Donnelly and Daniel J. Whelan, *International Human Rights* (Boulder, CO: Westview, 2018).

12 The Non Nil quotations that follow are taken from the text he read: "Summary of Judgment in Case 002/02 against NUON Chea and KHIEU Samphan," Trial Chamber, ECCC, November 16, 2018, www.eccc.gov.kh.

13 What follows is based on an author interview with William Smith, November 17, 2018, Phnom Penh. Smith also discussed my testimony in a conference keynote that was published as an article, William Smith, "Justice for Genocide in Cambodia: The Case for the Prosecution," *Genocide Studies and Prevention* 12, no. 3 (2018): 20–39.

14 "Statement by Adama Dieng, United Nations Special Adviser on the Prevention of Genocide, on the Conviction of NUON Chea and KHIEU Samphan for the Crimes of Genocide, Crimes against Humanity, and Grave Breaches of the 1949 Geneva Conventions by the Extraordinary Chambers in the Courts of Cambodia," United Nations Press Release, November 16, 2018, www.un.org.

15 On social movements and extremism, see Futrell, Simi, and Tan, "Political Extremism and Social Movements." See also Kurt Schock, *Unarmed Insurrections: People Power Movements in Nondemocracies* (Minneapolis: University of Minnesota Press, 2004).

16 Anthony F. C. Wallace, "Revitalization Movements," *American Anthropologist* 58, no. 2 (1956): 264–81.

17 Berger, *Extremism*; Donatella della Porta, "Radicalization: A Relational Perspective," *Annual Review of Political Science* 21 (2018): 461–74; Johnson, *Hateland*. If many scholars working in this literature use complicated processual and relational models of radicalization, the term has sometimes been used in a reductive fashion—such as by individualizing or exceptionalizing "the (often Islamic) terrorist" in ways that parallel "hater" discourses.

18 See, for example, Blee, *Inside Organized Racism*; Katrine Fangen, "On the Margins of Life: Life Stories of Radical Nationalists," *Act Sociologica* 42, no. 4 (1999): 357–73; Pete Simi and Robert Futrell, *American Swastika: Inside the White Power Movement's Hidden Spaces of Hate* (New York: Rowman & Littlefield, 2010).

19 Clifford Geertz, *The Interpretation of Cultures: Selected Essays* (New York: Basic Books, 1973). For a critical discussion of the experience-distant orientation of the prevention literature, see Alexander Laban Hinton, "The First Lesson in Prevention," *Genocide Studies and Prevention* 13, no. 3 (2019): 128–44. For a review of the small number of ethnographies of the hard Far Right, see Kathleen M. Blee, "Ethnographies of the Far Right," *Journal of Contemporary Ethnography* 36, no. 2 (2007): 119–28; Kathleen M. Blee and Kimberly A. Creasap, "Conservative and Right-Wing Movements," *Annual Review of Sociology* 36 (2010): 269–86.

20 Christian Picciolini, *White American Youth: My Descent into America's Most Violent Hate Movement—and How I Got Out* (New York: Hatchette, 2017); R. Derek Black, "Why I Left White Nationalism," *New York Times*, November 26, 2016, www.nytimes.com; Michael Kimmel, *Healing from Hate: How Young Men Get into—and out of—Violent Extremism* (Berkeley: University of California Press, 2018).

21 Mallory Simon, "How the Klansman Who Shot toward a Black Man in Charlottesville Ended Up at the African-American Museum," CNN, August 10, 2018. See also Adam Popsecu, "Why a Black Preacher Is Fighting for Control of a Neo-Nazi Group," *New York Times*, July 23, 2019, www.nytimes.com.

22 David Streitfeld, "In Amazon's Bookstore, No Second Chances for the Third Reich," *New York Times*, February 9, 2020, www.nytimes.com; Marantz, *Antisocial*.

23 "Rightwing Extremism: Current Economic and Political Climate Fueling Resurgence in Radicalization and Recruitment," Department of Homeland Security Office of Intelligence and Analysis, April 7, 2009, www.fas.org. My discussion of the 2009 report and the US response to the resurgence of white power extremism draws on a book written by one of the analysts who produced the report: Johnson, *Hateland*.

24 David McKenzie and Bent Swails, "They're Prepping for a Race War: And They See Trump as Their 'Ray of Hope,'" CNN, November 20, 2018, www.cnn.com.

25 Carolyn Holmes, "Tucker Carlson, Those South African White Right Activists Aren't Telling You the Whole Truth," *Washington Post*, May 15, 2019, www.washingtonpost.com. See also James Pogue, "The Myth of White Genocide," *Harper's Magazine*, March 2019, harpers.org.

26 Matt Pearce, "'This Is a White Supremacist Talking Point'; Anti-Racism Group Blasts Trump's 'White Farmers' Tweet," *Los Angeles Times*, August 23, 2018, www.latimes.com.

27 Lloyd Gedye, "White Genocide: How the Big Lie Spread to the United States and Beyond," *Mail & Guardian*, March 23, 2018, mg.co.za; Eyes on the Right, "Suidlanders Spokesman Simon Roche Has Deep Ties to White Supremacist Groups," *Angry White Men*, April 22, 2018, angrywhitemen.org.

28 McKenzie and Swails, "They're Prepping for a Race War."

29 McKenzie and Swails, "They're Prepping for a Race War."

30 "Special Section: Anthropology of White Supremacy," *American Anthropologist*, December 31, 2019, www.americananthropologist.org.

31 Farouk Chothia, "South Africa: The Groups Playing on the Fears of a 'White Genocide,'" *BBC News*, September 1, 2018, www.bbc.com.

32 Brenton Tarrant, "The Great Replacement: Towards a New Society," undated, https://archive.org/, accessed November 30, 2020.

33 Jackson, "'White Genocide'"; Moses, "White Genocide"; Teitelbaum, *Lions of the North*.

34 On the broader synergies between Trump and such views, see Bernard E. Harcourt, "How Trump Fuels the Fascist Right," *New York Review Daily*, November 29, 2018, nybooks.com.

35 Veronica Stracqualursi, "Mulvaney Defends Trump in the Wake of New Zealand Attacks: 'The President Is Not a White Supremacist,'" CNN, March 17, 2019, www.cnn.com.

36 Caitlin Oprysko, "Trump Denounces 'Horrible Massacre' in New Zealand," *Politico*, March 15, 2019, www.politico.com.

37 Brian Klass, "A Short History of President Trump's Anti-Muslim Bigotry," *Washington Post*, March 15, 2019, www.washingtonpost.com; Wajahat Ali, "The Roots of the Christchurch Massacre," *New York Times*, March 15, 2019, www.nytimes.com.

38 Isaac Stanley-Becker, "'They Hate White Males': A Norwegian Mass Murderer Inspired the Coast Guard Officer Accused of Inciting Terror, Feds Say," *Washington Post*, February 20, 2019, www.washingtonpost.com.

39 "California Man Indicted for Federal Hate Crimes Related to Poway Synagogue Shooting and Arson of Escondido Mosque," US Department of Justice, May 21, 2019, www.justice.gov; John Earnest, "An Open Letter," undated, https://archive.org/, accessed November 30, 2020.

40 Robert Evans, "Ignore the Poway Synagogue Shooter's Manifesto: Pay Attention to 8chan's /pol/ Board," Bellingcat, April 28, 2019, www.bellingcat.com.

41 Reproduced in Evans, "Ignore the Poway Shooter's Manifesto."

42 Pierce Alexander Dignam and Deanna A. Rohlinger, "Misogynistic Men Online: How the Red Pill Helped Elect Trump," *Signs* 44, no. 3 (2019): 589–612; Bharath Ganesh, "What the Red Pill Means for Radicals," Center for Analysis of the Far Right, June 8, 2018, www.radicalrightanalysis.com; Stern, *Proud Boys*.

43 Albright, *Fascism*; Staley, *How Fascism Works*; K. Biswas, "How the Far Right Became Europe's New Normal," *New York Times*, February 4, 2020, www.nytimes.com.

44 Katrin Bennhold and Melissa Eddy, "In Germany's 'Politics of Hate,' Even the Politicians Aren't Safe," *New York Times*, February 22, 2020, www.nytimes.com; Melissa Eddy, "Far-Right Terrorism Is No. 1 Threat, Germany Is Told after Attack," *New York Times*, February 21, 2020, www.nytimes.com. See also Shoshan, *The Management of Hate*.

45 Adama Dieng, "Street by Street: Systematic Dehumanization in Europe," United Nations Office of the Special Adviser on the Prevention of Genocide, October 2018, www.un.org; Tom Miles, "U.N. Genocide Expert Says Europe's Far Right Recalls Rise of Nazis," Reuters, May 1, 2019, www.reuters.com.

46 "Statement by Adama Dieng," United Nations Press Release, November 16, 2018.

47 "Strategy and Plan of Action on Hate Speech," United Nations, May 2019, www.un.org.

48 This definition is inspired, in part, by Mark Johnson, *Moral Imagination: Implications of Cognitive Science for Ethics* (Chicago: University of Chicago Press, 1994) and John Paul Lederach, *The Moral Imagination: The Art and Soul of Building Peace* (New York: Oxford University Press, 2010).

49 "Peace and Justice Memorial Seeks to Make Horror of Lynching Understood," National Public Radio, April 28, 2018, www.npr.org; Ezra Klein, "Bryan Stevenson Explains How It Feels to Grow Up Black amid Confederate Monuments," *Vox*, May 24, 2017, www.vox.com.

50 Ta-Nehisi Coates, "The Case for Reparations," *Atlantic*, June 2014, www.theatlantic.com.

51 Truth and Reconciliation Commission of Canada, *Honouring the Truth, Reconciling for the Future: Summary of the Final Report of the Truth and Reconciliation Commission of Canada* (Winnipeg: Truth and Reconciliation Commission of Canada, 2015). See also Woolford, *This Benevolent Experiment*.

52 "Greensboro Truth and Reconciliation Commission Report," May 25, 2006, www.greensborotrc.org.

53 Stephen Pomper, "Atrocity Prevention under the Obama Administration: What We Learned and the Path Ahead," United States Holocaust Memorial Museum, February 2018, www.ushmm.org; "Elie Wiesel Genocide and Atrocities Prevention Act of 2018," www.congress.gov, accessed October 31, 2020.

54 But see James E. Waller, "It Can Happen Here: Assessing the Risk of Genocide in the US," Center for Development of International Law, March 20, 2017, cdilaw.org; Max Pensky and Nadia Rubaii, "Warning Signs of Mass Violence—in the U.S.?" *Conversation*, August 21, 2017, theconversation.com.

55 Makau Mutua, "Savages, Victims, and Saviors: The Metaphor of Human Rights," *Harvard International Law Journal* 42, no. 1 (2001): 210–45; Hinton, *The Justice Facade*.

56 See, for example, Kamari Maxine Clarke, *Fictions of Justice: The International Criminal Court and the Challenge of Legal Pluralism in Sub-Saharan Africa* (New York: Cambridge University Press, 2009).

57 Rodriguez, "Inhabiting the Impasse"; Vargas, *Never Meant to Survive*; Mahmood Mamdani, "Responsibility to Protect or Right to Punish," *Journal of Intervention and Statebuilding* 4, no. 1 (2010): 53–67.

58 Sheryl Gay Stolberg, "At Historic Hearing, House Panel Explores Reparations," *New York Times*, June 19, 2019, www.nytimes.com.

59 Johnson, *Hateland*.

60 Samantha Capicotto and Rob Scharf, "National Mechanisms for the Prevention of Atrocity Crimes," *Genocide Studies and Prevention* 11, no. 3 (2018): 6–19.

61 Jack London, *The Iron Heel* (New York: Penguin, 2006); Roth, *Plot against America*.

62 Paul Kane, "Jeff Flake: The President Uses Words Infamously Spoken by Joseph Stalin to Describe His Enemies," *Washington Post*, January 17, 2018, www.

washingtonpost.com. For an illustration of how white power extremists similarly depict the media, see William Pierce, "Fear the Smear," *National Vanguard*, September 11, 2018, nationalvanguard.org.

63   Anonymous, "I am Part of the Resistance"; see also Bob Woodward, *Fear: Trump in the White House* (New York: Simon & Schuster, 2018).

64   Adeel Hassan, "Hate-Crime Violence Hits 16-Year High, F.B.I. Reports," *New York Times*, November 12, 2019, www.nytimes.com; Jason Wilson, "White Nationalist Hate Groups Have Grown 55% in Trump Era, Report Finds," *Guardian*, March 18, 2020, www.theguardian.com.

65   See, for example, Clark Mindock, "UN Says Trump Separation of Migrant Children with Parents 'May Amount to Torture' in Damning Condemnation," *Independent*, June 22, 2018, www.indepdendent.co.uk; Matt Steib, "Everything We Know about the Inhumane Conditions at Migrant Detention Camps," *New York Magazine*, July 2, 2019, nymag.com.

CONCLUSION. THE BIRD

1   William Branigin, "Nuon Chea, Khmer Rouge's Infamous 'Brother Number Two,' Dies at 93," *Washington Post*, August 4, 2019, www.washingtonpost.com; Lincoln Green, "World's Most Evil Man Dies; He Hated Education and Pushed Ethnic Supremacy," *Daily Kos*, August 6, 2019, www.dailykos.com.

2   "Chautauqua Institution," Chautauqua Institution, www.chq.org, accessed October 31, 2020.

3   "Our History," Chautauqua Institution, www.chq.org, accessed October 31, 2020.

4   "2019 Season: June 22–August 25," Chautauqua Institution, www.chq.org, accessed September 16, 2019.

5   Katie Glueck and Matt Stevens, "'Of Course He's Racist': 2020 Democrats Criticize Trump after Shootings," *New York Times*, August 5, 2019, www.nytimes.com; Peter Baker and Michael D. Shear, "El Paso Shooting Suspect's Manifesto Echoes Trump's Language," *New York Times*, August 4, 2019, www.nytimes.com.

6   Michelle Goldberg, "Trump Is a White Nationalist Who Inspires Terrorism," *New York Times*, August 5, 2019, www.nytimes.com.

7   Benjamin Weisner and Ali Watkins, "Cesar Sayoc, Who Mailed Pipe Bombs to Trump Critics, Is Sentenced to 20 Years," *New York Times*, August 5, 2019, www.nytimes.com.

8   Bianca Quilantan, "Mulvaney Defends Trump on Mass Shootings," *Politico*, August 4, 2019; "Remarks by President Trump on the Mass Shootings in Texas and Ohio," The White House, August 5, 2019, www.whitehouse.gov.

9   Editorial Board, "We Have a White Nationalist Terrorist Problem," *New York Times*, August 4, 2019, www.nytimes.com.

10   Steve Almasy, David Alsup, and Madeline Holcombe, "Dozens of People Have Been Arrested over Threats to Commit Mass Attacks since the El Paso and Dayton Shootings," *CNN*, August 21, 2019, www.cnn.com.

11 Devlin Barrrett, "FBI Faces Skepticism over Its Efforts against Domestic Terrorism," *Washington Post*, August 5, 2019, www.washingtonpost.com.

12 Charles M. Blow, "This Is a Warning about the 2 Sides of White Nationalism," *New York Times*, August 4, 2019, www.nytimes.com.

13 "U.S. State Department Official Involved in White Nationalist Movement, Hatewatch Determines," Southern Poverty Law Center, August 7, 2019, www.splcenter.org; Zolan Kanno-Youngs, "62 Border Agents Belonged to Offensive Facebook Group, Investigation Finds," *New York Times*, July 15, 2019, www.nytimes.com.

14 John Wagner and Colby Itkowitz, "Biden, in Iowa Speech, Says Trump Has 'Fanned the Flames of White Supremacy,'" *Washington Post*, August 7, 2019, www.washingtonpost.com; "Joe Biden Iowa Trump Rebuke Speech Transcript," Rev, August 7, 2019, www.rev.com.

15 Chris Riotta, "Republican Suggests 'Lack of Thoughts and Prayers' the Biggest Factor behind Mass Shootings," *Independent*, August 6, 2019, www.indepdendent.co.uk; David Montanaro, "'Fox & Friends' Says Oprah Is Right about Mass Shootings, America Missing 'Core Moral Center,'" Fox News, August 8, 2019, www.foxnews.com.

16 See Mark Goodale, ed., *Human Rights: An Anthropological Reader* (Malden, MA: Blackwell, 2009).

17 "On Being with Krista Tippett," The On Being Project, onbeing.org, accessed September 16, 2019.

18 Ilhan Omar, "Ilhan Omar: It Is Not Enough to Condemn Trump's Racism," *New York Times*, July 25, 2019, www.nytimes.com. On Baltimore, see Peter Baker, "Trump Assails Elijah Cummings, Calling His Congressional District a Rat-Infested 'Mess,'" *New York Times*, July 27, 2019, www.nytimes.com.

19 Sheryl Gay Stolberg, "Ocasio-Cortez Calls Migrant Detention Centers 'Concentration Camps,' Eliciting Backlash," *New York Times*, June 18, 2019, www.nytimes.com.

20 Charles Blow, "The Rot You Smell Is a Racist POTUS," *New York Times*, July 28, 2019, www.nytimes.com.

21 John Fritze, "Trump Used Words like 'Invasion' and 'Killer' to Discuss Immigrants at Rallies 500 Times," *USA Today*, August 21, 2019, www.usatoday.com; Thomas Kaplan, "How the Trump Campaign Used Facebook Ads to Amplify His 'Invasion' Claim," *New York Times*, August 5, 2019, www.nytimes.com.

22 Nikhat Noorani, "Rabbi Rami Chapiro Opens Interfaith Week with Jewish Understanding of Grace," *Chautauquan Daily*, August 6, 2019, chqdaily.com.

23 Nikhat Noorani, "Abdullah Daar Explores Grace in Islam: 'Manifestation of God's Mercy,'" *Chautauquan Daily*, August 8, 2019, chqdaily.com.

24 The details of his funeral are based on Taryn Wilson, "Fireworks Light Up Cremation of Khmer Rouge's Chief Ideologue," *Efe-Epa*, August 9, 2019, www.efe.com; Aun Chhengpor, "Nuon Chea's Family Remembers 'Pleasant' Father, 'Man of Secrets,'" *VOA Khmer*, August 14, 2019, www.voacambodia.com.

25 Donnelly and Whelan, *International Human Rights*.

26 "Nobel Lecture by Toni Morrison," Nobel Prize, December 7, 1993, www. nobelprize.org. On some of the key themes in Morrison's address, see Ernesto Javier Martinez, "On Butler on Morrison on Language," *Signs* 35, no. 4 (2010): 821–42. See also Toni Morrison, "Making America White Again," *New Yorker*, November 21, 2016, newyorker.com.

EPILOGUE

1 The following quotations from Trump's speech are from "Remarks by President Trump at South Dakota's 2020 Mount Rushmore Fireworks Celebration / Keystone, South Dakota," The White House, July 3, 2020, www.whitehouse.gov.

2 Levi Rickert, "American Indian Protesters Told to 'Go Home' by Trump Supporters at Mount Rushmore," *Native News Online*, July 4, 2020, nativenewsonline.net.

3 "Remarks by President Trump at the 2020 Salute to America," The White House, July 4, 2020, www.whitehouse.gov.

4 Annie Karni and Maggie Haberman, "Trump Travels to New Hampshire to Rally Republicans and Distract Democrats," *New York Times*, February 10, 2020, www.nytimes.com.

5 Harry Enten, "Trump's 2020 Position Is Improving," CNN, February 23, 2020, www.cnn.com; Stephen Collinson, "The President's Decision to Expand His Power Post-Trial Has Stunned Washington," CNN, February 13, 2020, www.cnn.com; Adam Serwer, "The First Days of the Trump Regime," *Atlantic*, February 19, 2020, www.theatlantic.com.

6 Donald G. McNeil Jr., "The Pandemic's Big Mystery: How Deadly Is the Coronavirus?," *New York Times*, July 4, 2020, www.nytimes.com.

7 Eric Cortellessa, "Conspiracy Theory That Jews Created Virus Spreads on Social Media, ADL Says," *Times of Israel*, March 14, 2020, www.timesofisrael.com; Sabrina Tavernise and Richard A. Oppel Jr., "Spit On, Yelled At, Attacked: Chinese-Americans Fear for Their Safety," *New York Times*, March 23, 2020, www.nytimes.com; "Weaponized Information Outbreak: A Case Study of COVID-19, Bioweapon Myths, and the Asian Conspiracy Meme," Network Contagion Research Institute, April 8, 2020, www.ncri.io; Hunter Walker and Jana Winter, "Federal Law Enforcement Document Reveals White Supremacists Discussed Using Coronavirus as a Bioweapon," *Yahoo News*, March 21, 2020, news.yahoo.com.

8 New Jersey European Heritage Association website, www.njeha.com; New Jersey European Heritage Association Gab website, https://gab.com/NJEHA.

9 Mary McCord, "Trump's 'Liberate Michigan!' Tweets Incite Insurrection: That's Illegal," *Washington Post*, April 17, 2020, www.washingtonpost.com; Ben Collins and Brandy Zadrozny, "In Trump's 'Liberate' Extremists See a Call to Arms," *NBC News*, April 17, 2020, nbcnews.com; "The Boogaloo: Extremists' New Slang Term

for a Coming Civil War," Anti-Defamation League, November 26, 2019, www.adl. org.

10 "Cyber Swarming, Mimetic Warfare, and Viral Insurgency: How Domestic Militants Organize on Memes to Incite Violent Insurrection and Terror against Government and Law Enforcement," Network Contagion Research Institute, February 7, 2020, www.ncri.io; Neil MacFarquhar and Adam Goldman, "A New Face of White Supremacy: Plots Expose Danger of the 'Base,'" *New York Times*, January 22, 2020, www.nytimes.com.

11 Salem Gebrekidan, "For Autocrats, and Others, Coronavirus Is a Chance to Grab Even More Power," *New York Times*, March 30, 2020, www.nytimes.com; Frances Z. Brown, "How Will the Coronavirus Reshape Democracy and Global Governance?" Carnegie Endowment for International Peace, April 6, 2020, carnegieendowment.org; Paul Krugman, "American Democracy May Be Dying," *New York Times*, April 9, 2020, www.nytimes.com; Nick Corasaniti, Jeremy W. Peters, and Annie Karni, "New Trump Ad Suggests a Campaign Strategy amid Crisis: Xenophobia," *New York Times*, April 10, 2020, www.nytimes.com.

12 Caitlin Dickerson and Michael D. Shear, "Before COVID-19, Trump Aide Sought to Use Disease to Close Borders," *New York Times*, May 3, 2020, www.nytimes. com; "SPLC Publishes Extremist File for White House Senior Adviser Stephen Miller," Southern Poverty Law Center, July 15, 2020, www.splcenter.org.

13 Derrick Bryson Taylor, "George Floyd Protests: A Timeline," *New York Times*, July 10, 2020, www.nytimes.com.

14 Maggie Haberman and Alexander Burns, "Trump's Looting and 'Shooting' Remarks Escalate Crisis in Minneapolis," *New York Times*, May 29, 2020, www. nytimes.com; Craig Timberg, "As Trump Warns of Leftist Violence, a Dangerous Threat Emerges from the Right-Wing Boogaloo Movement," *Washington Post*, June 17, 2020, www.washingtonpost.com.

15 "Assessing the Threat from Accelerationists and Right-Wing Extremists," Homeland Security Subcommittee on Intelligence & Counterterrorism, July 16, 2020, homeland.house.gov; Caitlin Dickson, "'Boogaloo' on the Loose: Experts Warn Congress about Extremism, on the Right," *Yahoo News*, July 17, 2020, news.yahoo.com.

16 "Statement by President," The White House, June 1, 2020, www.whitehouse.gov; Philip Bump, "Timeline: The Clearing of Lafayette Square," *Washington Post*, June 5, 2020, www.washingtonpost.com.

17 David E. Sanger and Helene Cooper, "Trump and the Military: A Mutual Embrace Might Dissolve on America's Streets," *New York Times*, June 4, 2020, www.nytimes.com; David Ignatius, "How Trump Came to the Brink of Deploying Active-Duty Troops in Washington," *Washington Post*, June 5, 2020, www. washingtonpost.com.

18 Felicia Sonmez, "Trump Declines to Say Whether He Will Accept November Election Results," *Washington Post*, July 19, 2020, www.washingtonpost.com;

Adam Weinstein, "This Is Fascism," *New Republic*, June 2, 2020, newrepublic.com; Sarah Churchwell, "American Fascism: It Has Happened Here," *New York Review of Books*, June 22, 2020, www.nybooks.com; Edward Luce, "How Things Could Go Very Wrong in America," *Financial Times*, June 4, 2020, www.ft.com; Michelle Goldberg, "Trump's Occupation of American Cities Has Begun," *New York Times*, July 20, 2020, www.nytimes.com; "Atrocity Alert No. 206: United States, Iraq, and Sudan," Global Centre for the Responsibility to Protect, June 3, 2020, www.globalr2p.org; Jeffrey Smith and Richard Ashby Wilson, "Researchers on Atrocity Prevention Warn: US on Path to Widespread Political Violence," *Just Security*, June 10, 2020, www.justsecurity.com.

19 Nate Cohn and Kevin Quealy, "How Public Opinion Has Moved on Black Lives Matter," *New York Times*, June 10, 2020, www.nytimes.com; Eugene Scott, "Majority of Americans Say Race Discrimination Is a Big Problem in the U.S.," *Washington Post*, July 10, 2020, www.washingtonpost.com.

20 See, for example, Allegra Frank, "What's in a Name?," *Vox*, July 9, 2020, www.vox.com; Samantha Kubota, "Here's How American Brands Are Changing and Facing Racial Reckoning," *Today*, June 24, 2020, www.today.com.

21 Christine Emba, "A Monumental Shift," *Washington Post*, June 17, 2020, www.washingtonpost.com; Sarah Mervosh, Simon Romero, and Lucy Tompkins, "Reconsidering the Past, One Statue at a Time," *New York Times*, June 16, 2020, www.nytimes.com.

22 Kendall Karson, "Broad Disapproval for Trump's Handling of Coronavirus, Race Relations: Poll," *ABC News*, July 10, 2020, abcnews.go.com.

23 "Remarks by President Trump at Mount Rushmore."

24 David Nakamura, "In Trump's New Version of American Carnage, the Threat Isn't Immigrants or Foreign Nations: It's Other Americans," *Washington Post*, July 4, 2020, www.washingtonpost.com.

25 "A Call to Defend Democracy," International Institute for Democracy, June 25, 2020, www.idea.int; Joby Warrick, "COVID-19 Pandemic Is Stoking Extremist Flames Worldwide, Analysts Warn," *Washington Post*, July 9, 2020, www.washingtonpost.com; "Warning Statement on the Potential for Mass Atrocities in the United States," Atrocities Prevention, July 1, 2020, www.medium.com; Madeline Holcombe, "Expert Warns the US is Approaching 'One of the Most Unstable Times in the History of Our Country,'" CNN, July 11, 2020, www.cnn.com; Jonathan Greeenberg, "Twelve Signs Trump Would Try to Run a Fascist Dictatorship in a Second Term," *Washington Post*, July 10, 2020, www.washingtonpost.com; Max Boot, "What If Trump Loses but Insists He Won?" *Washington Post*, July 6, 2020, www.washingtonpost.com; Eric Posner, "What a Second Trump Term Would Look Like," *New York Times*, July 13, 2020, www.nytimes.com.

26 Jonathan Holloway, "Message to the Rutgers Community," Rutgers University, July 1, 2020, www.rutgers.edu; Jonathan Holloway, "Our Plans for Fall 2020," Rutgers University, July 6, 2020, www.rutgers.edu.

27 "George Floyd Teach-In," *Daily*, June 3, 2020, https://thedaily.case.edu; Mark Whitaker, "For Publishers, Books on Race and Racism Have Been a Surprising Success," *Washington Post*, June 12, 2020, www.washingtonpost.com.

28 Bryan Pietsch, "Princeton Will Remove Woodrow Wilson's Name from School," *New York Times*, June 27, 2020, www.nytimes.com; "Scarlet and Black Project," Rutgers University, scarletandblack.rutgers.edu, accessed October 31, 2020; Kevin C. Collymore, "Colleges Must Confront Structural Racism," *Chronicle of Higher Education*, July 1, 2020. www.chronicle.com.

29 "An Interview with the Editor of *American Anthropologist* about the March 2020 Cover Controversy," *American Anthropologist*, June 29, 2020, www.americananthropologist.org; Ryan Cecil Jobson, "The Case for Letting Anthropology Burn: Sociocultural Anthropology in 2019," *American Anthropologist* 122, no. 2 (2020): 259–71; Kimberly D. McKinson, "Dear White Anthropologists, Let Not Symbolism Overshadow Substance," *Anthropology News*, July 2, 2020, www.anthropology-news.com; "Special Section: Anthropology of White Supremacy," *American Anthropologist*, December 31, 2019, www.americananthropologist.org.

30 Zeus Leonardo and W. Norton Grubb, *Education and Racism: A Primer on Issues and Dilemmas* (New York: Routledge, 2018); Gloria Ladson-Billings and William F. Tate, "Toward a Critical Race Theory of Education," *Teachers College Record* 97, no. 1 (1995): 47–68.

31 Omi and Winant, *Racial Formation*; Asley Mendoza, Jacob Amaro, Yeimy Gamez Castillo, and Jonathan Christie, "What We Learned in 100 Days of Life Interrupted," *New York Times*, July 6, 2020, www.nytimes.com; "Stories from the Pandemic," *Newest Americans*, www.storiesfromthepandemic.com, accessed October 31, 2020; Richard A. Oppel Jr., Robert Gebeloff, K. K. Rebecca Lai, Will Wright, and Mitch Smith, "The Fullest Look Yet at the Racial Inequity of Coronavirus," *New York Times*, July 5, 2020, www.nytimes.com.

32 Omi and Winant, *Racial Formation*; Bonilla-Silva, "Rethinking Racism"; Feagin, *The White Racial Frame*.

33 "The Brute Caricature," Jim Crow Museum of Racist Memorabilia, www.ferris.edu, accessed September 22, 2020.

34 Jane H. Hill, *The Everyday Language of White Racism* (Malden, MA: Wiley-Blackwell, 2008); Scottie Andrew and Harmeet Kaur, "Everyday Words and Phrases That Have Racist Connotations," CNN, July 7, 2020, www.cnn.com.

35 Frederick Douglass, "The Meaning of July Fourth for the Negro," July 5, 1852, Public Broadcast Service, www.pbs.org.

36 Moses, *Empire, Colony, Genocide*; Alexander Laban Hinton, "Critical Genocide Studies," *Genocide Studies and Prevention* 7 no. 1 (2012): 4–15.

37 Nikole Hannah-Jones, "What Is Owed," *New York Times Magazine*, June 30, 2020, www.nytimes.com; Emma Goldberg, "How Reparations for Slavery Became a 2020 Campaign Issue," *New York Times*, June 18, 2020, www.nytimes.com.

INDEX

AAA. *See* American Anthropological Association

Adios, America (Coulter), 122–23

Adorno, Theodor: *The Authoritarian Personality* by, 9–13, 16–17, 19–20, 59; Berkeley Public Opinion Study and, 9; critical theory and, 12, 27; *Dialectic of Enlightenment* by Horkheimer and, 11; "Education after Auschwitz" by, 12, 19–20, 27, 217, 227, 231, 233; on genocide education, 19; on language, 217–18; white power extremists and, 29

African Americans: reparations for, 192; under Jim Crow, 32, 46, 95, 99, 101, 112, 135, 139, 141, 191–92, 195, 228; US history of violence against, 139. *See also* Blacks

Africans, enslaved, 97–98

Albright, Madeline, 133

alternative facts, 25–27

Alternative for Germany, 187–88

alt-left, 39, 42

alt-lite, 40, 124–26

alt-right, 29, 183; AAA on, 23–24; alt-lite and, 40, 124–26; on anthropologists, 124; Bannon and, 152; *Breitbart* and, 40–41, 152; caricatures of, 125; on cultural Marxism, 107, 122–23, 152–53; *A Fair Hearing* manifesto, 121–26, 155, 184; KKK and, 105; memes, 123, 125; Miller and, 154, 156, 199; social media, white genocide and, 121–26; Spencer and, 38, 40, 122, 125, 185; Trump and, 39, 41, 123, 152, 154; Unite the Right

and, 40–41, 124–25; on white genocide, 149–50; in white power movement, 106–7

American Anthropological Association (AAA), 23–24, 31–33, 44

American exceptionalism, 8, 13, 17, 163, 194, 231; Manifest Destiny and, 143, 226

American Jewish Committee, 9–11

American Nazi Party, 109–10

American Renaissance, 155

analysis, in critical pedagogy and critical thinking, 29–30

Anglin, Andrew, 15, 42–43, 47, 51–52, 58; on Carlson, 157; on race war, 167; on Unite the Right 2, 86

Annan, Kofi, 137

anthropology: AAA, 23–24, 31–33, 44; on Cargo Cults, 123–24; Frankfurt School and, 20; race and, 44, 124; on white power, 44–45

Anti-Defamation League, 93, 111

anti-democratic ideologies, 9

Antifa, 24, 83–84, 87–89, 223

AntiFash Gordon (Twitter handle), 130–31

antisemitism, 7, 9–10; of Bowers, 90–92, 94, 129, 143, 151; of Ford, 103; hate crimes and, 93, 166; of Hitler, 61; Holocaust denial, 73, 75, 77; instrumental reason and, 11; intersectionality and, 83; of Johansson and Hovater, 73–75, 77; of Lindbergh, 103; "new world order" and, 105; *The Protocols of the Elders of Zion* and, 7, 61, 103, 108; Zionist conspiracy theories, 110, 114–15, 135–36, 198, 221

24; on Obama, birtherism and, 25, 91, 150; objectification of women, 14–15; Overton window and, 107; politics of fear, ahead of 2018 midterms, 18; populism of, 25, 106, 188; presidency as symptomatic of systemic white power history, x; race war and, 180; racism and, 3, 20, 42, 46–47, 51–52, 92; racist dog whistles of, 46, 127, 145–47; racist language of, 208–10, 217, 225–26; Sayoc and, 92, 148–49, 204; "shithole countries" comment, 46, 51–52, 73; "The Snake" story, at campaign rallies, 1–4, 15–16, 19, 150–51, 156, 185, 199, 218, 220; systemic white supremacy and, 121, 205–6, 231, 233; Tarrant on, 185; Tree of Life synagogue massacre and, 90–94, 148; on Twitter, 149–50, 158, 181, 210, 223; TWP on, 79; on undocumented immigrants, 76; on Unite the Right rally, "very fine people on both sides" statement, 18, 24, 36, 39–40, 42, 47–48, 51, 91, 180; Unite the Right rally and, 17–18, 23–24, 32, 36–42, 46–50, 121; as "very stable genius," 61; Vienna, Ohio, campaign rally, 2016, 1–5, 16; on violence at rallies of, 15–16; white genocide and, 149–51, 158, 220; white power and, 6, 25, 94, 149, 196, 199, 225; white power extremists and, 14–17, 20–21, 24, 41–42, 51–52, 94, 180, 185, 198–99, 204–5, 226

truth, distortions of, lies and, 24–27

Truth and Reconciliation Commission of Canada, 193, 233

Tuol Sleng Museum of Genocidal Crimes, 168–69

Turner, Earl (fictional character), 110–12, 116

Turner, Nat, 100–101

The Turner Diaries (Pierce), 109–17, 124, 132, 134, 155, 187

Twitter, 72, 74, 76, 106, 119–20, 224; AntiFash Gordon on, 130–31; Trump on, 149–50, 158, 181, 210, 223

two seedlines thesis, 113

TWP. *See* Traditionalist Worker Party

UN. *See* United Nations

United Daughters of the Confederacy, 40

United Nations (UN), 188; Commission on Human Rights, 10; "Framework of Analysis for Atrocity Crimes" booklet of, 136–38, 147–49, 159, 161, 163, 222; Genocide Convention, 10, 135–36, 138–41, 170, 190; on human rights, 10, 144–45; Office of Genocide Prevention, 173; Office of the Special Adviser of the Secretary-General on the Prevention of Genocide, 170; *We Charge Genocide* petition to, 139–47, 164, 190, 195, 227, 229–32

Unite the Right. *See* Charlottesville, Unite the Right rally, 2017

Unite the Right 2, 82, 91–93, 157; Antifa and, 83–84, 87–89; counterprotesters at, 83–85, 87–89, 179; Kessler at, 49, 83–89, 180, 191, 254n4; neo-Nazis at, 86–87; New Jersey hate group at, 129–30

Universal Declaration of Human Rights, 1948, 10, 32, 135, 214

Valle, Jovanni, 130

VDARE, 126, 135, 155–56

VICE News, 33–37, 40–42, 49, 54–55, 57, 73

Vienna, Ohio, Trump campaign rally, 2016, 1–5, 16

Vietnam: Cambodia and, 4–5, 65–66; North, 63, 65

Vietnam War, 112; US carpet-bombing of Cambodia in, 5–7, 13, 65, 143, 171; veterans, 105–6

ABOUT THE AUTHOR

Alexander Laban Hinton is Distinguished Professor of Anthropology, Director of the Center for the Study of Genocide and Human Rights, and UNESCO Chair on Genocide Prevention at Rutgers University. He is the author or editor of over a dozen books, including two books on the Extraordinary Chambers in the Courts of Cambodia, *The Justice Facade: Trials of Transition in Cambodia* and *Man or Monster? The Trial of a Khmer Rouge Torturer.*

In recognition of his research and scholarship, Professor Hinton has received a number of honors and awards. The American Anthropological Association selected Hinton as the recipient of the 2009 Robert B. Textor and Family Prize for Excellence in Anticipatory Anthropology "for his groundbreaking 2005 ethnography *Why Did They Kill? Cambodia in the Shadow of Genocide*, for path-breaking work in the anthropology of genocide, and for developing a distinctively anthropological approach to genocide."

Professor Hinton was listed as one of "Fifty Key Thinkers on the Holocaust and Genocide" and is a past President of the International Association of Genocide Scholars (2011–13). Professor Hinton has received fellowships from a range of institutions and, from 2011 to 2012, was a Member of the Institute for Advanced Study in Princeton. Most recently, Professor Hinton was a convener of the international "Rethinking Peace Studies" (2014–18) and "Global Consortium on Bigotry and Hate" (2019–2024) initiatives and, in March 2016, served as an expert witness at the Khmer Rouge tribunal. He has been invited to speak on six continents across the globe.